THE MECHANIC

THE MECHANIC

The Secret World of the
F1 Pitlane

MARC 'ELVIS' PRIESTLEY

YELLOW JERSEY PRESS
LONDON

1 3 5 7 9 10 8 6 4 2

Yellow Jersey Press, an imprint of Vintage
20 Vauxhall Bridge Road
London SW1V 2SA

Yellow Jersey Press is part of the Penguin Random House group of companies
whose addresses can be found at global.penguinrandomhouse.com.

 Penguin
Random House
UK

First published by Yellow Jersey Press in hardback in 2017
First published by Yellow Jersey Press in paperback in 2018

www.vintage-books.co.uk

A CIP catalogue record for this book is available from the British Library

ISBN 9781787290433

Printed and bound in Great Britain by Clays Ltd, Elcograf S.p.A.

Penguin Random House is committed to a sustainable future
for our business, our readers and our planet. This book is made
from Forest Stewardship Council® certified paper.

For Clare, Lexi, Leo, Rex and Ginger

CONTENTS

FOREWORD
BY DAVID COULTHARD

Marc Priestley, or Elvis as I know him, is the perfect example of an evolution of talent.

He started out getting his hands dirty as a mechanic in Formula Ford and British Formula 3 before rising through the ranks to the pinnacle of motorsport, which is where we first met when we both worked for McLaren's Formula One team. F1 attracts many, but few sustain in that rare air of competition where the correct answer to any question is 'Yes I can'. The relentless pursuit of marginal gains with many late nights and early mornings would break a mere mortal, but Elvis represents the pinnacle of a man's desire to constantly push to be the greatest version of himself.

No other sport relies on their backroom staff in the way that Formula One does. Yes, football clubs have their physios and coaches, and tennis players their psychologists and trainers; golfers use a caddy to strategise their way around the course. But within the fine margins of a Grand Prix, a pit crew can physically and decisively alter the outcome during a race, not only with the work they do in preparation, but with the consistency of their performances in pitstops too. Operating well for three out of four stops isn't acceptable if the fourth turns out to be a nightmare. Getting even the tiniest thing wrong might prevent the driver from taking a win, and so a team's support crew can be every bit as crucial as the guys behind the wheel.

Their in depth understanding of the car and its engineering, and my reliance upon them, became truly apparent when we had a freak technical failure right before the start of one particular race. It was the Canadian Grand Prix in 2001 and I remember leaving the grid for my formation lap ahead of the imminent race start, when I felt something rattling around in the cockpit. I couldn't look down to see what was going on because I was strapped in so tightly, but once I'd pulled up in my grid slot, I used what limited movement I had to scrape the mystery item along the cockpit floor towards me with my foot. It was what looked like a very big and very important gold nut.

I got on the radio straight away. 'Er, guys, I've just found something floating around in the car. It looks like a big gold ring.'

There was initial confusion on the pit wall. The mechanics and engineers were naturally concerned and wanted to know what it was, so I repeated my not-so-technical description.

'What do you mean a big gold ring? Can you describe it in more detail?' came the reply.

'It's bloody big, about two and a half inches across, circular, gold, and has small holes all the way around the outside. There's a fine thread in the middle . . . and a big crack through the centre!' I said as the remaining cars formed up noisily behind me.

As the mechanics and engineers rapidly worked out, using the spare car in the garage, what might have happened and what consequences it could have, someone suggested I throw it out of the car and over the pit wall next to my grid slot.

I couldn't believe it. There I was, attempting to ready myself for the start of a Grand Prix, all the while trying to throw what I hoped wasn't a vital part towards my mechanics. It was ridiculous, especially as I was strapped snugly into my seat and couldn't really move my arms over the sides of the cockpit. It must've looked hilarious from the outside. I jettisoned it from the car with all the might my forearms could muster.

I tried not to panic and almost instantly the team calmly reassured me the broken nut would not present a safety risk and I should prepare as normal.

Apparently, it was a retaining nut, which was supposed to hold the front rockers in place – a big part of my internal suspension buried deep at the front of the chassis, but the guys were able to explain, quickly and incisively, that its main job was to hold the rockers in during the build process or while the car was off the ground on stands in the garage. The dynamic loads going through the suspension on track were such that nothing was going to fall apart.

As ever, I had to put my trust in the guys who knew that car inside out, and as the five red lights began to light up one by one on the gantry to start the race, I confirmed I was happy to go for it and put any worry out of my mind. I had absolute faith in my team.

I did OK for the first few laps. The suspension, as predicted, was fine structurally, even if the balance of the car seemed a little strange. But halfway through the race my engine blew up, as they sometimes did back then with the extremes we were pushing them to, putting an end to any podium hopes. The failure was completely unrelated, but it showed just how stressful and chaotic life in F1 could be back then, and what an intense job the mechanics had when looking after such a complicated and technical race car.

Amongst all of this chaos over the years, Elvis was a dependable, reliable pair of hands and a great character to be around.

It's no surprise to me that after playing his part in securing Lewis Hamilton's first World Title, Elvis has moved on to his next challenge, still surrounded by engineering excellence and cars but now in his role as a TV presenter, where his easy, relaxed style makes it feel like he's putting his arm around the viewers' shoulders and taking them on a walk behind the scenes of one of the biggest sports in the world. I look forward to watching him continue to push the boundaries in this field whilst inevitably looking for his next great life challenge.

I hope you enjoy reading the book and joining him on his journey.

David Coulthard

1

ON THE CLOCK

The British Grand Prix, Silverstone

'Box. Box. Box!'

We heard the call across the team radio; there was a split second of free-fall, twenty mechanics charging towards the pitlane, dressed in fire suits, balaclavas, helmets and gloves, emerging from the garage at a pivotal moment; nerves, fear, excitement and pride take over. The noise of the passionate British crowd and the overwhelming scream of passing engines threaten to distract focus; a burst of radio chatter between driver and team as one of the most tactical, choreographed and adrenaline-fuelled procedures moves into action at The Fastest Show on Earth: the Formula One pitstop. Or as I lovingly called it for the best part of a decade, work.

I'm in the pack somewhere, anonymous to the millions of people watching on TV, waiting for our car to appear at the end of the pitlane. I did many jobs in pitstops over the years, but on this day I'm operating the right-rear wheel gun to remove and refit the retaining nut, while my teammates swap the wheels and tyres for me. It's a well-orchestrated routine that should take no longer than a few seconds with no fuel going in this time. A few seconds of technical, highly pressurised precision that takes place multiple times in every Grand Prix. But under high-pressure conditions, with zero margin for error, this pause in racing can often be the difference between winning and losing.

I can see him now: Lewis Hamilton, McLaren's World Champ-in-waiting, arcing into view and bearing down on us at 100kph. Several hundred kilos of pointy, sharp Formula One car moving in at speed as I kneel on a marked spot telling me exactly where he's supposed to land. I take a deep breath, fighting the urge to move back to a safer distance . . . Lewis's barely in-control car moves in hot, missing me by centimetres and screeches to a stop.

The timer starts . . .

I track the rear wheel as he arrives, my gun landing on the nut before the car comes to a complete standstill, both a test of trust and nerve. If Lewis were to overshoot his pit box, I'd almost certainly get dragged along with him, but he's one of the best and stops exactly where I need him. The gun unlocks the nut, trying to wrench itself violently out of my hands in the process, and my job's halfway done before I can even register the sights, sounds and emotions smothering me. I always loved the danger of pitstops. They delivered the adrenaline rush I needed to operate at the best of my ability, but the risks were high too. A fuel accident might engulf the crew and driver in a mini inferno; the heat coming off the brakes – a thousand degrees of glowing red carbon fibre – could burn instantly through my gloves and cook my skin.

One second . . .

The sensations quickly become intense. I lean back, switching the gun's direction of rotation as the rear wheel comes off. The new one goes on and I follow it in, pushing it on with the wheel gun. The acrid smell of burning rubber chokes my nostrils, as small marbles from the old tyre become dislodged and melt instantly on the brake discs, smouldering and catching fire.

Two seconds . . .

The nut's zipped back on with another high-pitched and violent whine. Then the noise explodes around me, the mind-blowing yelp of a 19,000rpm V8 engine flexing its muscles. Lewis is hard on the throttle now, the engine bouncing off its rev limiter, desperate to drop the clutch and get the car back into the race. I'm less than a metre away from the deafening scream and vibrations. I can feel it hammering my bones, my teeth, my muscles, like I've jammed my head into the launch pad of a lifting NASA rocket. It's overwhelming, despite my moulded earplugs and helmet. Behind the tyre I can see thick smoke rising; the brakes are being licked by flame, but there's no time to do anything about it. The fire will go out as the car moves away and the airflow returns. Instinctively, everything tells you a blaze like that's bad, yet I can do nothing but watch. Three seconds to change the wheels and tyres meant success. Five seconds was slow, and to hesitate was always to lose.

Three seconds . . .

As with every other pitstop, I do my job, hoping that everything else has gone to plan. It didn't always work that way: the occasional practice pitstop sessions where we'd sent cars away with cross-threaded nuts or dropped the car off the jacks before the nuts were tight had taught me that mistakes sometimes happened. In those relaxed practice situations I'd think, 'Shit, if that happened in an actual race it'd be disastrous . . .' Luckily, it rarely did, and trust, skill and nerve became the strengths my teammates and I relied on throughout my career.

I lean back, my arm instinctively raised in the air as the rear wheel shudders, clunking into gear, and the car drops hard onto the ground. My heart's racing and my senses are confused and disorientated by the incredible noise shaking my core.

My job's done.

Go! Go! Go!

Lewis wheelspins away from right under my nose as the sounds, vibrations and emotions reach new levels, and he's back in the game. Yes! We did it! High fives and fist-bumps all round as we rush back to the garage TVs, pumped on adrenaline, chests puffed out in pride, to see where he emerges back on the track.

*

During a career with the McLaren F1 team from 2000 to 2009 I've seen plenty of good and bad pitstops. I've watched as technical errors and bad strategy calls from the team have cost drivers their Grand Prix victory, even a Drivers' Championship, the ultimate accolade for any F1 racer hoping to prove their elite status. I've also seen how our good calls and quick thinking have delivered great success, and I've been involved in many races where the final results have come down to pitstop performance; there've been several occasions where the two leading teams pitted their drivers at the same time and I promise you there's no better feeling than watching your man stop at his box in second place, only to leave with a fresh set of tyres as race leader moments later.

The flipside, as always, were the critical failures, and I witnessed one or two during my career. Seeing another team sneak an edge on you after a particularly slow pitstop was always tough. At McLaren, a notoriously professional and fastidious organisation, we used to pride ourselves on being the best at what we did. To make a mistake was a painful experience, particularly because our actions were being played out and analysed in a very public way. The pressure of performing in front of worldwide audiences could bring with it real anxiety when I first started out as a young man, and I was always struck by the surreal nature of working in a job that I'd been fascinated by as a kid. Watching the British Grand Prix on the telly did nothing to prepare me, however. If anything, it only expanded the fear of failure, and I pictured the fans at home, quick to criticise the pit crew for making any mistakes during a driver's shot at glory.

Fortunately, I quickly got used to dealing with the pressure and was able to function at the highest level. Which was good because within those years at McLaren I experienced all kinds of drama: Grand Prix wins and soul-destroying losses; controversy and scandal; cheating and espionage. There were episodes of drug- and alcohol-charged recklessness; lavish parties and extravagant spending. I've also been at the frontline of technological advancement in a business that prides itself on pushing development and speed to the absolute limit, while working with some of the most talented and explosive drivers on the planet. It was a dream come true, and I thrived in this exciting sport during a period where the thrills, stakes and rewards were high; in an era when inflated tobacco sponsorship meant we were able to play with a seemingly endless reserve of cash.

From my position in the garage I was involved in some of the most dramatic moments in F1's recent history. I worked with world-class drivers like Mika Hakkinen, Kimi Raikkonen and David Coulthard, but I was also right there as the controversial battle between Lewis Hamilton and Fernando Alonso unfolded in 2007. It was fascinating to watch as Lewis developed from a young rookie into a potential championship-winning superstar; a potential that was realised not long after a damaging fallout with Fernando which would tailspin into part of one of the sport's biggest scandals: Spygate.

In his first months, however, the youngster was remarkably humble, and I remember a marketing event, I think for Hugo Boss, that we went to one evening, just after Lewis had come into F1. When Lewis emerged from the team's chauffeur-driven Mercedes to see his own face projected, in enormous scale, on the side of the building, he couldn't hold back the tears of disbelief and needed a moment to compose himself while the emotions around his life-changing role as an F1 driver hit him all at once. It was rare to witness a reaction like that from a top sportsman, especially when surprise, or vulnerability, is often viewed as a weakness in such a testosterone-driven industry. But Lewis was just a young man entering a strange new world for the first time, and his responses were genuine. I found it to be an endearing quality back then.

Inevitably things changed as his stock began to rise and the war between him and Fernando took centre stage. Both were brilliant in a car, probably the two most complete drivers I've ever worked with, but the rivalry, distrust and disrespect they developed for each other bred some characteristics in each of them that would leave many in the team falling out of love with their two star drivers.

At times, I had a ringside seat to some incredible bust-ups between the pair, some of them involving McLaren's iconic team boss, Ron Dennis. But once the dust had settled and Fernando had moved teams, Lewis began to flourish even more, and by 2008, after just two seasons in the sport, we were celebrating his first World Championship. It was a moment I'll never forget.

Elsewhere, I worked at the Monaco Grand Prix, where the bar bills were sobering and the super-yachts moored in the harbour were more costly than a whole street of homes in Beverley Hills. I've seen emerging drivers on humble wages transformed into overnight millionaires, and witnessed Ron Dennis and the team spend fortunes in the pursuit of technical perfection. But one small incident sticks in my mind that perhaps sums up the financial bubble we existed in: at a test, not long after I joined the team, McLaren chartered a helicopter . . . in a desperate attempt to *dry out a wet track*.

We'd exclusively hired out the Santa Pod Raceway drag strip in Northamptonshire to test a brand-new front wing on the car in private. Wind tunnel testing and computer simulations had shown that our developments, if successful, would give us a considerable performance advantage, but only real-world straight-line testing at high speed and in a controlled environment would deliver the technical data we required to confirm our predictions and approve the parts for racing. For that to work safely, we needed a dry surface, but during the morning the heavens had opened. A wet track not only meant that braking was difficult at the end of the straight (and driving through puddles at the speeds we needed to achieve would be dangerous), but the moisture had an impact on the airflow structures around the parts of the car that we wanted to measure, as well as on the sensors measuring them. To compare the data from the car on the racetrack to the one that had worked so well in our wind tunnel, conditions needed to be the same: dry. Meanwhile time was against us. We had a very small window, a matter of hours, to run the car and hopefully get the confirmation we needed that the wing was good. The parts then had to be signed off, manufactured, painted, assembled, and then packaged and flown out to the race team in time for the next weekend's Grand Prix. If we missed the opportunity, the wings wouldn't be ready for the race and the critical performance advantage they delivered would have to wait until the next round two weeks later – something we couldn't afford to let happen. The pressure was on.

With the tarmac showing no sign of drying and time running out, some bright spark suggested we charter a helicopter. At first I was pretty sure he only said it as a throw-away joke as we all stood around waiting, becoming more and more frustrated at the situation, but in the end some of the most brilliant engineers in the business began to raise eyebrows and become excited. His crazy idea was to instruct the pilot to fly up and down the length of the strip, just above the tarmac, so his rotary blades could scatter the surface water away with the downdraft. Such was the urgency in completing the test session in time, and the bottomless money pit financing our business model during that era, that the call was put in without hesitation or question. It turns out you can actually hail a chopper at pretty short notice for enough cash, like an Uber for the super wealthy, and shortly afterwards a bemused helicopter pilot was swooping in low over Santa Pod, his blades whipping up a typhoon of rain. It was quite a spectacle, but the reality was that while it did shift an awful lot of water into the air, 90 per cent of it fell straight back down onto the track . . . We never did manage to complete the test, though it did give us all a rather unusual anecdote to take away from the day.

Even after years in the sport, things like that still blew my mind, and as a normal bloke on the street, albeit one with a passion for working with cars and technology, I got to live out my dream job while dipping my toes into the lifestyle of the rich and famous. Just being in the bubble proved both infectious and disorientating at times. The adrenaline rush and the excitement of F1 is what entices and then traps a lot of people into the sport. They don't want to leave, and when they eventually do they often have a hard time finding a replacement for the emotional highs and lows. I was lucky and sidestepped the loss to some extent by moving from the pitlane to the paddock and into the F1 television media, working for Sky Sports, the BBC and other broadcasters over the last few years in presenting and reporting roles across Formula One and now Formula E. The excitement I get from operating on live TV, with no second chances or 'take twos', can sometimes be as big as a pitstop, and the deadlines and demands often match the pressure of a wheel change in the middle of a pivotal Grand Prix. It's also afforded me a privileged position: I'm able to watch the changes of an ever-evolving sport close up, while appreciating my time with McLaren for the thrilling, life-changing, slightly surreal and intensely challenging ride that it was.

2

THE FIRST STOP IS THE HARDEST

It was as if I was destined to work in motor racing.

As a kid, I grew up in a small village in Kent, which backed on to the world-famous Brands Hatch racetrack. At that time in the 1980s, the circuit shared the British Grand Prix with Silverstone in alternate years, and the sound of cars and motorbikes ricocheted around the village nearly every weekend. In Grand Prix week, the surrounding streets would overflow with fancy cars looking for parking spots, lots of them carrying unusual international number plates that fascinated me at that age. There were designs from all over the world and it piqued my imagination. 'Wow,' I thought. 'This must be pretty special if people have driven from Germany, Austria and wherever else to come all the way to my tiny village for these F1 cars.' To my mind, a glamorous circus had rocked up in town and I loved every second of it.

We didn't have a lot of money back then as a family, so I couldn't just pop over and buy a ticket, even though we lived next door to the track. Instead, it became a TV event and everybody in the house would crowd around to watch the start and the first few laps until, one by one, Mum, Dad, my brother and whoever else was in the house would drift away to make dinner, mow the lawn, or whatever. Not me. I would sit there transfixed, not just by the glitziness of the race, or the high-speed drama, which I obviously loved, but almost as much by the design of the cars and the teams involved. During F1's earlier years there were some pretty outlandish ideas on show. I remember the Tyrrell P34 had six wheels because the designers believed it would better transfer their huge engine torque onto the track; a Brabham had a huge fan on the back, designed to suck the car onto the racetrack and give greater downforce and grip. It was engineering ingenuity at its best and I loved it. And whenever a pitstop took place, the anonymous technicians running around in their fire suits and balaclavas fascinated me. I was in awe of how quickly they could change the wheels and how they were actually crucial players in helping the drivers to win a race.

'Forget being a Formula One driver,' I thought. (My karting skills, or lack thereof, helped me come to that conclusion.) 'I want to be one of *those* guys . . .'

As a kid, I was interested in building stuff and breaking things down and my bike was forever in pieces as I tinkered with the wheels and chain. I loved technology too, and whenever we got a new hi-fi or video recorder, I would pore over the manual until I understood the workings inside out. This practical curiosity translated to my schoolwork too, and while I think my dad was keen on me taking a traditionally academic route to university with subjects like English, I enjoyed and excelled in Craft, Design and Technology (CDT). I loved designing and making things.

I'd also had my racing cherry popped on the Brands Hatch track when one day, unbeknown to my parents, some friends and I snuck onto the property. There was a Historic Formula One car test day taking place, and a mate of mine lived in a house that backed onto the grounds of the Brands Hatch site. Having cycled round to his place and dug a hole under his fence big enough for a ten-year-old kid to crawl through, we made our way through the wooded perimeter until we found ourselves standing at the edge of the racetrack. 'We shouldn't be here,' I thought, feeling a little edgy, but undeterred, we watched, gawping, as a parade of high-speed, very noisy cars tore around the circuit in front of us.

Then I spotted a better vantage point: the infield grass at the Druids Hairpin at the top of the hill. The cars were braking heavily and coming so close to the apex of the corner I thought we'd get an amazing view of them as they went by, especially if we were over that side and tucked safely behind the low barriers. We waited for a pause in the action before, in somewhat suicidal fashion, we dashed across the racetrack and jumped behind the rubber tyre wall. It was a bloody stupid idea, but for a couple of laps we had the best seats in the house, crouching just a metre or so from the action. The noise was deafening and I could feel the draft as the huge cars with giant wings rushed right past us. I loved it. It wasn't long before we were spotted, though and once the session had been brought to an abrupt halt by red flags and the safety car had been sent out, our rag-tag gang was plucked to safety, by the ear if I remember rightly, and dumped at the Brands Hatch main gate with a scorching reprimand. When I realised they weren't taking me home to face the wrath of my parents, I quickly got over the telling-off. I'd just had one of the most exhilarating experiences of my life. What a day. In fact, the only thing I was now annoyed about was that we had to walk halfway back around the village for a mile or two to get back to my mate's house and pick up our abandoned bikes.

After my GCSEs, I tried to appease my family and embarked on A level courses in English, Design and Media Studies, but within a month or two, I knew I wasn't cut out for it – plus my head had been turned by a Mechanical Engineering course at the same college. After an awkward but ultimately encouraging chat with my parents, I was allowed to switch paths and I immersed myself in the world of cars and technology. Only then did I begin to think that instead of just dreaming about working in motorsport, I might actually try to do it. After a few weeks on the course, already thinking I knew it all, I started writing begging letters to the addresses of racing teams listed in the advertising sections of *Autosport*, the biggest trade magazine at the time. I wanted work experience and I would scribble pleas every week asking for an unpaid internship. Unsurprisingly, my letterbox was stuffed with rejection letters and notes telling me 'Thanks very much, we'll keep your details on file should anything come up in the future . . .'

Then, one day, somebody who lived in the village mentioned that he knew of a guy who worked with a Formula Ford team, pretty much the base rung on the single-seater motorsport ladder. 'He won't be able to pay you,' he said. 'But if you want, he'd be happy for you to spend some time working with them.' So, in the summer holidays of 1995 I decamped to Milton Keynes for a three-week adventure, where I slept in the spare room at one of the mechanic's houses and became a lackey in their workshop, sweeping the floors and satiating a seemingly never-ending thirst for tea.

I loved every second of it, and when I was eventually taken to a sportscar test day at the Mallory Park circuit in Leicestershire to help one of the privateers it felt like The Real Deal, even though a lot of the competitors were over-aged, overweight and under-talented drivers who were just doing it for a bit of a hobby. I'd been let loose with a proper racing car, on a proper track, with a proper team. It was all the incentive I needed – *I had to move up the ladder and get to Formula One.*

At the age of eighteen or nineteen, I used my limited experience to land an apprenticeship with a small team in London that built and raced Caterham 7s. I had the time of my life, building cars during the week and racing them on the weekends. I took it very seriously, learning as much as I could and using it as a springboard to gain experience and make contacts in the racing world, quickly trying to work my way up from there. I was soon on the doorstep of the big leagues. British Formula Three followed, then Italian Formula 3000, where I wore the team uniform with pride and lorded it around the paddock as if I was working at the Monaco Grand Prix. The level of professionalism was amazing and I really embraced it, wanting to be the best at what we did. I remember being so proud of my job – and my friends being super jealous. Then, after a couple more years of writing incessant speculative letters to every F1 team and continuing to receive an endless stream of rejections, McLaren responded to one. And it wasn't the standard copy-and-paste reply I'd become so used to. 'We'd love to talk to you,' it said. My head spinning, I read it over and over to be sure. *I had my foot in the door of F1 and I wasn't going to budge.*

Despite being only 22, I felt I had what was required to be an F1 mechanic. I was good at my job and very professional; I was keen on attention to detail, not quite to McLaren levels at that stage, but enough to have set me apart a little bit in Formula 3000. I was meticulous in my work and I knew how to behave around drivers, sponsors and team owners alike. After a terrifying phone call with the Test Team Manager, I was asked to come in for an interview at McLaren.

I remember putting the phone down and shaking like a leaf. An interview at McLaren! If nothing else, it meant I'd be visiting the McLaren factory and even that would be a dream come true. I thought about little else in the weeks that followed and when the day finally arrived I was as nervous as I'd ever been. I set off for the hour-and-a-half drive down to Woking from my home in Northampton at least three hours before my appointment time – there was no way I could risk being late. When I got there, I drove into the car park in my beaten-up old banger and found a spot tucked away in the corner, in an attempt to not draw attention to myself amongst the shiny new Mercedes cars filling most of the other bays. For an hour or so I sat there, worrying, wondering, imagining and dreaming, going over notes I'd written and trying to justify to myself why I should possibly be sat outside one of the most famous and successful Formula One teams in the sport's history.

Then the time came and I smartened myself up one last time, locked the squeaky car door and walked nervously towards the glowing red McLaren sign above the black glass front doors. The interview itself was all a bit of a blur. I met the Test Team Manager and the Chief Mechanic and was then shown around the factory floor where the team were building their cars for an upcoming test. It was amazing just to be that close and see what was going on, I was in total awe. When I left, I had no idea how it'd gone. I got on well with them both, but was sure I must've come across as a young, inexperienced, nervous, sweaty mess, because that's exactly how I felt. Why would a huge team like McLaren want someone like that to join their elite?

I went away having had an incredible experience and tried to take it as just that, but try as I might, I just couldn't think about anything else, dreaming of being one of those guys. Two weeks went by and I began to resign myself to the reality of not making the grade this time. It would never stop me trying of course, I would never give up and was sure that one day I would definitely make it, but for now I needed to continue my journey. I'd been offered a great job at Prodrive – not Formula One, but a big company who were hugely successful in the World Rally Championship (WRC), so I gladly took up their offer and proudly went to work for my first day in a top-flight motorsport team.

By lunchtime, things were going well. I'd met lots of people and been shown around the impressive factory and the equally impressive WRC cars. Then my phone rang. I answered it in a quiet spot and was shocked to find it was McLaren's softly spoken Test Team Manager. He calmly told me they'd seen lots of people over the last couple of weeks and would now like to offer me the position of Number Two Mechanic on the McLaren Test Team! *Oh . . . My . . . God!* I was beside myself. Desperately trying to sound in control, I thanked him profusely before ending the call and then jumping up and down on the spot, screaming inside. I'd accepted instantly, without thinking anything through, and now had to deal with the awkward situation of being on my first day in a great new job at Prodrive.

I went to my new boss, very gingerly, and bumbled my way through the explanation, trying to sound remorseful, when inside I was excited beyond belief. He understood, I think, and I left immediately without even completing a full day. I felt like I'd just found out I'd won the lottery and all my dreams had quite literally come true. I remember driving home in a complete daze and called my mum on the way. 'Mum', I said, trying to remain calm, 'I'm a bloody F1 mechanic!'

My inaugural year on the McLaren Test Team was incredible, everything I'd hoped for and so much more. Each day opened my eyes a little bit more to this mystical new world I'd longed to be part of for so long. It gave me plenty of much-needed experience in the workings of my new environment. I got to know the way things were done in Formula One and, especially, the way things were done in the team. I was working at tests, away from the pressure of being at a Grand Prix. That's a great place to start out, and from the team's point of view, a great way to bring people into the game and train them, fine-tune them and prepare them for life under the huge spotlight of Grand Prix racing. It's a luxury they don't really have today, with test teams having been disbanded, and tests reduced to a bare minimum in the regulations in order to cut costs.

Whilst I loved every minute of it, despite the relentless hours and punishing schedule, I was soon impatient to go racing. I still had my dream of being part of an F1 pitstop crew and wanted to move up. It dawned on me after some time, though, that if and when that moment came, how would I ever be ready? There were no pitstops while all I was doing was testing. Not once did I ever change a wheel in a hurry during that spell, which I was surprised at, and whilst, believe me, there is no set of circumstances that can fully prepare you for the reality of a real-time, heat-of-the-moment competitive pitstop, it would surely have helped to have at least been introduced to the process.

There was no mechanism for grooming the next generation of pit crew, which was something I found strange at the time. What happened if someone got sick or injured on the race team? Who took their place in the pitstops? Wait . . . there were no backups?! Being young and inquisitive, but not wanting to ruffle any feathers in my new role, I kept my questions to myself, but pondered them endlessly. If I did one day get the call to step up to the race team, how would I ever be ready to join the crew? Would they expect me to slot seamlessly into position? A precision, choreographed pitstop only works when every single element operated perfectly, in harmony. One slip-up could bring the whole stack of cards tumbling down.

Eventually I suggested to my Chief Mechanic that we should operate a backup pitstop crew on the Test Team and practice regularly at tests. It would give us all a taste of what was involved and we could have an understudy for each position should the Race Team ever need a stand-in. The idea was discussed for a while, but never implemented. Their reasoning was that the Test Team simply had no spare time to spend on something that was so rarely required. So, when I was eventually promoted to the Race Team at the end of 2001, after a year and a half of testing, I had no idea what would be involved.

The step up was a dream come true, of course. It was all I'd ever wanted for years. Getting my job at McLaren in the first place was one of the best days of my life, but as much as I loved my time on the Test Team, it wasn't racing, I wasn't attending Grand Prix, and wasn't part of the pitstop crew. I looked up to those boys, almost as idols, watching them as they came and went at McLaren's Woking factory, returning from successful races to the congratulations of the hundreds of people who worked there. *I wanted to be part of that experience.*

Joining the team for the final Race Team test of pre-season, before heading off to Australia for the opening Grand Prix of 2002, was my first experience with the crew. As the new kid on the block and a rookie youngster, the Team Manager, Dave Ryan, and the Chief Mechanic had given me a pitstop role that rarely came into play. My job was to replace the spare nose cone, which only ever happened if the driver suffered an accident in the race and damaged the original. That was a pretty rare eventuality, and given how nervous I was, I was quite satisfied with that level of responsibility.

Pitstops were a bit different when I first started, all those years ago. They were nothing like the slick, two-second spectacles of modern

Formula One. There just wasn't the same value placed on them back then by the team, and more impetus was given to making the car go around a lap as quickly as possible. The fact that we only practised them occasionally, and only ever at a Grand Prix, was a good example of their indifference, and if work on the cars ever slipped behind, pit-stop practice was the first thing to get bumped from our schedule. I got the impression it was viewed by management as an inconvenient necessity and a bit of a pain in the arse, rather than the game-changer it should have been, and later became. For me, though, there was nothing more important in the world that week than making sure my first competitive pitstops went well. So when we got to Melbourne and rolled the T-Car (or spare race car) out into the pitlane for practice on Thursday evening, I took it very seriously.

My role was to work like this: the car stops on its marks in the pit box and is manually lifted onto a small stand. Someone takes off the broken nose cone, then I seamlessly move in, swinging the new nose and the enormous front wing into position. I line the nose up with four pins on the front of the chassis and push it on, at which point two guys lock the catches, which secures it to the car. Once attached, I leap out of the way, allowing the front jack man to move in and lower the car back onto the floor.

At least that's what should have happened . . .

When my moment came the first time, I stumbled with the heavy nose and wing assembly, tripping and bumping into the guy taking the first nose off. I continually missed the four small pins on the front of the chassis, and in doing so damaged parts of the brake and power steering systems by heavily battering them with the nose cone. Once or twice I let go before the catches were completely done up and the nose cone dropped to the floor. On one occasion I even stood still, admiring my own work, preventing the front jack man from getting close enough to the car to do his job. Basically, it was a disaster. Everything that could go wrong went wrong, and I was so terrified it was going to happen on Sunday afternoon that I went to see the Team Manager after practice to express my concern over the situation. His reaction was telling about the way pitstops were viewed by the team back then.

'Oh, don't worry about it, Elvis,' he said, placing a reassuring hand on my shoulder. 'There're two things to remember here. Firstly, it's highly unlikely you're going to be needed anyway, so just chill out . . . Secondly, if we do need a new nose, it means the driver's had an accident, so his race is probably ruined. Just don't worry about it, it'll all be fine.'

His nonchalance was worlds apart from my paranoia, and as he waved me away with a pat on the back, I walked off to do exactly the opposite of his advice. *Worry.*

I was genuinely scared. I thought about little else for the next few days and even struggled to sleep on the Saturday night before the race. I went over and over the scenarios in my head, trying to visualise the perfect pitstop, but I was convinced my introduction into Grand Prix life would be a very public disaster. When race day finally arrived it was a mind-blowing experience. Our cars had qualified in fourth place (David Coulthard) and fifth (Kimi Raikkonen), so we were near to the front of the grid, right behind the two Ferraris. It felt surreal being on the track in amongst the scenes I was so used to watching on the telly. For a short while I was distracted enough not to think about the huge responsibility of my work and revelled in the addictive atmosphere of the first race of a new F1 season. I was in my element, strutting around David Coulthard's car with pride as the passing celebrities and TV cameras looked on. It felt larger than life.

Once we'd wished the drivers luck and strapped them in, they screeched off for their parade, or green flag lap, before the official race start. We headed back towards the pitlane, dragging the jacks, trolleys and equipment from the grid, so we were ready in case of any early pitstops. Eventually I heard the cars roar away from the start line, the lights going out as we rushed back towards our garages with the huge crowd of other fire suit-clad mechanics and engineers from every other team. The fear kicked back in and I zoned out from the rest of the world. All of a sudden I didn't want to feel larger than life anymore. Part of me wanted to be back home, watching it all on TV again, where I couldn't mess anything up. And then, my radio earpiece burst into life. It was Dave Ryan, the Team Manager. The Grand Prix had started but already he was delivering a message to the team with his usual commanding calm, but to my mind it was the sound of an impending panic attack.

'OK, boys, Kimi's been off at turn one and damaged his front wing,' said Dave. 'He's coming in for a nose change. Prepare for a nose change . . .'

My whole world stopped. My heart was pounding so hard I could almost hear it over the screaming noise of the cars echoing around the circuit. *Was I hyperventilating? Was I having a heart attack?* Flustered, I ran back to the garage, tripping myself up with the front jack and starter motor trolley I'd been dragging behind me. When I got there I threw the equipment carelessly into the garage, in among the VIPs and team management still watching the first lap on the monitors. My arrival certainly didn't go unnoticed. I'd made a huge mess, and was running around like a complete amateur in front of everyone.

I grabbed my balaclava, ran into the pitlane and picked up the replacement nose for Kimi's car, checking at least four or five times that I had the right one. Still overwhelmed with adrenaline, I leapt to the front of the pitstop box and prepared myself for the inevitable. But I was standing there alone. Turning back to the garage, I saw my more experienced colleagues clearing up the mess I'd just created in a fairly leisurely fashion. They knew we had around a minute and a half to set ourselves up while Kimi limped his way through the entire lap with a broken car. More worryingly, I could also see Ron Dennis, the team principal and a notoriously fearsome character, gesturing towards me as he chatted to one of the boys.

'Who's that?' I guessed he was saying. 'And why is he so out of control?'

I couldn't go back into the garage now, so embarrassingly I stood in the pitlane, shaking like a leaf in my fire suit, holding the spare nose and front wing in my arms. I prayed that nobody had noticed my arrival . . . *But they had.* My amateurish entrance had advertised to a TV cameraman the fact we were about to make a pitstop. He'd taken up position, no more than a metre away from my face with his camera. *The pressure was on.* I imagined the hundreds of millions of people on the other end of his lens all staring at me for the entire minute and a half. Clearly that's not what was happening – it would have made for terrible television – but paranoia had taken hold. I even pictured my friends and family watching back at home and instantly regretted telling them what my pitstop role was. I could've been completely anonymous with all my gear on, but now they were all about to see me screw up McLaren's race.

The noise of the other racing cars screaming past, just a few metres away on the other side of the pit wall, was enough to rattle my bones in those days, and with the sweat of anxiety running down my face and pooling into my stinging eyes, there was more than enough to put me off my relatively simple task. The truth is that most people are more than capable of picking up a nose cone and popping it onto a few pins. *That's easy.* But in that moment it seemed like the hardest job in the world. I imagined Murray Walker, up in his commentary box, talking viewers through the 'catastrophic mess-up in the McLaren pit'. The back pages of tomorrow's newspapers running the headline 'McLaren: Disaster!' with a picture of me underneath. Of course none of these things were actually going to happen, but that's what was going through my mind during these frantic moments.

The other members of the crew finally gathered around after what seemed like a lifetime, laughing at me for having stood there on my own for so long. I was humiliated, but at that point I at least felt a little less exposed, as Kimi eventually appeared at the far end of the pitlane and sped his way towards us. The pitlane speed limit back then was 120kph, just over 70mph. Watching him bear down on us, hoping, praying, that the car's front wing might stop at a spot just in front of my ankles, felt like standing in the fast lane of a motorway. The brakes on a Formula One car are so good though, that at around 15 metres from the pit box, a driver can still be doing 70mph! Still to this day it's the most terrifying thing I've ever done.

Kimi screeched to a halt, hitting his marks perfectly.

The broken nose cone came off and I shuffled quickly into position. I didn't hit anybody, or trip over, and the nose went straight onto the four pins. The guys locked the catches and I leapt out of the way and bounced back into the garage, buzzing. It was perfect! It couldn't have gone any better! My heart was racing. It felt like I hadn't gulped in a breath for minutes, I was so excited and relieved that everything had gone well. I must have been grinning from ear to ear as the balaclava came off – it was the best sensation ever. Suddenly it dawned on me that something was very wrong: I hadn't heard the car screech away, and when I turned around Kimi was still stationary in the pitlane. All sorts of frantic chat had been crackling over the radio, but to be honest, I hadn't heard any of it; I'd been so overwhelmed by my own emotions and stress.

When Kimi had gone off the track, a tiny stone from the gravel trap had kicked up, landing somewhere down between his back and the seat of the car. Drivers are tightly strapped into their cockpits, so anything lodged between them and the seat would have been incredibly uncomfortable and painful and he couldn't continue with it in there. He certainly couldn't reach to get it out himself so now the crew was clambering over the car, desperately trying to fish out a tiny little stone. By the time it'd been finally retrieved and the car had disappeared from view, he'd been stationary for almost a minute in what was possibly one of McLaren's worst ever pitstops. The contrasting reactions within the team couldn't have been more polarised afterwards: the very grumpy, experienced mechanics walking back into the garage, angry at the catastrophically slow stop and the over-excited, idiotic young rookie leaping around wanting to high-five everyone because his little bit had gone really well.

My reaction was naive but understandable. Getting through that first experience was a stress I'd never experienced before, but it was also the best adrenaline rush – *ever*. It also changed the way I looked at pitstops from that day forward. My minor role in the operation was just that – a tiny little part – but it took place in a grander scheme: it was a crucial responsibility. I could've easily made the whole thing a disaster on my own that day, and fortunately I didn't, but I was obviously never going to make the perfect pitstop alone. That can only happen when every individual, every piece of equipment, every process and all the planning and preparation comes together at exactly the right moment on a Sunday afternoon. Once the boys had got over their anger and frustration at the disastrous start to the race, my ridiculous schoolboy reaction became a source of some amusement to them and I was the butt of a number of jokes for the next few weeks.

I wasn't used again in that race, but I was already addicted; I wanted more. Somehow the pressure of such an anxious and difficult situation and the importance of what we were doing, twinned with the fact we could influence the race result for our team, was a feeling I thrived on. My next few pitstops over the early part of the season went well, and though I felt incredibly nervous before each one, I managed to remain more composed instead of acting like an accident-prone, overexcited puppy. Very quickly it became clear that the occasional involvement just wasn't enough to satisfy my cravings. I wanted extra responsibility. I needed to be at the centre of the operation. My life had been completely transformed by the drama and excitement of Formula One, and I loved every bloody second of it.

3

PARANOIA AND PLAYBOYS

Anarchy often ruled behind the scenes, despite the precision and quality of work taking place in the garages. I suspect McLaren would've loved a team of perfectly cloned, robotic mechanics and engineers that could meet the company's unique and constant demands for attention to detail; a crew that represented the company in a polished corporate manner. What Ron Dennis had instead was a group that worked impeccably in the team colours, but once set free from the shackles of the racetrack, enjoyed the liberal, lavish behaviour that Formula One insiders thrived on at the time. I soon learned that working in F1 brought with it an often debauched and hedonistic lifestyle.

I've found myself in the back of a stretch limousine as drugs were passed around freely, even though the teams obviously had a total ban on drug use. On one occasion an F1 driver was dangled out of the window of a moving car for accidentally knocking over someone else's line of cocaine. I visited parties where there was almost no attempt to conceal the class A drug-taking happening on the dance floor, and at others, high-class models and prostitutes were selected and paid for by teams to adorn their glamorous venues. I've heard of at least one F1 driver who was caught drink-driving in Monaco, but was let off because the officer who'd caught him was later very well 'looked after' at the next Grand Prix as a special guest, and the incident went undocumented.

There've been a long list of cover-ups and deliberately misleading stories over the years. I'm sure it's even worse if you go back another generation of the sport, but F1 was a wild and fun place to be during my time. Luckily, I managed to stay out of serious trouble, but was never far away from a bit of fun and a joke. I covertly appeared in the back of almost every celebratory Ferrari team photo throughout 2006, by running over at the last moment as the team were assembling in the pitlane and jumping up in my McLaren kit. I even ended up on the back cover of Michael Schumacher's biography, buried in amongst the red team shirts in one picture.

I jokingly threw a Bacardi and Coke into the face of a very drunk Schuey at a Mercedes celebration in Germany, and once rewired the horn into the brake pedal of our test driver Darren Turner's road car while he was out on track. We've been thrown out of bars and night-clubs and had to send letters of apology, together with signed team caps and merchandise, in order to be allowed to remain in certain hotels after more destructive incidents. We just couldn't help ourselves, but over time, I've managed to convince myself it was our way of letting our hair down and off-setting the high pressure, punishing hours and gruelling schedules during that era of Formula One. Whilst it's not an excuse, it might at least serve as an explanation for some of our more questionable behaviour.

As a young man in F1, I partied hard. On more than one occasion I remember my phone's morning wake-up alarm going off while I was still leaping around a dance floor somewhere. We became skilled at sneaking back into hotels undetected, usually through side doors, while our elder, more responsible teammates unsuspectingly had breakfast a few metres away. After a super-quick shower and change, we were back downstairs and ready to return to work again. Tiredness and hangovers were something I managed to deal with in my younger days (I guess we all do) and it wasn't uncommon to repeat the process night after night, something I couldn't even dream of doing today.

Despite playing as hard as we did, though, we always managed to find a way to focus on the job when it mattered.

Friday was normally a traditional night off from the booze, mostly because it was our longest day at the track. Having started around 7 a.m., if we were finished in the garages by 11 to 11:30 p.m., it was deemed a pretty good day and it'd guarantee at least seven hours of much-needed sleep and recovery time after the previous few evenings of partying. That said, I remember a particularly horrific occasion in Brazil, after two near-sleepless nights out, when at around 11 p.m. on Friday evening all we had left to do was push our car along the pitlane to the FIA garage and check its weights and measurements for legality – a mere formality. Imagine my horror when we wheeled the car onto the official precision flat plate, only to discover the measurements all pointed to some serious chassis damage. A significant crack was then uncovered beneath the driver's seat area. I couldn't believe it. I was exhausted, broken and already desperate for sleep. Back to the garage we went and the resulting chassis change meant I finally rolled into bed around 4 a.m.

Although I loved finally being part of the pitstop crew, I'd become desperate to move into a more permanent, active role than my occasional nose cone changes. Annoyingly, though, without someone actually leaving the team, key spots on the pitstop crew didn't open up very often. Still, I got variety, working in a number of fringe positions, starting with holding open the sprung 'dead man's handle' on the refuelling rig, which was a safety device to automatically shut off fuel flow in the case of an accident; I held the 'splash board', a long lollipop-type device, like a protective screen on a stick, which prevented the fuel nozzle from spraying potentially explosive fluid onto the hot exhausts and brakes at the rear; I steadied the car; I cleaned the radiator ducts; I adjusted the front wing; I topped up the engine's pneumatic system. I did all sorts of things when needed at different times over my first year, but I was adamant I wanted to get myself into a more regular, more senior position as quickly as possible.

Eventually, at the end of the 2002 season somebody left the race team and I was moved onto the right rear corner crew, initially as 'wheel-off man', and I loved it. I was involved in every single pitstop from then on, taking off the right rear wheel and dumping it on the ground behind me, then quickly turning round to pull on the release handle of the refuelling nozzle, in order to assist the fuel man. It felt like an added responsibility, which fed my narcissistic tendencies for a while longer. I was in my element.

Refuelling was a major part of pitstops at that time and it was generally the procedure that determined the total length of most stops. Once all four wheels were changed, everyone would wait for the fuel nozzle to detach, before releasing the car back into the race. As such, it was a job we worked on improving wherever we could, and one of my favourite technical pitstop tricks was in this area. Once the nozzle was attached to the car, fuel would flow through the giant, aircraft specification hose at 12 litres per second. When the system had delivered the required amount of fuel, a motorised butterfly valve inside the nozzle would close, and once completely sealed, the lights on the display would change from red to green. That was our cue to pull back on the safety and release handles before detaching the nozzle. Every team had the same standard equipment and it was strictly forbidden to modify or adapt it in any way.

Some years earlier, the Benetton team had removed a fuel filter inside the nozzle to speed up the flow of fuel into the car. The theory might have been correct, but the most infamous pitstop fire in modern history, on Jos Verstappen's Bennetton car in the Hockenheim pitlane in Germany in 1994, meant they were rumbled. Even tighter restrictions and checks on the equipment were immediately implemented.

Realising there was nothing we could do to enhance the rig, we focused on the human factor instead. There was always a moment of delay between the required amount of fuel going into the car and the motorised shut-off valve fully closing. That delay was then increased by the mechanic's reaction time in removing the nozzle from the car once the green light had flashed up. Our solution was ingenious: we rigged the fuel man with a stethoscope, which traversed up his sleeve and into a discrete earpiece. The other end (the bit the doctor normally presses to your chest) was pushed onto the fuel nozzle for each stop. The electric motor inside whirred into action when it was time to close the butterfly valve, and by listening in, the fuel man was able to react more quickly. He could start the process of pulling back on the release handles and by the time the valve was completely closed and the green light illuminated, the nozzle was almost detached. It might have only saved us a second or less with each stop, but those margins were sometimes the difference between us getting out ahead of, or behind, our main rivals. It was also technically legal, since we hadn't modified the standard fuel rig in any way, although we knew the FIA would have almost certainly frowned upon it, had they found out. We went to great lengths to keep the whole thing top secret.

I loved the technical arms race in Formula One, and pitstops had definitely become part of that game over the years. There was pride at stake, as much as it affected the race result, and people looked for any and every advantage. They were spending millions of pounds on technology in order to shave tenths of seconds off a lap time when the same, and much more, could often be achieved from within the pitlane. McLaren explored new ways to cover every possible eventuality and scenario, and whenever we found a potential advantage, it had to be shrouded in secrecy and kept away from the prying eyes of other teams for as long as possible.

We went to all kinds of lengths to protect our latest developments, but the cloak-and-dagger attitude was perhaps best summed up by an incident that took place later in my career. We'd developed a new front wing, which the wind tunnel and Test Team had shown to deliver a substantial gain in performance, but because the new design could, in theory, be easily replicated by other teams, it was imperative that we held off its public introduction for as long as possible. The FIA had banned the practice of putting covers onto wings to hide them, because they'd rightly wanted fans to be able to see the cars properly in the garages. In fact, it was a move almost certainly triggered by our own Chief Designer, Adrian Newey, who'd commissioned an enormous set of six-foot-high black screens that could be wheeled across the front of the garages when we wanted to hide the cars from view. I have to admit it was a bit ridiculous – we could barely see out, let alone anyone else see in. In fact it was so extreme and imposing, it got nicknamed 'Adrian's Wall' within the team. So with Adrian still keen to hide our game-changing new front wing from the prying photographers, he came up with a new plan. He instructed us all to completely ignore the front of the car, but make a huge fuss of the rear wing instead. Nothing had changed back there, but with us going to great lengths to form human walls and distract photographers, the ploy meant nobody paid a blind bit of notice to the real changes hiding in plain sight and it was only at the next event that people began to understand the truth behind our reverse psychology.

Every team was spying on everybody else, and they employed their own photographers with a brief, outlining what they wanted to see on every other car – wings, cockpits, floors and suspension. Every Monday morning after a Grand Prix, in our own drawing office, the designers would have a stack of pictures on the desks, all of them focusing on different detailed aspects of our rivals' cars. Today, of course, the photographs come through digitally and can be analysed almost immediately, even whilst the race is still going on. As pit crew, part of our role was to try to prevent anyone from taking pictures, particularly of the highly sensitive underside of the car when it was being craned on or off a recovery truck after a crash. Our biggest truckies would stand in front of the photographers, just to make their lives a little harder, a ploy that rarely worked, but one I got the impression they enjoyed.

We'd listen in to the other teams' radio chatter over a race week-end, in the hope of picking up information and clues as to their different race strategies. It was actually somebody's job on the team to scan all the frequencies up and down the pitlane in order to eavesdrop on anyone we liked. Everybody was doing it, not just us, so we invented coded methods of relaying our tactics and technical feedback without giving the game away, and I imagine most others were doing the same, which almost made the whole process pointless. So convinced were we that our main rival, Ferrari, was listening to every word we uttered on the airwaves that our routine morning radio check process would begin every single day with our systems engineer, Tyler Alexander, saying, 'Good morning, Mr Ascanelli,' as a little cheeky nod to the fact we knew the senior Ferrari man was hearing it. It wasn't long before expensive, military-grade encrypted radio systems had been introduced by most of the big teams.

That paranoia, particularly between us and Ferrari, fuelled by our fierce on-track rivalry over the years, took a number of twists and turns. The Italian team once invited us to come and test at their privately owned circuit, Mugello, in the heart of beautiful Tuscany. They were trying to encourage the big teams to start using the facility as a regular test track, presumably as an extra revenue generator. But such was our obsession with uncovering their 'underhand ulterior motives', that although we eventually agreed to go and test there, we sent a team of technical surveillance detection experts into the pitlane garages first to sweep for bugs and hidden filming devices. They didn't find anything.

In the constant battle to be prepared for any eventuality in pit-stops, a dedicated 'First Lap Crew' was formed. It came about after the team wasn't fully ready for an early first lap stop at the very short Austrian Grand Prix track. The cars came back round the one-minute lap so quickly and turned up in the pitlane whilst some people were still returning from the grid and sorting out equipment. The First Lap Crew comprised of people who didn't need to go to the grid for the Grand Prix start; it was a skeleton team, but one that was well drilled in dealing with any situation. Their mandate was now to handle any stop that happened during the first lap of the race, and after that they'd stand down and the full pitstop crew would take over. Smaller qualifying-only crews were formed for each individual car, whereas normally in a race the full pitstop crew would service both cars. It was their role to deal with quick-reaction tyre changes during the highly time-sensitive Saturday sessions, when it was common for both cars to pit for new tyres at the same time, and stacking them up in a queue one behind the other to wait for one pit crew could've left one at a disadvantage. The pitstop equipment was always under constant review to improve speed and reliability, and whereas before we'd just service the wheel guns, jacks and airlines at the end of each season, now they were given a formal, regular lifing schedule to ensure reliability, just like every part of the car. The whole thing was being taken to a new level and to be involved at the heart of such a high-tech, often clandestine operation was quite a privilege. Over the years my pitstop role changed and I moved through operating the wheel gun, fuel nozzle and front jack in different seasons, but all the way through, I was loving every minute, and quite literally living the dream I'd had for so many years, becoming central to the high-tech, cutting-edge development process. Pitstops are the thing I miss most today.

I wouldn't have classed myself as an out-and-out rebel, I wasn't necessarily one for making deliberate statements through my behaviour, but I did have fairly strong opinions about what I liked – and didn't like. So following the first race of the 2004 season in Australia, on a rare day off before we travelled to Malaysia for round two, I didn't go to the beach, or head out on a fishing boat with some of the other lads. I went to the hairdresser instead.

I was very conscious of my appearance back then – some have even rudely gone as far as to suggest I was vain (OK, I was vain) – but as the youngest in the garage and very different to some of the strait-laced guys on the McLaren team, it set me apart. I had coloured highlights at times; there were periods with long hair, short hair, and all sorts in between. Whenever I wore a cap, which I did a lot in the garage, it'd be back to front, which I know must have been annoying for McLaren's management. I enjoyed the 'sport' of trying to wind up the bosses, without causing too much trouble. I just wanted to be a little bit different and a bit more stylish than some of the older lads who had been around the garage much longer.

With reasonably long hair at the time (which I must've already known made the notoriously particular Ron Dennis twinge with rage) I decided a change of look was overdue. So, having spotted a funky-looking hair-dresser's in downtown Melbourne the previous day, I walked in and asked if they could give me dreadlocks. The shop was technically closed for a training day, but with a little persuasion, aided by my charming English accent, I managed to convince them to use me as a model for the trainees. A bunch of inexperienced stylists were to be let loose, just to see what they could come up with. It was a cool place, so I wasn't too worried; I knew I'd end up with something a bit edgy, which was exactly what I was after. What I hadn't expected was the pain. The process of continually back-combing, pulling and separating my hair, in the hands of various young apprentices, lasted for an incredible six and a half hours and is still the most painful experience of my life. I so wanted to cry, but it took every ounce of bravery and strength of mind not to give in before the audience of on-looking trainee girls.

Once the ordeal was finally over, I was very happy, not least because the attack on my scalp had finished, but also because I loved the new look. It was a bit grungy, a bit surfer, and a bit gangsta-rap. But above all it was different, and I thought it expressed some of the finer sides of my person-ality at the time. I walked out feeling like I'd made good use of my day off, even if I hadn't planned to spend it entirely in the salon, and headed back to the hotel to show the lads. I think most people genuinely liked it, although their overwhelming follow-up was less thrilling.

'Ron's gonna fucking love that!' remarked more than one of them.

We flew on to Malaysia and had a great few days by the pool, before preparing for the next race, and it was only when the Grand Prix weekend approached that I became slightly nervous of what Ron might think. I hadn't really thought about it at all until everyone else brought it up, but I always imagined that in Ron's ideal world, everyone at McLaren would have worn the same stock Lego-man hairstyle. It'd be cut to a standard length, using a precision-machined jig to ensure regularity. The colour, of course, would have to be black.

I spent the Malaysian GP keeping my head down, wearing a cap for as much of it as I could. Wherever possible I stayed well away from Ron, but did catch him staring over at me with his usual stern look from the other side of the garage on one occasion. Not once did he speak to me though, so by the time we headed back to England for a week at home between races, I assumed I'd been worrying about nothing. I was in the clear, I thought. Just a day or so into the relaxing break at home, though, having proudly displayed my new dreads around town, the phone rang. It was Dave Ryan.

'Elvis, we've got a problem and I need you to come into the office,' he said.

'Er, what is it, Dave?' I nervously replied.

'It's your hair, mate. We need to have a chat about your hair.'

When I arrived at the factory to see Dave, he was almost apologetic, even going as far as to tell me he thought my new hair looked pretty good. The problem was, Ron didn't agree. Apparently his exact words upon seeing me for the first time that weekend had been less than complimentary: 'What the fuck is that?'

I was told in no uncertain terms that I could not turn up to the next race with my dreadlocks as they were. 'I don't care what you do,' said Dave. 'But you need to do *something* with it.' So with little choice I agreed to cut them short, even though they hadn't had enough time to 'settle' and it went against all the advice I'd received from my Aussie salon. Still, a slightly smarter, shorter version, delivered by my local hairdresser, actually looked OK, but as soon as I put my motorbike helmet on to go out for a ride, it pulled all the dreads out. It looked terrible. Faced with a dishevelled mess in the mirror, the only remaining option was to reluctantly shave the lot off.

When I arrived at the next event, my hair had gone from around eight inches in length to just a few millimetres and everyone was pretty shocked. Dave was grateful and thanked me for my understanding, and when the senior management team arrived, McLaren MD Martin Whitmarsh called me out into the pitlane for a private word. At that time, I hadn't had much to do with Martin. He was the big boss of the company, below only Ron in terms of seniority, so when he asked for a quiet word with a cheeky young race mechanic, eyebrows were raised, none more so than mine. As we walked together out of the garage and into the pitlane, it felt as if the rest of the team had ground to a halt and was staring; I felt like a cowboy from out of town, walking into a saloon bar in an old western. I was nervous and hugely self-conscious.

Outside, Martin was full of smiles and friendliness. With his hand on my shoulder, he told me how incredibly grateful he and Ron were for the sacrifice and commitment I'd shown to McLaren by altering my look to align with the company's values. He poured out the compliments, saying how I'd been flagged as a rising star within the organisation by the management team and that they all agreed how lucky they were to have me there. This selfless act had cemented their faith and trust in me and both he and Ron wanted to show their appreciation.

While I did my best not to laugh at my idiotic colleagues, some of whom were now clowning around behind Martin, making blow-job gestures in my eye line, the words that came out of his mouth next were a promise that would save my career a few years later. 'So, Marc – Elvis – if there's anything that Ron, myself or the board can do to say thank you from McLaren, either now or in the future, please just come and ask,' he said.

I laughed, telling him I might take him up on his offer one day, whilst awkwardly trying not to breathe last night's alcoholic fumes into his face.

'No, do, seriously, I mean it,' said Martin. 'I may well forget this conversation, my memory's not what it used to be, but I want you to remember it. Remind me when you think of a way we can help you.'

The moment Martin had gone, everyone wanted to know what on earth had happened. There was an air of disbelief when I told them. 'Elvis, you are one seriously jammy fucker!' laughed one of the lads, and I had to agree. Suggestions on what I should use my 'golden ticket' for ranged from a personal parking space on the VIP driveway at McLaren's swanky factory, to helicopter transfers to and from the racetrack. Someone suggested a seat next to Ron on the pit wall on Grand Prix day. I figured it prudent to bank it as a get-out-of-jail-free card. A couple of years down the line, it would prove to be one of the smartest decisions of my career. With hindsight, Martin's pleasant overreaction was much more likely to be related to an HR-based concern about forcing an employee to have a particular hairstyle, rather than a genuine gratitude for my 'sacrifice' but hey, I took it and I'm glad I did.

The F1 paddock pass we had to wear around our necks at all times at the track was known at the time as 'The Key to the City', or 'Bernie's Party Pass', after the Godfather of F1, Bernie Ecclestone. In the right hands it could usher you straight into the hottest nightspots in town, even allowing the lowliest of mechanics to jump the most exclusive of queues. Of course, every now and then, we'd boldly walk to the front of a long line for a high-end bar or restaurant and nonchalantly flash the pass, only to be confronted and unceremoniously turned away by an unimpressed bouncer who had no idea what Formula One even was. You win some, you lose some I guess.

Partying was something that went hand in hand with F1 in those days, and most of the time it was the teams who were organising the most extravagant nights in a Grand Prix city. I've no doubt that in the eras before mine – in the seventies, eighties and nineties – there were even more extreme gatherings. But whilst the early 2000s were a hangover from those crazy days, there was now even more tobacco-funded cash to blow on the big nights out as the sport's budgets spiralled out of control. As a young man in my early twenties, I loved it, and took full advantage in the evenings, but very rarely was I ever late for work the next day. Despite feeling awful inside, I had a fortunate knack of looking half decent on the outside and often managed to disguise my hangover. It frustrated the hell out of my mates, some of whom weren't so lucky and looked like death every morning in the hotel lobby after a big one. Just occasionally, though, I slipped up and didn't quite make the call time.

Once in Monaco, after a huge night out following the race, I managed to wake up in the wrong hotel room, with my phone dead and the team bus having left an hour earlier for the forty-five-minute drive from Monte Carlo to Nice airport. *I was about to miss my first ever flight home!* Desperate, I ran around the upmarket Columbus Hotel, head pounding, gathering my belongings together, and decided my best and only hope of making the plane was to somehow blag a helicopter to the airport. I knew there was a helipad at the end of the hotel's garden, so I ran for it, dragging my half-open bag behind me. Once there, I begged to jump the queue by offering to pay double for an already very expensive ticket for the next chopper. It was way more than I could afford but crucially got me into the air around twenty minutes after waking up. At Nice airport, I jumped from the helicopter and ran into the terminal, still half dressed and certainly not in the immaculate Hugo Boss team travel uniform that everyone else was wearing. Miraculously, though, I made my flight with minutes to spare. Looking back, it was pretty rock'n'roll, but it did cost me yet another company reprimand for 'not representing the team in the manner McLaren expected of its employees'.

Then, at the last race of the 2005 season I went one better, missing the only flight of my career, although I like to think there were some mitigating and frankly quite terrifying circumstances on that occasion. Red Bull had put on a spectacular end-of-season party on a floating pontoon on the river Bund in Shanghai, and that night I was one of the last to leave. I'd been separated from most of my teammates, having lost my phone at a party the night before, so I spent much of the evening with friends from the Williams team. I was having a great time, but as the sun came up, everybody realised we needed to get back to our respective rooms for the flight back to London. The Williams lads headed to one hotel, I jumped in a cab to mine.

I remember drunkenly trying to put my seat belt on, but it was broken, so I gave up on the first rule of road safety and promptly fell asleep. The next thing I knew, I was being thrown around violently in the back seat, my head smacking against the window as I landed awkwardly on my crumpled neck. The car had tipped onto its side and was sliding along the highway, where it screamed with the most awful noise to an eventual halt. I had no idea what had just happened. I was covered in glass. I felt numb. There was a cut on my shoulder, but the driver, who was now in a heap on the passenger side, had blood smeared across his face and was far worse off.

Some people helped to get us both out of the car and we sat by the side of the road in shock, staring at the overturned car until an ambulance arrived and took us to hospital. I slumped down in a waiting room for half an hour without being able to understand or communicate with anyone, before deciding I was fine, suddenly realising it was far more important for me to get back to the hotel.

By the time I arrived in the lobby, the team had left for the airport, and without a phone they had no way of getting in touch with me – or vice versa. I looked a mess, with cuts, scrapes and blood on my shirt, and although a number of concerned hotel staff tried to help me, I didn't have the time to explain what had happened. Instead I ran to the room for a very quick change and splash of water on my face, before grabbing everything and running down to the foyer to jump into another cab to the airport.

When I arrived my worst fears were confirmed. The flight was closed and everyone was gone. I was on the other side of the world all alone, I didn't have enough money for another flight, no way of contacting anybody and no idea what to do. I argued with the British Airways staff, pleading my case to board my flight, but got nowhere – it was too late.

Booking another ticket was going to cost well over a thousand pounds and I had no credit card on me. I was panicking.

Then, all of a sudden, way off in the distance, like a shining beacon of light, I saw our travel company rep walking through the terminal. I ran towards him and after almost collapsing at his feet, explained the whole sorry situation. He managed to get in touch with the team and got me onto the next flight home via Germany, without me having to dig into my own pockets, which was a minor miracle. When I finally arrived back home and was able to check my voicemails on another phone, I was bombarded with a series of panicked messages. Apparently the guys had got onto the plane, and having heard about my situation, spent a small fortune on the airline's satellite phone to warn my family. I don't think they were too surprised, which probably says a lot about my behaviour back then.

Despite all of this, I took my job as a race mechanic and member of the pitstop crew very seriously at McLaren. All of us were well aware of the potential consequences of getting something wrong, but we'd been brought up in an environment that fostered, and even encouraged, a work hard, play hard mentality. As the sport grew more and more corporate and mobile phones and social media grew in sophistication and popularity, teams had to start protecting their public image more and more. Even Red Bull, the team who'd burst onto the F1 scene with an open-door policy to their bar-raising parties, the team who'd branded themselves very deliberately as the wild, fun and extremely social players in the game, changed their ways. By 2007 a conscious decision was made to cut back on their extravagant events and the focus switched to winning races. A year and a half later they did, along with the first of four championships in a row for Sebastian Vettel and the team.

The wild and crazy days seemed to be over. For a while.

4

RON'S HOUSE

Presiding over all this madness, unknowingly at least, was Ron Dennis, McLaren's eccentric yet formidable team principal, and a man who'd overseen seven Constructors' Championships with McLaren and, in the end, ten Drivers' World Titles by the time he stepped down in 2016. Knowing what I did of him back then, I imagine my extra-curricular antics over the years must have been a source of constant irritation, although I could have said the same about his unusual behaviour on many occasions. Still, I'd like to think there was a mutual respect buried somewhere deep beneath our very different working practices.

When I first arrived at McLaren in 2000, Ron was as famous and idolised as any driver, in my mind at least. His name was synonymous not only with the team, but with Formula One as a whole, and the success he'd achieved over the years was unprecedented. I felt privileged to be wearing the uniform, walking through his immaculate factory in Sheerwater, Woking, and to be mingling with the best of the best in motor racing engineering. For those first few weeks on the job, I worked at the team HQ, still dazed and in awe of my new surroundings, without ever seeing Ron Dennis in the flesh. His presence was everywhere though, even if not physically, and it was pretty obvious from talking to people that things had to be done a certain way because *that's just how Ron liked it*. The old McLaren factory was part of an ageing industrial estate and, from the outside, it blended in with the other innocuous, run-of-the-mill companies sharing the site. Walk through the black glass doors, though, and you entered Ron's World.

For someone like me, who'd grown up in motorsport and always dreamt of making it to the hallowed halls of F1, that building was like a cross between Buckingham Palace and Willy Wonka's Chocolate Factory. Everything was impressive, spotless, futuristic, intriguing and expensive. I was scared to touch anything, but wanted to touch it all. It felt like I shouldn't really have been in there in the first place. Ron had created an enigmatic, mysteriously secretive and impenetrable facility that matched the glamour and exclusivity of the F1 paddock, and when I finally got the privilege of being allowed inside, I was as impressed as anyone could be.

That's exactly what Ron wanted, of course: to impress people. He truly believed he was the best at what he did and his team should be a reflection of that. From day one, it was very quickly drummed into me that the standards were high at McLaren, the highest of any team in the sport, but never high enough. It was a giant leap from the Formula 3 and Formula 3000 racing categories, where I'd always prided myself on personally raising the bar when it came to attention to detail.

Ron demanded excellence from everyone and his undisputed OCD-like tendencies filtered down through the entire organisation. This was a guy who had the gravel on his own driveway cleaned regularly and apparently demanded the slots on screw heads be lined up the same way on various fittings around the building. This fussy, fastidious attitude rubbed off on everybody and after spending nearly a decade in Ron's environment, I now drive my wife crazy by incessantly reloading the dishwasher in the most efficient way possible and get unreasonably annoyed if even the tiniest bit of a black rubbish bag pokes out from under the lid of the kitchen bin.

It takes a certain type of character to be able to work for Ron, and I've seen many talented people arrive only to find themselves unable to cope with his demands. But I strongly suspect that most people at

McLaren would also agree that he was a brilliant man, albeit uniquely quirky; a man with a vision well beyond his years and a man who cared deeply about making the company the best it could be. Anyone who worked for him usually had their eyes opened to a new level of perfectionism. I thought of that as being a good thing, but it's not always easy to appreciate when you're immersed in his universe day in, day out.

When I finally did get to see him in person, I thought he was an impressive man. He marched around purposefully and regally, sometimes with an entourage of minions alongside him, taking twice his number of steps just to keep up. His appearances on the factory floor were often preceded by a warning of his imminent arrival and the already ridiculously tidy facilities would be given a panic-stricken once-over, with anything that wasn't absolutely imperative to proceedings, or nailed down, hidden away in a cupboard until he was gone. I wasn't sure if it was fear or respect that people had for Ron, but whilst I was definitely frightened of him in the beginning, that was transformed into undoubted and unrivalled respect over the years.

Recently, I tried to recall the first time I ever actually met him, but having thought about it, I don't think I ever really did *meet* Ron. I was never introduced to him, not formally anyway. Throughout my time at McLaren, I only spoke to him a handful of times in person, and most of those exchanges weren't anything more than a sentence or two. I never went to his office, though on reflection, I'm sure that was a good thing. I'd have had to *really* screw up for that to happen, and I often imagined the space as a large circular room with Ron sat in a giant black leather chair, stroking a white cat perched on his lap. In reality, though, having learnt a little more about him over the years, I now know there's no way he'd allow a filthy animal to make contact with his pristine dark suit. (And if he did ever have a cat, it would have been McLaren grey, not white.)

He wasn't a hands-on people manager, but he did have a very capable and authoritative lieutenant in Race Team Manager Dave Ryan. Dave ran an extremely tight ship and enforced Ron's unprecedented high standards, both at the factory and the racetrack. He was exactly the right man for the job and he made sure the team stood out in terms of presentation and preparation. At times, Ron's pedantic requests drove us all crazy, but he was forever making sure that McLaren looked and behaved like McLaren.

Funnily enough, some of the things that made Ron's McLaren so brilliantly impressive were also the same things that made it such a bloody difficult place to work. When I think back to the old factory, I remember having a constant battle with management about whether or not I could have a radio on the worktop in the race bays. I couldn't bear not having something to break the silence during the day, but for them it went against the team ethos. To have something as ugly and un-McLaren-like as a radio on display, along with the unordered, uncontrollable noise it would produce was a definite no-no. On more than one occasion I snuck the radio on when working late at night in the factory and forget to put it away when I left. The next morning, the radio would be gone, confiscated, and it would take another grovelling visit to a senior manager's office to get it back.

Everything had to be meticulously clean. Whenever we stripped a car in the race or test bays, normally without a huge amount of time to complete the job, we had to wipe down every part that came off. I mean, that was fine, until someone had the temerity to dirty the benches and the rules were changed. Then we'd have to take each item off the car and carry them right around the corner to another area of the factory, where we could clean them out of sight, before bringing the offending parts back to the bays to start working on them properly. It was so frustrating and often felt like we spent more time keeping the cupboards and worktops spotless than we ever did working on the cars themselves.

However, if the old factory had some annoying rules and procedures, it was absolutely nothing compared to the futuristic, spaceship-like showpiece that became our new HQ: the McLaren Technology Centre (MTC). Make no mistake: MTC was Ron's baby. Opened in

2003, it encapsulated everything he stood for and was a direct extension of his personality and characteristics. It also showed just how
tenacious and driven he was to see his futuristic vision right through
to reality, and for that I have nothing but total awe. The old Sheerwater factory was as good as it could have been given it was a rented
building on a Woking industrial estate. It served a purpose and the
team won Formula One World Championships from within it, but
Ron needed to have total control and he couldn't do that while at the
behest of a landlord.

I remember first hearing of the new factory shortly after I'd started
at the team and I was excited at the prospect of a new base; it was
always going to be pretty special. Then one day, we were presented
with an architect's model for the vision of McLaren's future and everyone was blown away. (The well-known architect Sir Norman Foster
was responsible for the design – he was also behind such famous buildings as the Supreme Court Building in Singapore and Wembley
Stadium.) It looked incredible, like a giant spacecraft in the middle of
Surrey. These new plans were a massive upgrade from what we were
used to, especially the setting, which comprised a lake and acres and
acres of beautiful countryside. It looked picture perfect and space age,
but it seemed such an ambitious project that many people believed its
completion would be years, maybe a decade, into the future. A few lads
joked they wouldn't be around to see it. Luckily, Ron had other ideas.

It all seemed to happen pretty quickly for such an enormous project, and before we knew it, the team was being taken for construction
site visits to the new location about a mile up the road. The surrounding area was beautiful, nestled away from the traffic in one of the
greenest, quietest parts of the Surrey countryside. It was hard to
believe we were so close to the uninspiring, industrialised zone of our
current building. Amazingly, we were locating our new factory on
greenbelt land, which tells me that Ron probably used his persuasive
powers to get an exceptional deal, with conditions. One of the planning restrictions was that the buildings couldn't go over a certain

height, or be visible from the road. So not to be outdone, or overly restricted, he decided we'd build *underground*.

Inside, although it was still a building site, we couldn't help but get excited about our new surroundings. The building gleamed. Vast boulevards ringed the outside of the structure, which was made up of huge glass-fronted areas and miles of shiny, perfectly tiled flooring. I loved it, and I remember thinking it was just so Ron Dennis. He'd publicly justified the enormous investment with one of his typically enigmatic quotes: 'Put a man in a dark room, he's hot, it smells bad, versus a guy in a cool room, well lit, smells nice . . .' he told the press one day. 'When you throw a decision at those two individuals, who's going to be better equipped to effect good judgement and make a good decision?' It was true, and I felt very proud to be part of this futuristic, innovative company.

Of course, the doomsayers at McLaren predicted it would be a difficult place to work, a building that was so focused on looking good, neglecting that it was actually a place to design, manufacture and build Formula One cars. For me, I thought the state-of-the-art facilities and equipment, together with the beautiful and inspirational environment, would be enough to outweigh any impracticalities. In the end, when we finally moved in during the 2003 season, both camps could actually claim to have made an accurate assessment.

The day we moved in, a lot of the older guys were really sad to be leaving the Sheerwater factory. They'd worked there for a long time; a lot of them had experienced a number of dramatic chapters in the McLaren story and enjoyed some major success at the old place. Change came hard to some of them; they were comfortable with what they already had. I was different, a cheeky young whippersnapper who'd only been with McLaren for a couple of years. I couldn't wait to get up the road and unpack.

The completed MTC was huge, pristinely white inside, and futuristic. We had space, storage, and brand-new equipment all around us – I couldn't have asked for more. Everything was shiny and spotlessly clean and, ultimately, bloody impressive. It felt like we were working on a magazine shoot, or a film set, with a series of spectacular views from the race bays that overlooked the lake outside and acres of manicured grounds beyond. There was a lot that was aesthetically so much better, and we had to be hugely grateful for that. Very quickly, though, the challenges of working in a giant, pristine showroom began to present themselves.

There were simple things: for example, the sheer size of the building meant it took longer to get anywhere than it had before. The departments we needed to visit regularly, either to deliver or collect parts, or even just to talk to people, could be a long way away. It slowed the whole working process down, when we were often up against the clock. Meanwhile, new rules meant there was to be no more coffee in the race bays. All desks and workbenches had to be completely cleared each evening before going home, even if you were halfway through a job. Packing everything up and putting it all away at night (just to get it all back out again before picking up where you left off the next morning) became a very frustrating part of everybody's working day – we could lose about an hour a day to this seemingly futile exercise.

I'd assumed that with a brand-new, purpose-designed facility our race trucks would be housed inside the building, not only to allow them to be easily prepared in all weathers, but to keep them close to the race bays where there was a constant need to load and unload cars and spares. As it was, the trucks couldn't have been further from where the cars were being built, and furthermore, in order to remove the fully assembled cars from the race bays, they had to be lifted onto a trolley and manoeuvered through a series of tight gaps and right-angle corners before travelling the entire length of the factory to get outside and into the transporters. It took for ever, and I recall one or two very costly accidents when heavy machinery was dropped, shattering the pricey tiled flooring in the process. On another occasion, a piece of kit was shoved enthusiastically into a glass elevator, smashing the frontage to pieces. This being McLaren, those incidents of wear

and tear were normally repaired within hours and rarely spoken of
again.

The place was a maze, and one thing that used to drive everyone
mad was the car park. From day one it was too small to accommodate
the staff that worked there, but more annoying was the fact you
couldn't just pop out to your car if you needed something during the
day. To get from the car to the race bays meant walking across the car
park and into a rotunda, down a deep stairwell underground, through
three sets of doors, along an almost endless white corridor which ran
the entire length of the building, until another stairwell brought you
up to ground-floor level; this was followed by a walk through Mc-
Laren's various departments and into the annexed race bay area. If
you forgot something: *tough*. Chances were, you weren't going back for
it unless it was really important; the journey was just too far. I'd feel
dizzy just thinking about the logistics sometimes.

For all its nuances and impracticalities, the MTC was, and is, a
stunning building to look at, which was exactly what Ron had set out
to achieve. He wanted to be able to show off the premises to impressed
clients and sponsors, and as with everything he did, he wanted the
MTC to be the best in the business. It's always easy to criticise ideas
that don't work well, or any projects that might have deviated from the
norm. But the reality was that McLaren's new HQ was a marketing
tool as much as it was an engineering facility and that function, in the
end, was just as important to the business.

Shortly after moving in, the Queen (yes, Her Majesty) came to
officially open the factory, and while the place was locked down by the
biggest security operation I'd ever seen, I was chosen as one of a handful of people to meet her as Ron gave The Grand Tour. After a formal
briefing on how to address Her Majesty and the strict list of dos and
don'ts of royal etiquette, I promptly forgot the lot. As she arrived in
the race bays for our official handshakes, I moved towards her, extending both hands like a crazy person (a definite *don't*). I'd become
completely and utterly star-struck. I couldn't tell you what we said to

each other, it's all just a blur, although I do remember there were a number of furious stares from her close protection security staff. It's a wonder I wasn't arrested on the spot.

The fact that the United Kingdom's ruling monarch came to open Ron's new factory (and then a few years later, the British prime minister, David Cameron, opened McLaren Automotive's new building next door) says a lot about the kind of man Ron was, not to mention the kind of business he was leading. We were highly respected. People regarded McLaren as being the most professional team in the business; we were considered to be one of the most innovative too, and having a successful spell at McLaren on your CV did you no harm at all. What had begun years ago as just a small F1 team was now a group of market-leading global technology companies. And every part of it was based on Ron Dennis's personality and values.

Ron Dennis also led the way in the paddock and pitlane, too.

Take the McLaren Brand Centre as an example, a huge, mobile, head-turning, three-storey glass-fronted building where the team is fed and their guests wined, dined and entertained at races. Each team's paddock base first started its evolutionary journey years ago as a double-decker bus, or 'motorhome', with an awning off to the side. By the time we'd finished with its design, it had become a purpose-built temporary building, which was so far advanced and so much more impressive than everything else that the other teams had little choice but to join the revolution, or look second-rate by comparison. The McLaren Brand Centre is the latest iteration and even today, nearly ten years on from its initial introduction, it still stands out from the crowd. You can argue all day that the modern palaces lining the paddock are overly extravagant, or even vulgar, but that's the glitz of Formula One. The wow factor has been one of the sport's selling points for years now and Ron's been instrumental in taking that pizzazz to new levels – over and over again. His motorhome was an extension of our factory, with the same design philosophy; and high fliers from different sponsorship companies couldn't help but have their heads turned by it. He once justified the enormous expense of his latest architectural masterpiece by reminding us that hundreds of millions of pounds worth of business deals had taken place inside its predecessor. When you thought about it that way, it made some sense.

Ron's vision didn't stop there, though. We revolutionised everything from the garage layout to our pit equipment, each time going bigger, better, or just better-looking. Eventually he decided that if we were really going to stand out as a team, then the people working in it needed to stand out too . . . and so began the clothing revolution at McLaren.

Traditionally, every team in F1 – and even every team in most types of motorsport – wore trousers and shirts as the basis for their working uniform. Colours and sponsors varied endlessly of course, but at McLaren we'd been pretty lucky, for a few years having Hugo Boss supply us with smart black trousers and a selection of grey or white shirts. There was always a mutual sympathy up and down pitlane, as well as a mutual mickey-taking obviously, for any team unlucky enough to be forced to wear outrageous, day-glo colours whenever a title sponsor changed. While we never ended up wearing some of the vile shades of pink, green or yellow that some teams did, we definitely got our turn at being the butt of the paddock jokes, most notably with McLaren's introduction of the pitlane 'onesie'.

I'll never forget the day Ron called the race team together at the factory to unveil and explain his thinking behind the upcoming year's mechanic team clothing. It was always a slightly nervous moment at the start of each season, finding out what had been chosen for us to wear at every Grand Prix, but that year rumours had been swirling for some time that our look would be very different. The fact Ron felt he had to personally convince us to buy into the concept put everyone on guard.

We were right to be concerned. We all gathered in the race bays and Ron arrived with Dave Ryan. A speech followed about how McLaren worked at the forefront of innovation, pushing boundaries in every area while reflecting the company's vision of how we presented ourselves. Ron wanted us to stand out from the crowd and to once again lead Formula One with our innovative technologies. And then the model walked in.

I didn't know whether to laugh (which I did nervously) or cry (and I was definitely weeping inside). The model, clearly embarrassed, was dressed in an all-in-one shiny black silk zip-up jumpsuit. It was like nothing I'd ever seen before, apart from on a toddler. Ron went on and on, explaining how the suit represented the future of F1 and how they were a technical, as well as stylistic, collaboration with our partners at Hugo Boss. He revelled in the model's demonstration of the zip-off arms and legs (for hot weather climates), and the advanced materials installed in the accompanying underwear (which apparently kept us warm at the colder races, but also cool at hotter ones). Ron made the outfit sound amazing, but it most definitely was not amazing. It was bloody awful.

Our disappointment must have been obvious, because he quickly assured us that once we were over the shock of seeing something so new and revolutionary, we'd end up loving it. More than that, he was convinced the rest of the teams in Formula One would all be wearing something similar the following year. I'm not sure if it was just to butter us up a bit after presenting us with our shiny black Babygros, but Ron then went on to talk about his vision for transforming McLaren's pitstop crew into stars, just like the drivers. He said he wanted to draw out the characters behind the masks; he reckoned an official website featuring our profiles would encourage McLaren fans to connect with the pit team. Ron even wanted to produce merchandise and trading cards, a bit like Top Trumps, for each member, so that people could collect and swap our mugs like football stickers. Thankfully, that idea quickly died on the vine.

When it came to wearing the suits at the racetrack, sartorial shame proved to be the least of our worries. Hugo Boss's state-of-the-art material didn't breathe. The onesies were heavy, so we sweated. The fabric wouldn't stretch and ripped daily, especially on the bigger-boned members of the team. The removable legs and their exposed zips, which sat just under the knee, were terribly placed and every time we knelt down on the ground to work on the car, it was like kneeling on a piece of Lego. There was also a big zip that ran up the front of the suit, which scratched the car's paintwork whenever one of us leant over to work on the chassis, which Ron hated. Crucially, the all-in-one design meant that whenever there was a certain call of nature it meant getting almost fully naked in a cubicle to be able to sit down on a toilet.

I hated it, we all did. I was embarrassed to wear that suit, whereas before, in my shirt-and-trousers combo, I'd felt proud. Still, looking back, the change was indicative of Ron's ambition. He was gradually building and reshaping the image of McLaren, a company that's since been renamed the McLaren Technology Group. Thanks to him, the team had become an exceptional brand, representing high technology, disruptive innovation and microscopic attention to detail. Ron was forever finding a way to push the envelope in every direction.

It wasn't long before the F1 Babygros mark two had arrived. There was elastic flex in key areas, repositioned zips, and even an arse-flap for those pressing toilet breaks. It turned out that the cutting-edge designers at Hugo Boss had decided the answer to our lavatory issues was to install a zip right across the backside which, when opened, provided the freedom required for all our personal admin. I suspect the fashionistas and Ron had been pretty pleased with their innovation, right up until the moment somebody pointed out that – bum flap or no bum flap – we still had to strip everything off anyway if we were to pull our underwear down before performing our ablutions.

5

WEIRD SCIENCE

It wasn't just the MTC that was breaking new ground. In a behind-the-scenes program that looked at the human element of what we were doing, McLaren was hoping to maximise our performance as a team. Under the inspirational leadership of Dr Aki Hintsa (now sadly deceased), an expert in 'the science of human high performance', the McLaren Lab was born.

Primarily Aki's first-class facilities and expertise were for our drivers, but he soon convinced Ron that there was some merit in focusing on the pitstop crew too. Unlike most sports, where the backroom staff do their work before a game or event, a Formula One pit crew play a crucial and active role during each and every Grand Prix. Aki believed the explosive, physical and critical nature of what we did meant our well-being should be nurtured and invested in. If we were slow to react, it impacted on the race. If we were poorly prepared, injured or sick, our performances might diminish, which could be the difference between losing or gaining vital split seconds. If we were serious about looking for improvements, no matter how small, and in every single area, the enhancement of the pit crew was something we couldn't ignore. More importantly, none of our rivals were doing it, so it represented an immediate competitive advantage. That was all Ron needed to hear to make it happen.

Initially we began physical training programs and, unsurprisingly, not everybody warmed to the experience. Some of the old guard believed they were already the best at what they did; they didn't need to work out, or become fitter to prove it. But as time went on, and the competitiveness within the team grew, that all changed. A sixteen-stone middle-aged truckie working on the pit crew just couldn't cut it anymore. All of us had to be in shape, and to improve our technical skills we began practising almost every day, and in an increasingly structured way. We even created a pitstop practice 'mule' car so we could train for our specific roles in the factory when the race cars weren't there, or were still under construction.

In 2006 we undertook the first of our annual trips to the sports science facility at the Finnish Olympic Training Centre in Kuortane, where we went through in-depth analysis of our individual physical strengths and weaknesses, using biometric testing to help formulate a personalised and truly bespoke program for each of us. If our role on the crew meant we had to quickly lift a heavy rear tyre, for example, emphasis would be placed on strengthening the core muscles used in that task. A correct posture (in positions where standard health-and-safety advice like bending at the knees with a straight back just wasn't practically applicable) helped to maintain balance and, importantly, prevented injuries. This was vital. If one of us did get hurt, it messed with the continuity of the team and somebody else would have to stand in. Consistency was the key to dependable, fast pitstops.

We spent time in classrooms, learning ways to improve our mental reactions and focus our abilities; there were Pilates classes, and we went through recovery sessions in the aqua therapy pool. But as much as any of those things, we used that first week away at Kuortane to bond together as a team before the season started. It was a relaxed trip and Aki ended up taking us to his nearby lakeside house for a special dinner and, memorably, to take part in what he assured us was a trad-itional Finnish pastime.

In the evening, I remember him disappearing from the house for a while. Everyone wondered where he'd gone. It was pitch black outside, but Aki reappeared at the rear doors of his beautiful home carrying a burning flame torch. He told us all to come outside, where it was freezing cold. The ground was covered in snow and Aki, along with his daughter, had lit a path of burning candles that stretched down towards his private lake. The water was frozen over, the ice was a foot thick, but he'd cut a big square hole with a chainsaw around 15 feet from the edge and surrounded the gaping maw with more candles. The idea was to undress, leap into the icy black hole before being lifted out. We then had to race over to his hot tub in the garden. It was crazy, but of course, we did it over and over again, daring each other to endure the cold one more time as our manhoods shrivelled to nothing, along with the feeling in our fingers and toes. Apparently, this ritual was good for the circulation.

We weren't the only ones to have physically suffered at the whims of Aki. He was also punishing our drivers, pushing them hard in training and tracking their body temperatures to study how it affected performance levels. In doing so, he'd found a real advantage in lowering a race driver's core temperature at the hot events before and even during a race – it improved their reaction times and decision-making ability considerably. Keeping the body as close to normal operating temperatures became a focus, and the drivers were soon wearing frozen vests, right up until the point of getting into their car; their heads wrapped in cold towels as they waited to drive away. Inside the cockpit, special pouches were moulded onto the back of the race seat and it was my job to fill them with dry ice just before the driver buckled in. As well as cooling the seat, this had the added benefit of keeping the driver's on-board drinks bag chilled for longer. With all this attention to detail bringing human performance enhancements to the drivers in their cars, it wasn't long before keeping the pit crew cool became the next big focus.

It being McLaren, Ron wasn't just going to buy a new air conditioner for the garage and be done with it. If we were going to revolutionise the world, we'd go big and PR the shit out of it along the way. At a time when F1 budgets were seemingly bottomless, we went to the European Space Agency (ESA) for help, and before we knew it, tests were being done on a new, specially designed pitstop suit, using ESA temperature-controlling technology and cutting-edge materials. The suits were covered with a tiny network of flexible tubes that fed chilled liquid around the entire body. The liquid was then refrigerated through a cooling unit that we 'plugged' into in the garage and circulated around the suit via a pump, housed in a backpack we all had to wear. When it came to pitstops, the idea was to disconnect from the cooler and run into the pitlane looking like spacemen, albeit pretty cool ones.

When the crew first got wind of the idea, it was met with the usual mix of eye-rolling despair and intrigue (the onesies were still fresh in the memory after all). But as soon as we heard that one of the prototype suits had arrived in the factory for analysis, no one could resist taking a look. As part of the 'scientific' testing, a model, or guinea pig, had been chosen to conduct some temperature-controlled experiments, and it was at that point that we all rocked up to see what the fuss was about. What we saw was quite extraordinary. The test subject, a poor young man from the marketing department, had been dressed up in a full set of existing standard pitstop gear – fireproof underwear, multi-layer race suit, balaclava, gloves, boots, helmet and goggles. Even in the cooler weather systems of Woking those garments were enough to raise a person's temperature considerably, but this was testing, which meant McLaren had to simulate extremes. The unfortunate lab rat had been rigged up with thermocouples, or temperature sensors all over his body. He was then made to climb into the enormous autoclave, the giant industrial oven used to cure carbon fibre components for the race cars, for an extended period of time.

After emerging half baked, he was allowed to cool back down as several boffins pored over the data, before getting into the new gear and doing it all over again. I never saw the actual results, other than my own visual analysis, which was that he looked like he wished he'd never volunteered for the job in the first place, but they must have been favourable. The suits were signed off and were taken to the very next race, the British Grand Prix at Silverstone, which ironically was possibly the coldest venue we visited on the calendar and, as was somewhat typical of Ron Dennis at the time, a big song and dance was made about the whole thing, even before we'd had a chance to try the suits on. This was to be a public promotion, Ron boldly explained, a show of McLaren's innovative thinking and attention to detail. Disappointingly, it didn't work out quite that way.

A photocall was announced in a press release ahead of our Thursday-afternoon pitstop practice, in which the world would be introduced to our revolutionary new system, as would we, for the very first time. Out of sight at the back of the garages, we struggled into our new gear; some of it fitted, some of it didn't. Chairs were set up for us at the front, as they would have been for the race, and the pipework and cooler unit was installed. *We were ready to plug in.* Everything was new, so there were some inevitable teething issues, but with a bank of photographers waiting for us in the pitlane, there was no time to change anything. We moved to the front of the garage, sat down and plugged into the pipework running along the floor between the rows of chairs. The system was switched on and the cameras began clicking away.

Our normal pitstop practice ensued and we were soon called into action on the radio by Dave Ryan. Leaping up from our chairs, we unplugged the pipes, or at least most people did, and ran into the pitlane. Unfortunately, one or two forgot and there was utter chaos as loops of piping became entangled in chair legs and ankles, with several people tripping up on their way out of the garage. Outside there was a ripple of excitement at what we were wearing, not least for the fact we all had futuristic backpacks on. No one had seen anything like it before, but we continued with our very real pitstop practice session with the photographers clambering over each other to get their dramatic action shots. I could hear onlookers talking, speculating whether the packs contained a compressed gas unit for adjusting the tyre pressures, or blowers for cooling brakes and radiators. All of the theories were wide of the mark, but it was amusing to hear them nonetheless.

Unfortunately, because we hadn't been able to try the system out in private, some of the suit's flaws (a few of them teething, others more serious) were being discovered live, under the glare of the world's media. They were heavy and uncomfortable; the backpacks restricted movement and took up too much space in what is already such a crowded environment around the car; the futuristic helmets and visor design impaired our peripheral vision and almost comically, the whole lot was all so bulky and cumbersome, it ended up making us feel hotter than the original outfits had. It took some time to persuade Ron that we couldn't use the suits and he only backed down once the question of them adversely affecting pitstop performance was mentioned. They went quietly back in a box, never to be seen again. Despite all the best intentions, that photocall hadn't been our finest hour. Still, I think Ron genuinely loved innovating and being able to stake a claim in shaping the future. But as is the case throughout history with some of the world's most successful entrepreneurs, there are victories, but there are also disasters.

My job changing the wheels in the pits was the focus of an equally exciting surge in technological development as the pursuit for everfaster and more consistent pitstops continued. We began using high-speed cameras, mounted on the overhead gantries, which allowed us to play back the individual elements of each stop in super slow motion. We focused on the guys working at a particular corner of the car and compared their wheel changes to the guys doing the same job on the other side. If they were repeatedly faster or slower, perhaps just in the early part of the process for example, we could study them and discover why. Sensors placed on the equipment and even the personnel around the crew helped us to build a data set for each stop that we could then analyse at meticulous levels; attention to detail was everything. The fine-tuning continued, over and over and over.

One of my good friends and a former McLaren colleague, Rhodri Griffiths, had left the team years earlier to set up a small company which looked at commonly used motorsport equipment and how it could be improved. Having been groomed in the forensic environment McLaren tends to foster, he began taking off-the-shelf products, like the Italian-designed pneumatic wheel guns that almost every team in the pitlane used, and found ways to specifically tailor them to the unique needs of Formula One. It soon became clear to him, and to us, that if we were spending so much time and money designing and developing the cars to be the best they could be, we should be doing the same with our equipment, particularly when it could have such a big impact on the race result. Knowing well in advance that refuelling was to be banned in the regulations from the 2010 season onwards, work began on making wheel changes the main focus of pitstops. The game had changed completely.

So, with the help of Rhodri's one-man operation, we began re-engineering the standard wheel guns that'd been used for years, as did a number of other teams. Together we designed and manufactured new components, including a completely new back section for the gun to increase the flow of compressed air (essentially it made the guns spin quicker). This was simple stuff, but no one had looked at this area before, not in detail. Faster, more reliable and automated methods of changing the gun's direction in between taking the wheel nut off and putting the new one on were developed. By removing the traditional need to take a hand off the gun and manually slide a small shuttle valve across to reverse the gun's rotation, it took away one element of the human process. Today, that action has been seamlessly designed into our equipment and is now part of the gun's natural operation, saving valuable split seconds. It's almost foolproof. Fast pitstops are as much about outright speed as they are consistency, reliability and repeatability. After all, it's no good having two stops in a race at 1.9 seconds, if the third takes 4.8 seconds.

Lightweight, flexible airlines on the guns later gave us far more manoeuvrability than the heavy, rigid ones we'd always used previously. They carried huge pressure, which meant they needed to be of an extremely high quality, but giving more scope for the mechanics to move with the new cutting-edge materials allowed the process to be a bit more user-friendly. Until it was banned in the regulations – on environmental grounds – we were using highly compressed helium to power the wheel guns, as its low density and lack of moisture gave an even faster flow through the system, meaning the gun could spin a little bit faster. The advantage over regular compressed air was tiny, but even a tiny improvement was still an advantage, and we were looking for anything we could get.

Elsewhere, the front and rear jacks received a major overhaul and developed from very basic steel-framed items, to the complex machined aluminium and carbon fibre technical masterpieces we ended up with. By going back to the drawing board and designing something specifically for the purpose, rather than using something we already had (and modifying it for the task), we transformed the speed and efficiency of every operation. Today's swivel-front jacks remove the need for the operator to move out of the way before the car leaves. Instead, he can be doing it while the wheels are being changed and can just release the jack to drop the car at the very last moment. Some jacks can now drop themselves when they see a dedicated electrical signal from the wheel guns to say the nuts are tight. This eliminates the time-consuming need for a gunman to take a hand off the gun and raise it in the air (along with the time it took the jack man to react to it, as was previously the case).

It didn't stop there. Laser positioning devices mounted on the over-head gantries helped the guys to hold their guns at exactly the right height for the wheel nuts, before the car even arrived in the box; digital 'traffic light' systems replaced the old lollipop man in releasing the car once the job was finally done to eliminate further human reaction time. Anything and everything was analysed meticulously and improved using the technological advances our sport was famed for. The equipment used around the pitstop was now on a par with the engineering that went into the car itself.

While we were looking at the equipment in this much detail, we had to look at the way it interacted with the car, not just the person using it. Could we design the car and jacks together? Rather than just making a rear jack to fit somewhere under the existing gearbox or crash structure, perhaps there was a better way if we integrated the design of them both? Could we redesign the wheel nuts to help them work more effectively with the new, faster guns? Could we come up with a new axle design for the car, allowing the nuts to engage quicker and more consistently? Could we make them from different materials? The answer to each of those questions was a resounding 'yes', and so we changed it all.

Jacks that needed less accuracy in their positioning tended to minimise delay. Wheel nuts became lighter and had more 'teeth', which better engaged the gun for faster torque transfer and easier location. The threads on the hubs became coarser, which required less of them, and therefore fewer turns of the nut to tighten or loosen it. In the end, the nuts themselves were permanently retained with clips inside every single wheel, so they were automatically located onto the axle as the wheel itself went on. It also reduced the need for the gunman to consciously think about retaining the nut in his gun during the change, something that had cost us time in the past.

Everything was being looked at in minute detail. Minuscule improvements were made in almost every area of the operation. Together with the work we'd been putting in at McLaren in the years leading up to the refuelling ban (which eventually took place in 2010), it gave us a number of tiny advantages that added up to some great results at times. Of course, like anything in Formula One, it didn't take long before other teams were doing the same as us and we had to find the next little improvement, wherever that might have come from. That could have been adapting an idea from someone else, or looking even harder for advancements that no one else had thought of. Either way, it was, and still is, an ongoing challenge.

As is often said in this game, 'If you stand still in F1, you get left behind.'

6

TESTING THE LIMITS

Life on the Formula One circuit, particularly during the peak, tobacco-sponsored days of the late nineties and early 2000s was both a wonderful and vulgar place to exist. The sport had thrived on a fruitful, and at times monopolistic, business model, which resulted in extreme wealth for a number of key stakeholders, the like of which they'd never enjoyed before. The sport was awash with cash, and as is often the case in entertainment industries – football, Hollywood, pop music – overflowing bank accounts drew out a number of different characteristics in people, not all of them altruistic.

I remember thinking how arrogant some of my colleagues were when I first arrived at McLaren. One or two of them clearly thought they were the best at what they did, and they weren't afraid to tell me that either. At the same time, they were so dismissive of people outside of F1 – the mechanics operating in Formula Three and Formula 3000, where I'd arrived from – that I got the impression these blokes didn't think too much of my background and that my experience didn't count for a lot in their eyes. They were spoilt too. In Formula Three I'd have to sweep the floor, load the trucks, build the garage and make the tea, as well as work on the car. I'd do everything because there were so few of us working on the team. It was very different in F1. I heard people moaning about anything and everything and I remember thinking to myself, 'I hope I don't ever end up acting like that lot.'

Formula One was going from strength to strength and those within it were swept along for the ride. An arrogance and sense of superiority developed within the heart and soul of the industry; ordinary, hardworking individuals and organisations were drawn into thinking they'd become untouchable. Unfortunately, I could count myself in that category on occasions and my garage mates and I, along with those at every other team, were exposed to leadership and industry practices that convinced us we were big hitters in The Most Important Show on Earth; misdemeanours were covered up and a blind eye turned to certain incidents of bad behaviour. Before very long, we were believing our own hype, flouting the rules and running around the world like we were invincible. I'm not proud of many of the idiotic things I was involved in during this period, but feel I should include an example or two to deliver a fuller picture of Formula One during a time when almost anything could happen (and if anything went wrong, as it sometimes did, there was normally a way to bury it from public view).

Life on the road started for me within weeks of joining McLaren's Test Team in 2000 when I was flown out to Spain for F1 testing. David Coulthard, or DC as everybody referred to him, and Mika Hakkinen were our two race drivers that year, but I was in awe of everyone and everything around me back then. The Formula Three and Formula 3000 championships had been great fun for sure, and during my time in F3 there weren't many Sundays when most of the mechanics on the grid before a race weren't still wobbly from the Saturday night before – it was just the way it was back then. Such were the differing levels of professionalism, compared to the very highest echelons of motorsport, that it was commonly the mechanics' mission to head out to the bars of the local town on a Saturday evening to 'snare' a young lady either 'hot enough', but more commonly just willing enough, to take on the task of being grid girl the next day. It was quite remarkable how often one of the team managed to convince somebody to stand on a cold, wet grid and hold a sponsor board in front of our cars on Sunday afternoons.

Having stepped up to Formula One, I imagined things would be a bit different. There was so much more at stake, both financially and professionally, and the entire world was watching what we did. Well, on some levels. As I learnt in my first few weeks on the job, when it came to testing, the media weren't necessarily watching. In fact, nobody was. Sometimes we'd work at a group test, with other teams sharing the track alongside us, but quite often we'd hire out the entire circuit for ourselves and do the test behind closed doors. Private security kept out the press, photographers and fans while we performed our 'top secret' work to an audience of none.

Testing was a pretty brutal experience as a mechanic. Before health and safety became fashionable, and the F1 powers-that-be began introducing curfew regulations or night shifts to ease the workload on staff, Test Teams used to graft hard – *seriously hard*. There were very few restrictions on when or where we could test, so the thinking was that the more we could run a car, the better. The McLaren Test Team was an entirely separate entity to the operation people saw on television at a Grand Prix, but we wore the same uniforms and built an identical garage at whichever track we worked at. We operated what looked like the same McLaren F1 cars driven by DC and Mika Hakkinen; we transported them around in what looked like the same McLaren trucks. In reality, though, it was a completely separate set of kit – a huge operation running in tandem with the Race Team, but rarely ever crossing paths.

Our attention to detail extended to our preparation, too. Wherever possible we'd test at a Grand Prix track two weeks before the race was due to be held there, preparing while the Race Team competed at the preceding event. If we couldn't go to the actual GP track, we'd go to the one we decided was most representative of its characteristics and worked like hell, keeping the cars running all day long, collecting data

and feedback from the drivers. Because parts were often experimental, or we were trying something new, we'd have to strip the cars down
every evening, crack-checking and meticulously inspecting everything. Part of our job was to prove that certain car parts would last the
race mileage without failing. To do that, we had to push them to
destruction, monitoring their responses all the way there, which
required a hell of a lot of work. It was perfectly normal to start work at
6:30 or 7 a.m. and not leave the racetrack until well into the early
hours, before doing it all again the next day. Occasionally, we just
never made it back to the hotel if something had gone wrong and it
was a particularly time-critical test.

Those kinds of relentless hours, night after night, meant we were
physically and mentally destroyed by the end of each shift. Whatever
sleep I could grab seemed like a bonus in those early days; I sometimes
felt terrified I wouldn't be able to perform to the exacting standards
that Formula One, and particularly McLaren, demanded. So I was
later surprised to learn that one or two of the more experienced
members of our team were working those hours and still somehow
heading out on the booze. Their short window between leaving the
track and heading back in the morning was often spent in a nearby
nightclub.

Despite our punishing schedules there was a great sense of fun and
camaraderie among the guys. At the end of a test we'd always let our
hair down, and I think the team gave us some allowance for that, what
with the efforts we put in to our work. But with the underlying,
ingrained egotism in F1 this led to some pretty disrespectful shenanigans. The sport seemed to lack much in the way of morals during
those times, and pit crews often operated on the fringes with their off-
track behaviour. There were a number of what should've been
shocking incidents involving drunk driving, assault, and even arrests in
dodgy establishments, but many of them barely raised an eyebrow at
the time. These scandals were always kept well away from the public
eye by the various teams involved. As far as I could tell, throughout

the testing fraternity it was very much a culture of 'What happens on tour stays on tour.'

This attitude extended to our own infrastructure. I remember initially being appalled at the treatment of our hire cars, often from the moment we'd collected them at the airport. The mechanics, who were split over two or three vehicles, would brazenly race each other on the public roads, often colliding deliberately. At junctions, the car behind would drive into the one in front, trying to push it out into the oncoming traffic, egged on by the occupants of both vehicles. Tyre burnouts and handbrake turns were ritualistic and once in a while, whenever we had a minibus, a chant would swell up from the back seats, gaining support and volume as it moved down the rows.

'Reverse to first! Reverse to first!'

Our designated driver would respond in what was a well-rehearsed stunt: having located a convenient spot to get the vehicle going as fast as possible in reverse gear, he would then forcefully jam it into first while keeping the throttle flat to the floor. The resulting extreme wheelspin might have been hilarious fun, filling the minibus with smoke and laughter, but it was occasionally terminal on the tyres, transmission and engine and on a number of occasions the pranks ended up killing hire cars, which we'd end up finding even more funny.

News of our hire car pranks often made it to the race drivers, and I remember even Mika Hakkinen laughing his head off whenever we detailed the latest 'accident'. After each eventual hire car failure, we'd all squeeze into the surviving minibus, or as we did on one occasion, flag a lift to the track from the passing Italian Ferrari team (who I don't think quite understood, or believed, the alarming regularity of our various transport failures) and call the hire company. We'd tell them their rental had broken down, and because they were so keen to keep the mighty McLaren as a happy customer, they'd apologise profusely and send another one. Dents in bumpers and broken front grills were normally glossed over for the same reason. Eventually we began to feel like we could get away with almost anything. In our minds we were bulletproof, and that flawed sense of invincibility only encouraged us to misbehave in new and increasingly reckless ways.

During December's winter testing in Spain at the end of my first year with McLaren in 2000, our Team Manager announced there'd be a reward for all our hard work on those sleepless nights. Somehow, he had managed to get a plane to take us all home for the night of McLaren's highly anticipated Christmas party. This was a big deal. We thought we were set to miss the glamorous event as it fell halfway through an important test. I was excited – all of us were. The company's Christmas parties were legendary, extravagant affairs and in other years they'd been staged at Alexandra Palace and Battersea Power Station in London. Full funfairs had been built inside, Cirque de Soleil put on shows for McLaren's staff, and at the height of their fame the Spice Girls had performed an exclusive gig. On this occasion, the entire Royal Albert Hall had been booked and we knew that a pretty special evening lay ahead.

The agreement was that the Test Team had to complete the day's work, turn the cars around as per normal that evening, and jump on the plane home the next morning before readying ourselves for the big night. Then, the morning after the party, we'd jump back on the plane and get back to the test. It was a real treat for the team and something we'd never expected to happen, so most of us were very grateful. As often seemed to be the case, though, we'd been given an inch, so we duly grabbed a mile and nearly spoilt it for everyone.

Knowing we had nothing but a flight home to do the following day, a few of us went out to a club and hit it hard after finishing at the track, with the one non-drinker in the team installed as a willing minibus driver. Around 4 a.m. we'd had more than enough and piled back into the luxury Mercedes people carrier and headed back to the hotel. We were in high spirits and things soon became rowdy. There was singing; people jumped around and hung out of the windows, shouting at other drivers in traffic like football hooligans, while the bloke in the front passenger seat began emptying the glove box contents into the road while everyone else egged him on. With so many drunk, competitive guys in such a confined space it didn't take long before things got *really* out of hand.

A gang mentality had taken grip where every destructive action had to be bettered by the next person, despite our sober driver's attempts to instill some calm. Once the car's manual and rental paperwork had been lobbed from the window, somebody climbed through to the front and ripped the entire glove box door off its hinges. That went into the road too. It was chaos. We went wild and threw headrests onto the highway; arm rests were stripped from the seats; it was a collective frenzy of destruction that damaged everything in its path: the parcel shelf, sections of carpet, wing mirrors, the roof lining, interior lights; I remember someone swinging from the wiring looms normally hidden behind them. It wasn't until the driver's seat was attacked (and he absolutely lost it, screaming at everyone to stop) that we suddenly had a long-overdue moment of sobriety. *What the hell have we just done?* In the space of fifteen minutes the car had been wrecked, the mood shifting to one of somber realisation. We pulled into the hotel forecourt and all I could think was, 'How the hell do we get out of this one?'

Still hammered, the group consensus was that we should take our Mercedes round the corner and burn it out – *literally*. It was madness, but what else could we do? The minibus was ruined beyond repair; we could write it off in the time frame we had available to us . . . *and it would probably add to the fun*. None of us were in the mindset to spot the risks: we were a danger to ourselves and others, so it was probably a saving grace that our now shellshocked driver had decided to seize control, angrily demanding we all just go to bed. He pointed out the security cameras watching us from the front of the hotel and furiously explained he would deal with the anarchy we'd unleashed. He was very cross and we obeyed like naughty puppies, trotting off to bed with our tails between our legs for an hour or so, before rising again for our flight to London.

The trouble with an hour's sleep is that a person can feel ten times worse than when they fell into bed. My head was bad, really bad, the reality of what had happened the night before slapping me around the face. I wasn't the only one, but the guys who hadn't been out with us, the ones who were now about to travel to the airport in the vehicle, were unsurprisingly horrified at the damage we'd caused to the van as it rattled and wobbled its way towards them in the hotel car park.

'Just keep quiet and get in,' we hissed, conspiratorially.

At the airport, the vehicle was left in the hire company's parking zone. The keys were deposited in what was left of the glove box and abandoned.

We got on the plane, the drunken fog lifting, an uneasy sense of guilt and paranoia settling into all of us. I was so ashamed of myself. I loved to muck about, often pushing the boundaries of acceptable behaviour whenever I did, but the wrecked Mercedes wasn't simply pushing the boundaries. I'd smashed right through them in an act of insane vandalism. Had I read a newspaper article about a rugby team or a band pulling the same stunt, I'd have probably turned my nose up in disgust. I imagine that's exactly what you're doing right now and I can't blame you.

As we took off, we knew we were up to our necks in trouble; alibis and escape plans were hatched. *Could we just deny it?* Unlikely, someone would know it had been us. *Should we get together and make up a story?* That would never work. *Or should we go, cap in hand, to the Team Manager and confess before he got the inevitable call from the hire car company?* There was a collective shrug. It seemed like a nuclear option, but the fact we were taking responsibility for our actions might somehow play in our favour. So back at the factory we sucked it up and knocked on the Test Team Manager's office door. He looked fairly happy to see us at first, but as one of the lads explained what we had done, his mood swiftly changed.

'I'm afraid we've let you down and damaged one of the hire cars . . .'

A look of concern spread across his face. 'Oh no, is everyone OK?' he asked. 'Was it a big accident?'

'Well, it wasn't actually an accident . . .'

He raised an eyebrow. We came clean with a slightly watered-down version of the story, and explained how sorry we were, that we realised the Christmas party was a special occasion and we'd let everyone down, not least McLaren. We must have resembled a line-up of shamed kids, barely able to look up from the floor. We then listened silently as he expressed his disappointment. The potential outcome didn't look good.

'I can't pretend this isn't going to cost you your jobs,' he said, calmly and quietly but in a manner that showed he was clearly annoyed. It was like your dad saying, 'I'm not angry . . . just disappointed.' Somehow it felt worse than just being straight-up shouted at.

I felt sick. I'd only just got my dream career off the ground and I was now about to lose it. We all went home feeling like we were preparing ourselves for a wake, not the biggest party of the year. When I finally did get to the Royal Albert Hall and took my seat for the pre-show, the funereal vibe only increased. The seat allocations had put me in the chair next to the Test Team Manager. It was a tense part of the evening.

Now we just had to wait for the fallout. It was in the hands of our bosses and we had no idea how they, or the hire company, would deal with it. We headed back to Spain the next morning for the final few days of testing before packing up for Christmas. My mind was in bits: *I can't pretend this isn't going to cost you your jobs*; my growing guilt; the threat of unemployment at Christmas; I could barely think about anything else.

I figured our punishment would be tough, but we'd also need to find a way to pay for the vehicle. It wouldn't be cheap, tens of thousands in cash, and there was no way we could stump up the funds to replace an expensive Mercedes between the few of us. So after much desperate discussion we settled on an absolute last resort: one of us would speak to David Coulthard. He was considered one of the lads, and if anyone would understand the mess we'd found ourselves in, it would be him. Reluctantly, fearfully and ashamedly, we decided to see if he might be able to help out, temporarily at least, and our most senior mechanic was tasked to broach the sensitive subject with him.

'I don't like to do this,' he stammered. 'But we managed to destroy a hire car the other day and there's no way we can afford to pay for it. We're expecting a pretty serious bill and I wondered if we could ask you for a temporary loan?'

'Bloody hell, is everyone OK?' said DC.

When the sordid tale was relayed back to him, and that we thought the cost could be in the region of twenty grand, he began laughing.

'Wow, good effort, boys!' he said. 'Of course I'll send you the money, no problem at all. Just call me whenever you get the bill, any time apart from Christmas Day. If you call then, you'll get nothing. But any other time I'll transfer the money to you.'

We promised to figure out a repayment plan and return the loan in double quick time, but he nonchalantly waved us away.

'Ah, don't worry about it,' he said. 'We all make mistakes and I think it's fair to say I owe you all a lot more than that for everything you do . . .'

I was amazed. DC was an idol to me, he had been for a long time, but I was even more impressed at how easily he took our call for help and how funny he thought it all was. Most of all, I'd been stunned at his attitude and generosity, but as Christmas came and went we'd still heard nothing of our inevitable, career-wrecking fate. None of us wanted to probe too much, so we just waited nervously, until one day, in mid-January, we were called into a meeting with the Team

Manager, where each of us were handed two white envelopes, one of which would contain news of our fate from the company, the other the bill from the hire car company, which McLaren obviously expected us to pay in its entirety.

The first envelope contained a very serious-looking letter from McLaren and I skimmed over the necessary HR introduction to read the line 'Formal Written Warning'. I'd kept my job. Somehow. The relief was overwhelming, yet I couldn't show it. Then my heart sank as I tentatively opened the second envelope. I was convinced the cost would put us in a nightmarish financial spot, requiring us to lean on our world-famous driver for a handout. But when I opened the folded paper, I had to double-check the numbers. The invoice, written in Spanish, only charged €147 to each of us, a tiny fraction of the cost we'd been expecting. There was clearly some mistake. I was so confused, yet elated at the same time and had no idea how to react. Our biggest problem now was tempering the excitement with the sober period of introspection that was expected of us after our bollocking. None of us could work out what the details of the bill said, so I took a photo and sent it to my Spanish brother-in-law to translate. Minutes later his response came back.

'Elvis, those costs were to cover a new radiator grill and wing mirror.'

That was the bill for some damage incurred to the other of our two crew hire cars that week – the general bumping and scraping that had become normal shenanigans on overseas trips. *How could that be? Where was the other bill?* It's not like the poor guy with his checklist inspecting the returned vehicles at the airport could have missed the damage. The car was absolutely wrecked; vandalised from top to bottom.

We paid the costs, waited a day or so, but there was no mention of any further charges. As far as McLaren were concerned, the matter had been closed and I couldn't have been more relieved. The world's biggest weight had been lifted from my shoulders; it felt as if I'd been cured of an incurable disease, and if we couldn't believe it, nor could anyone else on the team. We'd somehow escaped from Death Row. For most people, an incident like this would've highlighted the need to rethink, to establish a more mature set of working values, but not us. We were invincible; *this proved it* and our escapes from authority only fuelled the anarchic self-belief that we should party harder. And faster.

7

THE PRICE OF PERFECTION

For all of his image-defining characteristics and consummate professionalism, Ron knew how to enjoy himself away from the glaring eyes
of the paddock. And though it wasn't too often that I'd end up at the
same social event as him on a night out, it did happen a few times.
On those occasions, he was always very generous and up for a laugh,
though I never saw him out of control, not like some of the other high-
ranking members of the F1 hierarchy. But then I suspect Ron simply
doesn't do 'out of control'.

There was one occasion, however, when our paths crossed in the
most unusual fashion. It took place at the inaugural Singapore Grand
Prix in 2008, where we were all enjoying the benefits of remaining on
a European time zone, while working the unusual hours of the first
ever night race in F1 history. Saturday, by then our earliest finish of
the week due to the post-qualifying *parc fermé* rules (whereby all cars
were impounded to prevent changes being made between qualifying
and the race), was a good chance to get out and see the city's nightlife.
At a normal race, we'd leave the track around 6:30 p.m., but in Singapore, we finished in the early hours of the morning. So after a quick
shower and change, we headed out to a nearby island where a swanky
party we'd got wind of was just hitting full swing.

We had a great time and the lunchtime start the following day meant we could still bank some sleep even if we stayed out until way beyond the normally acceptable time. So we did. Ron was going through a bit of an understandably uncharacteristic time after the difficulties of splitting up with his long-standing wife, Lisa, and had been 'enjoying himself' a little more than usual while on the road. At some point in the early hours of the morning he'd arrived at the same party as us, and when I spotted him and his entourage, I thought it best to keep a low profile. We stayed at opposite sides of the venue wherever possible, because much as I had respect for Big Ron, I imagined our social circles, and the acceptable behaviour within them, to be pretty different.

It was only as the sun rose high up in the sky on race day morning that we realised we really ought to travel the considerable distance back to our hotel, in the heart of the city. Heading out of the venue, we quickly realised we had an issue – and a fairly big one. The party was shutting down and the queue for taxis was a mile long. We had little choice but to join it, even if the rate of progress was disastrously slow. After a good hour of queuing with very little movement, time became increasingly pressing and there was no obvious solution to the problem. It was then that I felt a firm tap on my shoulder. I turned to see Ron towering over us, casting a shadow over his minions from the bright morning sun behind him. For a moment I was in shock.

'Hello, boys,' he said. 'What are *you* still doing here?'

We looked at one another and blurted out an explanation that wouldn't make us look overly irresponsible. 'We left the party ages ago,' I said, guiltily. 'We've been waiting here ever since, but there're just no taxis!'

Ron nodded sceptically. But realising our predicament, and with a mutual acceptance that neither of us should still be in a nightclub at that time of the morning before a race, he made a quick call on his mobile phone.

'My driver's on the way here,' he said. 'He'll take you back to your hotel, then send him back for me when you get there.'

It was the unlikeliest scenario. I wasn't sure what to do. We were incredibly grateful, but equally well aware that we should've been tucked up in bed hours ago ahead of race day. I wanted to jump up and hug him, but as with my previous encounter with the Queen, there were too many protocols involved, and I'm pretty sure a cuddle would have contravened a number of them. Instead, we tried to remain as calm as we could, but made sure he was aware of just how grateful we were. Back at work that evening, we crossed paths and I made an effort to smile at him and say hello, but the relationship had definitely returned to the strict professional status – order restored. Neither of us ever spoke of the incident again.

That wasn't our first social meeting, however. Years earlier, at the Monaco Grand Prix, we'd been told of an exclusive party on a super yacht to celebrate Ron's birthday and one of the McLaren marketing guys had suggested we should swing by. Having found the jaw-dropping venue, a boat in the glittering Monte Carlo bay, security attempted to stop us on the harbour wall.

'This is a private party,' came the slightly aggressive introduction. 'Sorry, no one else is coming aboard.'

We attempted to explain that we were McLaren employees, before somebody decided to exaggerate our status: 'We've been invited by Ron.'

The two security guards suddenly had a dilemma. I'm sure they didn't want to bother Mr Dennis with a bunch of jokers trying their luck with a made-up invite, but what if we really had been asked to come along by Ron and they had turned us away point-blank? Whilst one remained stony faced and kept us well away from the gangplank, the other sheepishly sloped off onto the upper deck to ask approval. A minute or two later he returned with our boss, who was in high spirits by that point.

'Do you all work for me?' he said contemptuously, looking us up and down in the most disrespectful manner.

'Yes, Ron, we're all race team mechanics,' I said, resisting the temptation to roll my eyes.

He nodded. 'Oh, OK. Then come aboard and take your shoes off,' he said, already on his way back up the gangplank to the party. There wasn't even time for us to wish him a happy birthday, although I definitely found a moment to give the grumpy security guards a little wry smile and a cocky wink on the way past.

Ron's dismissive demeanour wasn't in any way inspiring, or motivating to the lads. Somewhere along the line, though, someone must have bravely explained that to him, because in the build-up to one season I remember he'd asked the Chief Mechanic to print out a contact sheet with headshots of the entire race team. Our pertinent details (name, job and so on) were even listed underneath. It was his awkward way of learning our names and faces in the garage and trying to appear more in touch with the team, and while the intention had been well meaning, I don't think he ever called any of us directly by our names in all the years we were under the same roof. I'm not even sure how much he studied it – or if he did at all. When it came to social niceties within his own workforce, Ron's attention to detail was very un-McLarenlike.

His successes were huge, enviable in the ferociously small world of Formula One where every other competitor was trying to either outdo you, have you over, or steal your ideas. Securing the services of the best drivers in the world; partnering with the biggest blue-chip brands on the planet; winning races and World Championships; building the MTC and then paying off the huge debt in record time; taking McLaren from a small race team to a global technology group . . . The list goes on and on. What stood out for me, though, in later years (that hadn't necessarily done so while I was on the constant treadmill of the F1 circuit) was that these scores were all part of Ron's master plan. None of it happened by accident and one led almost directly into the other. The world-leading McLaren Technology Group of today wasn't built by committee, or just by board members relying on focus groups and market research studies to make decisions. It had been built by Ron Dennis and his single-minded vision, plus a thousand employees, give or take, who were either convinced, or coerced, into following him along the way.

Ron's failures (though I doubt he'd ever call them that) were part of the journey too. He tried things that didn't necessarily work out, but each one became a valuable lesson and part of the constant development process. These included engine deals that proved fruitless, business deals that collapsed before they'd even begun, and design schemes that people just didn't buy into. But the most common reasons for any setbacks Ron encountered along the way were often relationship-based.

There's a paddock legend that in 2007, just after McLaren had been fined an unprecedented $100 million for being found in possession of confidential Ferrari information (we'll get to that later), during a staged photo call on the steps of the team's Brand Centre – which had been designed to give an appearance of there being 'no hard feelings' between the team and the governing body – FIA president Max Mosley reportedly leant over and whispered into Ron's ear.

'$1 million was for what you did, Ron; the other $99 million's for you being a c**t.'

In a way, that comment, if indeed it's true, summed up many of Ron's relationships in and around Formula One. He'd earned huge respect for being so successful over the years, but there were a lot of people ready to pounce on him when things went wrong, perhaps none more so than Max Mosley. He also had a habit of rubbing people up the wrong way. They included his own staff; some well-known drivers; the FIA and, in the end, his own business partners and shareholders. Ultimately he lost control of the one thing he needed to have total control over: *his* McLaren.

Having watched the bitter endgame play out through late 2016 and early 2017 as McLaren's shareholders turned against him and forced his exit from the company, I couldn't help but feel unexpectedly sorry for him. Many would argue that a change at the top was long overdue and it was time for the old guard to make way for the next generation of leadership, in whatever form that would take. But the one thing I told everyone at the time was this: yes, there may be a number of reasons to criticise Ron Dennis, and I'd done it many times myself, but you will never find anyone in this world as deeply passionate about McLaren – past, present or future. That's something no board, committee or chief executive could ever replace.

When the news broke that he'd lost his fight to remain in control of the company, I was shocked and saddened. But I was even more surprised to see the outpouring of emotion and support that he received from within the ranks of present and former employees – I'm a member of various groups, comprising 'old boys' and current-day staff, and almost unanimously the feeling was that, yeah, Ron had been a pain to work for at times, but McLaren would never be the same again. Difficult though he might have been, those who loved McLaren had a soft spot for him and an appreciation for what the company meant to him. They loved everything he'd done to make it, and its employees, what they are today. His qualities stretched far beyond the business world, but perhaps only those on the inside ever really got to see them.

What a lot of people also didn't know was that Ron's a very generous man. I'd heard all manner of tales of his extraordinary charity donations and of him looking after loyal colleagues who'd fallen on hard times. These were only whispers from around the factory, mind you; rarely did that kind of news ever see the light of day outside, and that was very deliberate. Ron might have enjoyed the public spotlight and craved recognition for his achievements in sport and business, but he was deliberately understated when it came to his generosity. I've been in restaurants, both when working for the team, and since, as part of the F1 media, where unannounced, the bill for our entire table has been paid by Ron from across the room as a thank-you gesture.

When a dear friend and colleague of mine and Ron's, Tyler Alexander, fell seriously ill towards the end of his life, I know the support and friendship Ron gave him behind the scenes was a great comfort and help to him and his loved ones. He went way above and beyond the call of duty to look after him because loyalty meant a lot to Ron, and Tyler had been loyal to McLaren for over forty years. It may have been an unbusinesslike act, uncharacteristic even, but only if you believed in Ron's cold, hard public persona. For the people who really knew Ron, it wasn't a shock for him to behave like that. I can't honestly say I knew him well, despite working for him for so long while being in the same race garage; and through some incredible ups and downs together, but I got a rare insight that most people didn't get.

It felt pretty special to have witnessed it.

8

THE ICE MAN COMETH

Back in 2000, when I'd finally got my break in F1 with the McLaren Test Team, Kimi 'the Ice Man' Raikkonen had only been out of karting for little over a year. Having then made immediate waves in the Formula Renault series, he began competing as a Formula One driver when Peter Sauber, owner of the Sauber F1 Team, opted to take a punt on his prodigious talents after an initial test. Such was their confidence in the young Finn that in 2001 Sauber pleaded with the FIA to give Kimi his super-licence – the qualification required to compete at the highest level. This hunch was later proved to be correct. That test drive with Kimi displayed enough talent to secure a place in F1, but it almost didn't get off to the best of starts.

On what was surely the biggest morning of his life, after a career of just twenty-three car races so far, the Finn showed up late. His absence in the hotel lobby at the arranged departure time could have been taken as an ominous sign; a dose of stage nerves maybe, or perhaps a complete turnaround on his new career calling entirely. In reality, what eventually unfolded was a moment that perfectly reflected Kimi's persona: he was still hanging out in his hotel room, and a panicky phone call from his nervous and frustrated manager was greeted with a typically lethargic response.

'Yes, yes, OK,' yawned Kimi. 'I'll be down in a minute.'

Having watched some personalities change considerably over just a period of months in F1, it was nice to see Kimi remain pretty much the same person over the fifteen years or so he's been involved. Top-level sport, and perhaps indeed the fame and fortune that generally comes along with it, can easily shape the characters inside, and not always for the best. Egos get inflated; real friends can be forgotten in favour of a celebrity crowd, and there are many, many unpleasant examples of people going off the rails. With Kimi, though, there's never been an ego, let alone an inflated one, and the celebrity lifestyle just wasn't his way. It's the same today.

After an impressive first season with Sauber, in which he was fast asleep under a bench in the garage just thirty minutes before his first ever Grand Prix in Melbourne, Ron Dennis snapped him up. Kimi was brought in to replace our outgoing Finn and double World Champion, Mika Hakkinen. They were big shoes to fill for a kid after just one year in the sport, but he was clearly a talent. Meanwhile, we still had the experienced head of David Coulthard in the other car to show him the ropes, and I eventually met Kimi at the pre-season tests ahead of the 2002 season with a handshake and a mumbled hello – nothing more. I was now a Number Two Mechanic on the T-Car, or third spare race car, for that year and when our crew ran Kimi's car at one of the early tests, we weren't particularly surprised by his minimal way with words, having worked with Mika previously.

Mika used to say things like, 'Car feels OK,' in an unmistakably robotic Finnish accent, when it was really feeling quite good and he'd been asked for his feedback, or, 'We go now,' when he'd had enough of listening to his race engineer in the garage and wanted to get back out on track. When questioned whether he wanted to run again before lunch, or stop early, the response was invariably, 'Flat out: let's go.' Any description of the car's behaviour would be accompanied by a twisting, flat-handed gesture to depict understeer or oversteer. Kimi was much less authoritative in those early days, but the simplicity of his English language was very similar.

From the go, Kimi's speed was unquestionable, and despite the low word count, there was little ambiguity in what he wanted from the car. If the engineer asked the right questions, the answers wouldn't leave much room for further questioning. He soon developed an effective working relationship with Mark Slade, or Sladey, his race engineer, who'd previously worked with Mika and so was well prepared for life with another Finnish racer. He was also someone I respected hugely and grew to become good friends with over the years. Sladey was one of the most passionate engineers I'd known, throwing everything into whatever he did. The explosive release of joy he displayed whenever we got pole position in qualifying, or fought past a rival in a race, was similar to a football fan celebrating a goal. We could see how much success meant to him and it was something that inspired me greatly when I later began working alongside him on Kimi's race car crew.

The obvious flip side of this heightened emotional state were the outbursts of frustration and disappointment, even anger, whenever things didn't go to plan. It was a case of 'stand well clear', especially if a mechanical change hadn't worked, the car had failed, or, worse, somebody in the crew hadn't done their job properly. In those dark moments, Sladey's frustrations were usually taken out on the nearest laptop, garage wall, or, in a best-case scenario, just a pen. He'd hold his head in his hands, eyes shut for a moment or two as the internal pain subsided. Kimi would find those moments quietly hilarious from inside his crash helmet, looking over from the cockpit as he waited to leave the garage while Sladey had a meltdown, or shouted at somebody on the radio. During our years working together, it became a running source of amusement between Kimi and I, even if neither of us would have ever dared let Sladey catch us sniggering.

That first year with the team was both good and bad. Kimi's car and engine were terribly unreliable, failing to finish eight of the seventeen races, usually because of one kind of mechanical failure or another. This meant he'd often have to fall back on our spare T-Car for races, as bits fell off or broke on his race car most weekends. In those days we had an extra track session at each event, known as the Sunday Morning Warm-Up. It was a practice and an opportunity to test the cars one last time ahead of the afternoon's race, particularly as they'd been substantially rebuilt after qualifying the day before. Race engines and gearboxes would replace qualifying ones. Sensors, removed to save weight in qualifying, were fitted for the race to monitor as many parameters as possible. Brake ducts, wings, cooling, and any adjustment to the car's ballast (to compensate for the weight changes) would all have been replaced or adjusted overnight, so the Sunday Morning Warm-Up was a chance to check that everything was operating correctly.

Just like the two race cars, we also did a single installation lap with our T-Car, which would be set up for one of our two drivers at each race. Prior to Kimi's arrival, Mika and DC would decide between them who would have the spare McLaren assigned to them for which Grand Prix. They worked out before the season started the races they each thought might give them the best opportunity for a good result, or where one of them felt they were most likely to have a crash and might need the back-up. The T-Car crew would then work to the designated driver's specifications, all the while mirroring the constant changes being made to their race car that weekend, so it was always ready to go in an instant. When Kimi arrived, though, he didn't seem to care too much about the races in which our T-Car was his, a sign of his utterly relaxed and apolitical nature. In the end he left it up to DC to decide the ones he wanted it for and he took the rest.

My job that year was to look after everything from the cockpit forward on the spare car, which meant making sure all the control and comfort settings were correct for the driver. I'd make sure to sit DC or Kimi in it on the Thursday before a race, just to check they were happy with the pedals and steering wheel positions; mirrors, seat and belts were adjusted to their liking, as we made sure it generally felt as close to the race car as was possible. None of them liked spending too much time 'mucking about' with the spare, as it was just that: nothing more than a back-up. But I'd have to insist they went through the laborious process, because if they did need it, it was likely to be in a hurry when something had gone horribly wrong with their race car, usually at the last minute. Plus, it would be my fault, not theirs, if something wasn't right.

During those 2002 sessions, I gradually came to know Kimi a little. I tried to make light of the tedious task when dragging him over to our car to carry out the checks each week and he began to play along. On Sunday mornings, whoever had the T-Car assigned to them would do an installation, or single exploratory lap in the race car, before returning to the pits and working with me, where I'd strap them into our car for the same process. DC liked his belts done up as tight as anyone had the strength to physically muster, whereas Kimi hated to feel too constrained and preferred them looser. I later came to realise this was a perfect metaphor for Kimi's personality.

No matter how much I'd bled the brakes to shift any air in the system and ensure the pedal was rock solid – as Kimi liked it – he'd always climb out of the T-Car and shrug his shoulders. 'It's OK,' he'd say, walking off before shouting back, 'Maybe we should just bleed the brakes?' It happened with such comical regularity that I'd often jokily shout it out with him in anticipation as he walked back towards his race car. One day, knowing the same routine would play out, I even wedged a hammer between the pedal and front of the chassis, meaning there was absolutely no movement at all when he pressed down on the brake pedal. Kimi got out, laughing to himself.

'The pedal could still be a bit harder,' he shouted. 'Maybe you should give the brakes a quick bleed, Elvis?'

The step up from middle-of-the-grid Sauber to championship-contending McLaren wasn't something that phased Kimi; he just loved being behind the wheel of a Formula One car. Despite his aggression on the track, he was quite a shy character. I don't think he enjoyed the huge numbers of people on the McLaren team, but that might have been the reason why we eventually ended up building a tight spirit amongst our small race car crew within the team. Kimi kept himself to himself most of the time. If he wasn't required in the garage, or the engineering truck, while we made changes to his car, you could almost guarantee he'd be asleep somewhere, either in his private room in the team 'motorhome', under a bench or on a tool cabinet, in the team kitchen, or the back seat of his hire car. It was always wise to check before removing a pile of coats off the work-top in the spares truck, just in case Kimi was curled up asleep underneath . . .

Something I know he hated about his move to McLaren was the substantial number of press and sponsor appearance days Ron had made him commit to in his first contract with the team. He never enjoyed that side of the job and despite it being a responsibility of the modern-day F1 superstar, Ron's drivers definitely did more work than most in that regard. At the time, the role of F1 drivers was quite different to today. Track testing was a regular part of the sport, so much so that most teams had a dedicated Test Team, a full two-car set up, with their own cars, trucks, equipment, support teams, mechanics and engineers. The race drivers would often go from race to test, test to race, race to test, for much of the year without any of the testing restrictions we have in place today. To add in a significant number of days of PR work on top was pushing them to the absolute limit.

These commitments took place because Ron wanted to give value to his partners by offering them something that no other team could. The result was that he could charge a premium to those companies who were involved, and it didn't just extend to time with the drivers. In fact, some of the PR stunts we did at the time broke new ground. In 2000, McLaren chartered a zero-gravity – or parabolic-flight – aircraft with Mika and DC and one of our cars. I've no idea what it must have cost the company, but for our money we did several runs, with the plane achieving seven seconds of weightlessness on each as our two drivers floated around in the air with their car for a photo shoot for West, our tobacco sponsor at the time. I remember thinking it was completely and utterly insane.

Reluctantly Kimi would turn up to those events where the team had guaranteed their sponsors his presence, but his reluctance quickly became his trademark. An awkward and uncomfortable style on stage, twinned with his blunt, monosyllabic quotes in front of a microphone should have been a PR nightmare, but it ironically turned into the thing most people loved about him. Even today, fans can't get enough of it, and he's now famed for his indifference to media work. The more he hated and wanted less of it, the more public loved him, but as his value to the team became clear, and expanded over time, so did his contract-negotiating power. The PR days gradually dwindled to more manageable numbers, even if only by McLaren standards.

The persona was never an act with Kimi, that's how he is. He got into racing because he loved driving and was good at it. Karting allowed him to do just the basics: turn up, drive fast, and then go home. Even in the lower categories of car racing, that's pretty much what the job entailed. It's only when a driver gets to Formula One, with no prior training, that they're usually expected to be TV personalities, actors, presenters, public speakers, models, ambassadors and leaders of a thousand men. For some it comes naturally; they enjoy the responsibility and are good at it. For others, like Kimi, it's the worst part of being an F1 driver. The reason he'd been hired was because he could drive fast. He didn't understand why he needed to be good at all those other things when actually he hated doing them.

After that first year with McLaren, as Kimi showed us just how good he was (in between the car breaking down) with three podium finishes, there was a shuffle behind the scenes. One of the crew had retired, and I was promoted from the T-Car onto Kimi's race car. It was a dream move from my point of view. The T-Car had been a great introduction to the race team and life on the road at Grand Prix events, but it was still only the 'spare car', which meant I was part of the 'spare car crew'. Nevertheless, I had a lot of fun, working really hard and loving my job, but I never quite felt central to the task of winning races, I was more of a fringe player. The race car was where I wanted to be: one of the few key guys working with a driver in order to achieve success; part of the small circle of trust I'd seen celebrate their victories before. I felt envious knowing how much winning meant to them and I'd looked up to those guys for doing it. Now I was part of the actual event.

It was an exciting time. For the 2003 season, our designers had come up with a radical new car, the MP4-18, employing some revolutionary concepts in aerodynamics, but it was decided to hold back its introduction to racing until the inevitable teething issues were sorted out on the test track. We were to begin the championship with an updated version of the MP4-17 (the MP4-17D), which, having been used throughout 2002, was now well tuned and understood by us all.

It transpired as a lucky escape. The MP4-18 turned out to be, without doubt, the worst racing car I've ever worked with and I was fortunate to only go on one test with it. The poor Test Team spent a dismal few months wrestling with it, trying to tame it, hone it, and polish what was fast becoming known as a turd on wheels. Not that any improvements arrived easily. It was difficult to work on because the radically tight packaging of the bodywork around the rear end was so restrictive we couldn't get enough access to adjust or install anything. It broke down regularly and for more reasons than I'd care to remember, and most of the time it never left the garage because something had failed before it even got moving.

If ever it did manage to turn a wheel and complete an entire installation lap, the '18 was guaranteed to be on fire by the time it returned.

The V10 exhausts ran unconventionally underneath the gearbox and through the car's carbon-fibre floor, and to improve the aerodynamics they were designed with very little space around them. That meant everything was cooked in their vicinity because the cooling airflow that traditional over-the-top exhausts benefitted from just wasn't there. To make matters worse, the engine overheated and the chassis repeatedly failed to pass the FIA's stringent safety crash tests; it had a number of unexplained and slightly strange accidents in the hands of Alex Wurz, our test driver – and it wasn't even that fast.

Having been on the McLaren Race Team for a year myself, I already knew everyone and was friendly with Kimi's crew. I also understood what I was doing with the 2002 car, which we were continuing to use. Just as importantly, I'd figured Kimi out to a certain extent, so all I had to do in my new role was fit in with everybody's way of working while learning the procedures and protocols of a race car crew. I realised pretty quickly that a Grand Prix weekend is a very different experience as part of a driver's race crew, but in a good way. For starters, being responsible for a car that would race felt different to being responsible for one that *might* race. Actually, putting the car together and preparing it was pretty much the same process, but the pressure to make it perfect seemed greater. Everyone knew that if there was a problem with the front end of Kimi's car, I'd built it, I was responsible for it, but somehow I enjoyed that extra pressure. I felt important and thrived on the responsibility. And so the 2003 season began: the dawning of a new, exciting, and slightly more stressful era.

McLaren got off to a great start and our updated MP4-17D car looked very promising, despite having a few fragility issues: DC won the season's first Grand Prix in Australia and we came third with Kimi. It was an amazing feeling to climb the pit wall fence, hanging over the track and cheering our two drivers across the finish line in style. What an opening weekend! I felt hugely proud of myself and of our team and experienced a new level of emotion I'd craved and yearned for while working on the T-Car the year before.

My first actual experience of winning had been when DC unexpectedly took the Monaco Grand Prix back in 2002. It was my first season on the race team so when it happened the experience was incredible. It was amazing seeing his car crew being so overjoyed by the experience. Everyone was congratulating them and they felt like heroes. I ran out of the garages with DC's mechanics, this young kid, new to the team, soaking up every last drop of the moment. I knew then that I wanted to be part of it for real; I wanted to be one of those guys one day. It was such a big deal I still have the newspaper cuttings detailing the win at home.

If Australia felt good and forged an inspirational path for us all, then the next round in Malaysia would give us memories I'll never, ever forget. With two drivers on the podium in the previous race, we had total belief in ourselves and felt good going into that weekend, despite the intense heat and humidity at the Sepang Circuit outside Kuala Lumpur. I strapped Kimi into the car on the grid, dripping sweat all over him as I leaned in to buckle up the belts, and when he made a joke about it I knew he was feeling relaxed at that point, which I assumed was a good thing. Then, casually, just a few seconds before I had to leave the grid ahead of the race start, he asked me how many laps the race lasted for.

'Er, well, its fifty-six, but . . . Shouldn't you know that by now?' I replied, double-checking I wasn't the victim of some elaborate prank.

It later turned out that Kimi hadn't a clue how long he was supposed to be racing for and that this would become a common occurrence. It had been no joke.

DC's car had an electronics failure in Malaysia and had to retire, but Kimi kept on going and going. The rate of technical development back then was so relentless and extreme that F1 cars and their engines were never the same two races in a row, which resulted in a lot of experimental parts and inevitable mechanical risk. So when Kimi was leading one of the hottest and toughest Grand Prix in the world, having never won one before, either as a crew or even by himself, we were all tense. I couldn't take my eyes off the garage monitors; my fingers were crossed and my knees bounced with nervous energy as I sat watching on, *hoping*.

Management wanted Kimi to slow his pace towards the end and I could understand why. We had a huge thirty-second lead over the car behind and with just a few laps to go everybody was concerned about the engine holding out. It turned out that Kimi didn't do 'slow' very well and went on setting faster and faster lap times, ignoring our advice on the radio and extending his lead to almost forty seconds with two laps left. It drove our Chief Engineer, Steve Hallam, mad – a man who was so straight-as-you-like, well spoken and ethereal that the garage had nicknamed him 'The Reverend'.

'Kimi, we've got a forty-second lead, I want you to back off now and bring the car home?' said The Reverend on the radio.

Silence.

Another half a lap passed. 'Kimi, this is serious now,' warned The Reverend. 'We really need you to back off and lower the engine mode on the steering whee—'

The comms suddenly exploded into life. *JUST STOP TALKING – I KNOW WHAT I'M FUCKING DOING!'*

When Kimi eventually passed the McLaren garage to begin his final lap, everybody charged across the pitlane, cheering him towards the finishing line. I still felt nervous, though. I figured it was too premature to celebrate, and as I stared at the TV screens, taking in the exciting scenes, I couldn't quite allow myself to believe that we might actually be achieving the ultimate: a Grand Prix win. Then, realising the giant spectator viewing screens outside would still enable me to see the closing stages, I allowed myself to break away from the garage monitors and ran into the pitlane to join the gang. Finding a gap among the melee of black pitstop suits crowding around for a glimpse of F1's newest race winner was hard work, but somehow I wriggled through. I wasn't going to miss this moment for anything: Kimi took the chequered flag and won his, and our, first ever Formula One Grand Prix. The relief; the adrenaline; the emotion. It was a moment I'll never forget.

9

CHASING GLORY

The amazing experiences just kept on coming.

At the very next Grand Prix, in Brazil, we were crowned victors again, or so we thought. A rain-soaked and chaotic race ended prematurely with a spectacular crash for Mark Webber in his Jaguar, which Fernando Alonso then slammed into, *hard*. Kimi had been leading the race moments before the accident, when a slight mistake allowed Giancarlo Fisichella to slip into first place. With the crash causing a real mess on the track, the red flags inevitably came out shortly afterwards, ending the Grand Prix, which was when the chaos began.

F1 rules stated that the result should be taken from the order of cars on the lap *before* the race was stopped, and there was some confusion about whether it was Fisichella's Jordan team or ours that had actually won. Even as we waited under the podium, none of us really knew what the hell was going on and there was a slightly surreal moment, the McLaren crew standing shoulder to shoulder with our rivals dressed in yellow, all of us waiting to find out the result. When the news came over our team radio from Dave Ryan, we went crazy: Kimi had been awarded first place. Of course, no one else had heard the message from Dave, so we must have looked like right idiots as we leapt around on our own, with everybody else still none the wiser.

Much as we felt for our confused friends at Jordan, we were delighted to be celebrating another win.

Our celebrations soon turned out to be premature though. Several days later, after further review, it emerged that Fisichella, while briefly leading the Brazilian race, had actually crossed the line and started a new lap in first place, just before the red flags had been waved to end the Grand Prix. That meant the final result was to be taken from the lap *after* the one the track officials had originally registered. With the parameters altered ever so slightly, it turned out that Giancarlo Fisichella had actually won the race, not us, and at the next round in San Marino we had to give the trophy back.

Kimi moved on from there. Finishing in second place at three of the next four races was brilliant, yet slightly frustrating at the same time, but I guess that was a sign of our unbound ambition – we were taking on the mighty Michael Schumacher and Ferrari after all. The last of those four races was Monaco (the other podium finishes being San Marino and Austria) and we'd headed there while leading the Driver's Championship, something none of us could have dreamt of before the season started. To take a race win on the streets of Monte Carlo was something very special indeed, and we'd be lucky enough to experience that sensation two years later. But in 2003 we finished less than a second behind winner (and future teammate) Juan Pablo Montoya, though any bad feelings about missing out on first were tempered by the fact that we'd extended our lead over Schumacher.

This was a big deal. My time in F1 coincided with Schuey's most successful years and he was the one we were always trying to beat. He was our arch-nemesis, particularly through the Mika Hakkinen years. Mika beat Michael to the World Championships in 1998 and 1999; Michael defeated him in the remainder, and a rivalry had formed between the two teams as well as the two drivers, but in the pitlane we had huge respect for one another. Michael set the standard and he was a nice guy too, though he had a reputation of not being well liked by some of the public. In reality, he was hard and tough in a racing car and may've done some questionable things on the track, but he was a lovely bloke to be around.

Kimi, under McLaren, had established himself as a genuine and exciting title contender. We were consistently beating our teammate, DC, which was the only true benchmark to measure oneself against in F1, given the difference in other teams' equipment. As a crew we were as close as I've ever been to a group of colleagues. We relied heavily on one other; we trusted each other, knew each other inside out, and despite the exhausting schedule and long hours spent working at the racetrack, we still found time to play together too. As a team we were all truly dedicated to winning the championship, and with Kimi we really believed we could do it.

Our faith was about to be tested to the limit.

Sure, Kimi could make mistakes at times. In Spain and Canada, he went off the track during qualifying and had to start his races from the back of the pack. Thankfully, those errors were pretty rare. He was always racing at the edge, which was why he was so fast, and if ever he started a Grand Prix in last place, it was actually a joy to watch him as he tore through the field towards the front. Obviously we'd have preferred not to have any mistakes at all, but in a team of people, of which he was one key player, they happened. We learned that how we actually dealt with those setbacks was what would define our crew, not any mistakes themselves, and after a brief door-kicking, or laptop-slamming blow-up from Sladey, we'd gather together to formulate the recovery plan.

In those moments, Kimi would usually walk back into the garage after a crash or a spin in qualifying to apologise. Sometimes he'd simply shrug his shoulders, as if to say, 'Shit happens.' We'd smile and call him a wanker and move on. Despite years of trying to get him to help me clean or fix his broken car after an accident as punishment for his cock-ups, only once did I ever persuade him to pick up a cloth and wipe the dust from the chassis. And that only happened after I'd screamed at him like it was an emergency. With my hands hidden and contorted inside the cockpit where he couldn't see them, I pretended I was stuck, in trouble and urgently needing his help. Once he'd rushed over to me with the cloth with a worried look on his face, I started laughing.

'Ah, thanks very much,' I said calmly, knowing I'd reeled him in. 'Give that a quick polish will you mate?'

We won together and lost together, and despite the car failing on occasions, the team understood there was rarely anything we could have done about it. Kimi knew it, too. The MP4-17D was a fragile animal and we pushed it all the way, all the time, in our desperate chase for success. The decision had now been made not to introduce the troubled MP4-18 into the McLaren line-up, and having spoken to some of the Test Team mechanics about their experiences with it I couldn't say I was disappointed. After numerous brake and suspension failures, plus several big shunts, our test driver, Alex Wurz, had finally refused point-blank to drive it again, something the race drivers had done some time ago. He called the Test Team Manager after one particularly horrific crash, where the engine had ended up detached from the car, landing alongside him on the tarmac. Enough was enough, said Alex, he wasn't getting in it again and I couldn't blame him. It was the last time the MP4-18 ever turned a wheel.

On one hand, that decision would have seemed sensible and a win-win, particularly given our championship position with the established car. But because the arrival of the MP4-18 had been promised, and delayed, for such a long time now, when it was finally shelved for good, development had already stopped completely on the engine for our ageing MP4-17D. The focus had been for some time on the all-singing, all-dancing brand-new model as its anticipated replacement, rather than improving what we already had. As the season went on, we fell behind Ferrari, both in terms of pace, but also in points as they out-developed us during our stunted technical progression. As a team, though, we never gave up. We worked harder with what we had, looking for any small improvements, no matter how tiny they might have seemed at the time. Between our amazing spirit and determination and Kimi's unfeasible knack of dragging the car around the track faster than should have been possible, we managed to stay in touch of the championship right to the very end.

Where we lost out in speed, we made up for it with clever race strategy, and we kept Schuey and Ferrari looking over their shoulders all the way. Heading into the final round in Japan we had a slim outside chance of becoming champions. We needed to win the race with Schuey finishing outside of the point-scoring positions. However unlikely this scenario, the Japanese Grand Prix still felt like the biggest of my career so far. Qualifying had been chaotic, with rain affecting some drivers more than others, and we eventually only qualified eighth, which wasn't great. But Kimi had won from seventh in Malaysia, so we knew success was possible. More importantly, Schumacher was only fourteenth.

It was *on*.

The morning of the race felt different to any other. There was a greater pressure than before and I was nervous, terrified I'd forget something, or make the mistake that might let Kimi and the boys down. And if I did, the whole world would know about it instantly. My mind drifted back to a chat I'd had with an experienced colleague when I first joined McLaren. He'd been Mika Hakkinen's tyre man for years, but was retiring at a relatively early age. I remember asking why he was leaving his incredible job, not understanding how someone could want to walk away from something I'd dreamt of being part of for years.

'I was on the grid in Mika's last championship-deciding race of 1999,' he said, 'waiting to remove the heated tyre blankets before the race started and I was shaking with fear.'

Something had clicked in him. 'I thought, "If I'm so scared of making mistakes, wrapping up the wrong race tyres in their blankets, or setting the wrong tyre pressures for such a big occasion, that it means I'm going to work in utter fear, then I need to get out," ' he explained.

He'd decided to do something less stressful. 'There were more import-ant things in life to be worried about,' he'd concluded. It was a fair point, but I was a long way from giving up my privileged position.

Still, in Suzuka, I could empathise with those emotions. I kept recalling his words while working on the grid. I found myself walking around our car and looking at every part, questioning myself whether I'd actually done up the fixings in the garage, or calculated the correct amount of ballast to ensure the car made the minimum weight limit. In that moment I understood exactly what he'd been talking about.

There was so much at stake; every single one of us on the crew wanted to win the championship more than anything else that day, and if we didn't, I couldn't bear us failing because of something that I'd either done or hadn't done. But in some strange twist of maso-chism, instead of wanting to get away from the situation like my esteemed colleague had done years before, I wanted more. I realised that I loved it. The fear was put firmly in its place by the adrenaline coursing through my veins and I thrived off its buzz. For years I'd watched these moments on television, in awe of the guys around the cars, lining up on the starting grid before a race, wondering if one day that could possibly be me. Call it egotistical, but I thought I was one of the most important people in the world that afternoon. Something Formula One had a bad habit of doing to a person.

Michael Schumacher's Ferrari crew, further back on the grid, had been dominant in the sport for so many years and here we were, little old us, taking them on. The TV crews were all over Kimi. He was the new kid on the block, an underdog, but a talent everyone was sure would be a champion one day, even if not today. Meanwhile, Kimi was as pragmatic as ever. He'd give it everything, it was the only racing style he knew, and after that? Well, we'd have to see what hap-pened. If we won, amazing; if we didn't, we'd try again next season. There was never any politics with Kimi, there were rarely any demands or fuss. He was an easy guy to work with and his attitude rubbed off on us all.

The driver in any crew's always the figurehead, the leader and the guy the mechanics and engineers look up to, so that's partly why we all worked so well together with Kimi. He was level-headed, always relaxed, and an absolute pleasure to be around, so we gave him everything we had. Simultaneously, we knew he was doing the exact same thing for us: giving it his all. Together, we knew the result of the 2003 Drivers' Championship could be decided by something, or someone, beyond our control, but our task was a simple one. We had to win the Grand Prix.

Whatever transpired, we knew we'd become a stronger crew as a result of what we'd been through that year.

Everything happened in that race.

We moved forward from eighth to second; at one point, Schumacher fell from fourteenth to the back of the pack after two separate collisions, one of which cost him his front wing. The gods were teasing us, *tantalising* us, with the hope that the unlikely could actually occur. I was gripped to the edge of my seat, adrenaline surging through me for the entire race, peaking with every pitstop. I remember coming back into the garage after each one so pumped that my entire body trembled with excitement.

With a handful of laps to go, we were still second to Schumacher's teammate, Rubens Barrichello. He was fast, very fast, and some way ahead of Kimi, so we really needed him to have an issue if we were to get close or past him. Schuey, meanwhile, had worked his way towards eighth, the final point-scoring position in those days. Kimi chased and chased and never stopped believing, but in the end Barrichello won the race, we came second and Michael snuck into eighth position, taking his sixth World Title by just two points.

We were gutted, but at the same time so proud of what we'd achieved together during our first season as a new crew. There were handshakes, hugs and commiserations all round, but the overwhelming feeling was a positive one. We'd done our absolute best and against the odds, working with an underdeveloped car, which had pushed F1's legendary megastar right to the wire – *we'd made him work hard for that one*. I went straight to the Ferrari boys in the pitlane and without knowing a single word of Italian, showed them my appreciation. We embraced and ran to the podium together. It felt like we'd all been part of something very special. Kimi was now a true F1 frontrunner and the respect he had amongst the paddock was more than deserved and we all felt honoured to be part of his success. When he finally got back to us at the garage, the five mechanics, three engineers, Kimi's trainer and Kimi himself crowded together in a team huddle. It was a moment that summed up the special unity our little group had built over the year.

That night there was the traditionally wild end-of-season party at the Suzuka Circuit Log Cabin karaoke venue. I'd exhausted myself during the race, the adrenaline had faded, and now the sustained expenditure of nervous energy was taking its toll, I was knackered. But the idea of *not* partying wasn't in our nature; any despondent thoughts were long gone, and by 4 a.m. I was singing 'Easy Like Sunday Morning' with a slurring Norbert Haug, the motorsport boss of Mercedes Benz, on one arm, and Michael Schumacher, so drunk he could hardly stand, let alone sing, hanging off the other. He was wearing a shirt from the Toyota team, soaked with beer, ripped and barely clinging to him. At one point I remember Schuey falling through a window and onto the grass outside. Fortunately, it was a ground-floor building.

He'd been determined to celebrate his championship win in style. Earlier in the evening he'd stolen a forklift with a bunch of guys from Toyota and driven around the paddock with about eight passengers holding on for dear life. When we bumped into him later, also in high spirits ourselves, the union resulted in a rock'n'roll-style trashing of the team's hospitality offices in the paddock and I have an ever-lasting memory of a large table being thrown through the window.

At around 6:30 a.m., when I finally realised I had to return to my hotel to catch the 7 a.m. bus to the airport, I panicked. It was at least twenty minutes away and there were no taxis anywhere in the usually sleepy little town. There were three of us, so I did what I'm sure any unscrupulous, unprincipled and shamelessly drunk F1 mechanic would have done in that situation: I went straight across to the Suzuka Circuit Hotel reception, pretended to the ever-so-polite receptionist that I was back-of-the-grid Formula One driver Justin Wilson, and asked if they could give me the keys to his scooter. All the drivers stayed at the Suzuka Circuit because of its proximity to the track so I guessed I had a fair chance of at least getting that bit right.

To my amazement, despite the fact that I appeared nothing like Justin (I'm nearly a foot shorter) and, at the time, resembled an extra from a zombie movie, the receptionist asked me to sign for the keys. I couldn't believe it. Desperately trying to contain my excitement, I walked back outside to my two teammates who were waiting, neither of them believing there was any real chance of success. Even more amazing was the hotel staff member offering to unlock the bike and raise the security barrier as we departed, bowing politely all the while as he did. Like three comedy inmates escaping from prison, not wanting to blow our disguise, we all stacked ourselves onto the tiny scooter, waved goodbye to our unknowing accomplice, and rode unsteadily off into the sunrise.

Another fairly standard end-of-season night out then.

10

RULES, RULES, RULES

It's no secret that Kimi partied hard at times. There are enough videos on YouTube to back that up, and we got into a number of close calls and scrapes during our time together. Amazingly, though, a number of people have asked me over the years, 'Is it true that Kimi used to turn up drunk on race days?' And while such a stupid question barely dignifies an answer, I can assure you that of course he didn't – *ever*. Apart from the obvious fact it would be a career-ending move for a professional racing driver and would definitely be discovered, he took driving very seriously indeed. He rarely left his hotel room on any night during a race week, watching TV and ordering room service most of the time instead. But when it got to Sunday evening, with the race over, the gloves were off and when our worlds collided and we all ended up at the same post-race party, things could get pretty messy.

The dates are a little fuzzy, but I can recall one Sunday night after the race in Melbourne when I'd bumped into Kimi and a few of his Finnish mates after a party (one of them was a pro ice hockey player and was built like a brick outhouse). A few of our crew and the Finns ended up going back to Kimi's suite at the Crowne Towers for a late drink. Naturally, it got out of hand. Various items of furniture were broken, drinks spilt, and one of the lads cut his head open on a table edge. At about 6 a.m., Kimi called reception and ordered ten full English breakfasts and some beers. When they arrived, we thanked our nervous and slightly confused waitress, took the cart and closed the hotel room door behind her. All was calm.

Ten plates of steaming hot eggs, bacon, sausages, beans and all the trimmings were divided among the group and within thirty seconds, the first hash brown had been thrown at someone across the room. For the next half an hour or so, the place was turned into a war zone. I had baked beans in my hair, my white shirt was covered in ketchup, making me look like the victim of a serious injury; the walls and expensive carpets were peppered with food and the curtains were ripped down as somebody tried to wrap themselves up in a makeshift protective cloak. My lasting memory as I left for the airport to fly home was of Kimi cowering in a corner of the room, using his laptop as a pathetic shield, while eggs and slices of toast rained down upon his head.

I thought no more of it, apart from the occasional chuckle on the flight as memories began to surface through the hangover, but less than an hour after landing in England, my phone rang. It was our officious team coordinator.

'Er, Elvis, were you out with Kimi at the Red Bull party last night?' he said accusingly.

Technically I hadn't been, as we'd been somewhere else and had only met Kimi after he'd left the Red Bull party.

'No, why?' I replied angelically, biting my knuckles as I awaited his response.

He sounded sceptical, maybe even a little disappointed. After confirming again that I hadn't gone to the party, he went on to explain that a huge amount of damage had been caused in Kimi's hotel suite. He wanted to be absolutely sure none of the mechanics were involved. I calmly assured him once more, without having to cross the line into outright lies, that I wasn't at the Red Bull bash and my friends and I had all been out together elsewhere in the city.

I got off the phone, panic-stricken that I was about to get busted for something major and immediately called Mark Arnall, Kimi's trainer and my best buddy. Most of the time Mark knew almost everything about what Kimi had been up to, often because he was the one hiding the tracks or covering up the latest misdemeanours on Kimi's behalf. Mark confirmed that, yeah, the hotel had been furious the next day, understandably so, but Kimi's manager, Steve, had managed to calm them down with a substantial sum of cash to redecorate the suite, and I imagine some kind of signed memorabilia. Mark assured me that everything had been taken care of and there shouldn't be any comebacks. Apparently that's just how things rolled with multi-millionaire sports stars, and on that occasion I was very happy to have been bailed out by the celebrity high rollers.

Kimi loved an impromptu party, but none of them were more impromptu that the one he got into during the 2006 F1 Monaco Grand Prix. Yes, you read that correctly: *during*. With his car stopping halfway through the race due to a heat shield failure, Kimi parked up, got out and walked around the harbour wall to where his super-yacht had been moored. Still wearing his gloves and crash helmet, he then climbed aboard. I remember watching him from the garage, despondent because we'd had another failure in a season full of them, but laughing, wishing I could have climbed onboard with him.

We never heard another word from him all race. Comms were lost as he stepped away from the car, but the cameras had spotted him. A few laps later, they zoomed in on Kimi, de-clothed and relaxing in his hot tub on the yacht's upper deck. He didn't return to the garage for his debrief and the party started right there as the rest of the field continued to race around the streets of the principality in front of him. We finally caught up with Kimi sometime later, but by then he was well beyond the point of no return and any form of sensible conversation about the race had to wait until the next day.

Whereas we all lived and worked under the intense scrutiny of our enigmatic, Bond villain-style boss and rarely did anything to seriously wobble the perfect corporate balance he created, Kimi did what he wanted and the people around Ron would have to repair any 'damage' or come up with creative statements to divert attention away from whatever it was Kimi had done or said that week. He'd then come into the garage at a race weekend and we'd all have a little laugh together about what the team had said to the press versus what he told us had actually happened.

Whenever Kimi misbehaved, Ron would inevitably call Mark, who lived nearby and trained with him most days. Together, they went to the same events and worked closely at every Grand Prix. Not many people knew Kimi like Mark did, so whenever a newspaper report or photograph emerged, or a reporter phoned the McLaren front desk asking for a comment on a story about Kimi's latest alleged antics, Ron would pick up the phone to Mark. Mark then had to hope that the story either wasn't true, or, if it was, convince Ron that it was a journalistic mistake and that Kimi was fine and training hard, not in fact recovering from some mythical event such as a three-day bender involving public nakedness and damage to a well-known nightclub, as was once fairly accurately reported.

Then there was the occasion when Ron called to enquire about the legitimacy of a wildfire rumour that Kimi had broken his arm in an off-season snowmobiling competition. Mark explained to Ron that he'd just spoken to his driver and that they were about to train together. The minute Ron had been assuaged with a believable alibi, Mark then phoned around Kimi's mates to get the real story. This was followed by a call to the best doctors in Finland for urgent, but discreet, treatment to a fractured forearm.

Throughout much of the early part of the 2004 season our car was rarely on the track, because of various technical issues. If the MP4-18 had been a horror show of near catastrophic proportions in 2003, then its successor – supposedly the phoenix to rise from the ashes of Chief Designer Adrian Newey's ill-fated works – was hardly an upgrade.

Don't get me wrong, Adrian's an undisputed genius when it comes to car design. His record of championship-winning success is unparalleled in the sport and he's long been considered an F1 guru in aerodynamics. He can also be a stubborn character, and if there's an idea he believes in, like he did with the MP4-18, he won't let go of it until he's proved its effectiveness.

Part of our problem in 2003 was that Adrian refused to accept that his new car wasn't the right way to go. It was a radical design and much of its aerodynamic principles eventually became commonplace in Formula One, but not until years later. The MP4-18 was simply ahead of its time and we couldn't make it work in that era. Likewise, the MP4-19 began 2004 with all sorts of reliability problems. Of the first seven races, Kimi failed to finish five and DC retired in three – one of the worst records I can remember and a pretty depressing way to start the year. Having come so close the season before, we all thought our momentum would help us to go one better and finally dethrone the great Schumacher, but it wasn't to be.

The trouble with a poor car wasn't just the terrible results, since for a mechanic it generally translates into more work. We were forever taking it apart and putting it back together; fixing it or, when it did manage to run, trying even harder than ever to find new ways to make it go quicker. This was well before the days of any such thing as a paddock curfew (which the F1 mechanics of more recent times enjoy) so all-nighters were commonplace in our garage during the early part of that season. Rival teams would leave the circuit for their hotels and walk past our garage while shouting hilarious comments.

'Don't forget to turn the circuit lights out when you leave, will you!'

'Would you mind popping next door and turning our engine heaters on around 5 a.m. for us, please, so we can have a lie-in?'

We laughed through gritted teeth but it wasn't funny for us at all.

It's amazing to think about the kind of work we were doing come race day: making strategic decisions, doing pitstops and strapping drivers into cars we'd assembled with only a handful of hours sleep all week. The consequences of getting any of it wrong could have been considerable, but that was just how it was in those days. It certainly wasn't just at our team; it was a symptom of the era in general. Although that year we were having a particular nightmare, and before the days of health and safety regulations in F1, no one got much more than about two or three short nights of sleep across the entire five days when we were working at a race.

Our car was so poor in the first half of the year, a journalist for the *Daily Express*, Bob McKenzie, even wrote in his column that he would 'happily run naked around Silverstone should McLaren win a race this season'. The situation was serious. Ron soon put his foot down and told Adrian and the design team to come up with a new car, and just after the mid-season point, it arrived. The MP4-19B was born in July 2004 and it was definitely an improvement, in that it was a fast car and inherently simpler and more reliable. A welcome podium followed for us at the 2004 British Grand Prix, and by the time we'd got to Spa that August, we'd started to understand its characteristics and nuances a little better. Tenth place wasn't a great qualifying position, but in a busy race and with a number of fortuitous safety cars helping us, Kimi somehow hustled it into first and we won the 2004 Belgian Grand Prix.

It felt like we'd won the championship, such was the outpouring of built-up frustration from the rest of the season. The podium at Spa in those days was quite a run from the pitlane, but we sprinted there, none of us quite believing we'd tasted victory again during such a desolate year. I remember rushing to get a good spot when one of the FOM TV cameramen shoved his lens in my face. I was so excited I grabbed the end and screamed a celebratory obscenity straight down the barrel. I don't think they ever broadcast the footage.

The boost was just what we needed and the whole team celebrated the result. The irony, though, and one very indicative of our tragic season, was that while we were celebrating Kimi's one-off victory in Belgium, Michael Schumacher's second-place finish behind us had sealed a seventh and now record-breaking World Title for him, and with four races still to go. He and his team thoroughly deserved it of course, but we'd failed to put up any sort of fight and that was a real shame. On the plus side, *Daily Express* journo and good sport Bob McKenzie did indeed run a lap of Silverstone the following season, wearing nothing but some McLaren branded body paint and an embarrassed smile on his face.

Without the pressures of a championship fight, we managed to enjoy ourselves away from the racetrack a little more freely. Kimi shoulder-shrugged his way through the numerous mechanical failures and the rest of us followed suit: there was nothing much more we could have done with the car we had. Kimi went as fast as he could until it broke each time, and that was how he treated every race car. The idea of nursing one home just didn't figure in his repertoire, he went flat out or bust, and we came to accept that M.O. because *his* flat out was so blisteringly quick. Once a race was over, whether at the chequered flag, or parked by the side of the racetrack on lap one, there was nothing more he could do. In his mind he left each disaster behind, psychologically moving on almost immediately, often to a party or nightclub, and as soon as the garage had been packed away, we were normally right behind him.

I loved being on the Race Team, although working at a test could actually be much more fun than being at a Grand Prix sometimes. There was far less pressure to behave, for starters. The reporters weren't there in force, likewise the paparazzi. Most importantly, Ron was often missing too, so the drivers were relaxed and so were we.

At one test in particular, Kimi was late getting to the French Circuit Paul Ricard in time for the beginning of our planned private test. We'd booked the entire track exclusively to try some new parts without the prying eyes of the media or other teams watching on, but at 8 a.m. he was nowhere to be seen. Out of the blue, the Test Team Manager got a phone call. It was Kimi. Driving to the track in his own custom DTM (German Touring Car)-inspired Mercedes road car, he'd been a bit late, so pushed the speed limits a little (probably a lot). The local French police coming the other way spotted him, flashed the blue lights and turned round to have a word, but instead of stopping and becoming even later for the test, Kimi had taken the split-second decision to keep it flat out along the long deserted French motorway and . . . well, he gave them the slip!

The cheeky but still super-relaxed phone call came to ask if we could open up one of the spare garage doors further down the pitlane so that Kimi could drive straight in, close it and 'hide' the rather distinctive car he was driving, just in case anyone should come looking for it. We did just that and the car remained there for two days before he carefully drove it home once the test was over. It was like something out of the Dick Dastardly playbook.

In many ways, the following season in 2005 was a similar year to 2003. We had a fast car and won plenty of races, but we were too often denied the chequered flag because something had broken or failed. Our crew was stronger than ever, especially after the ups and downs of the previous campaigns together, but the opposition had changed. Schumacher's Ferrari and their partner Bridgestone had struggled to adapt to the all new tyre regulations, which required a very different technical approach.* Meanwhile, the Michelin runners, which included us, were experiencing a tyre advantage for a change. The new man of the moment, and our new biggest rival, was Fernando Alonso and Renault.

Nevertheless, the year was a lot of fun for me, and it was great to be back to winning ways. Kimi later won Grand Prix races in Spain, Monaco and Canada. DC had left the team after many years at McLaren and we'd given him a send-off in the only way we knew: everybody got hideously drunk and caused havoc in a local nightclub

---

* These rules stipulated that a car could use only one set of tyres for qualifying and one for the race.

somewhere. In loving homage to his trademark, incessant moaning about his rear view mirrors not being adjusted properly *every time he stepped into his car*, we presented him with a beautiful plaque-mounted McLaren MP4-19 mirror assembly, which was fully-customised, adjustable and complete with remote controls. There were tears and an emotional speech and we were all genuinely sad to see him go.

From his point of view he'd always been the consummate professional, winning thirteen Grand Prix, but never quite regularly matching up to the machine-like Mika Hakkinen. Then, perhaps frustratingly for him, Kimi had arrived as a young hopeful who quickly proved himself as another excellent driver, and DC couldn't consistently reach the standards he was setting either. He was finding it so hard at times that, at one point, he turned to a sports psychologist for help, which I thought was indicative of his desire to win and a very brave move at the time, but it just didn't work out for him. Nevertheless, it was a testament to his character that we were all sad to see DC go – believe me, it doesn't always work out that way.

In his place came the highly rated Juan Pablo Montoya as teammate to us and Kimi. Meanwhile, Alonso emerged early as a very strong contender for the title as Schumacher struggled, and Kimi, as ever, forced some impressive results from our fragile car. Montoya had to pull out of the third and fourth races of the season due to an injury sustained while away from the track. He'd told Ron he'd hurt his shoulder playing tennis in between races and so that was exactly what the team's press release stated, but rumours quickly began whizzing around that it may not have been strictly true. When Kimi turned up to Bahrain, with Pedro de la Rosa standing in in the other car, we were chatting at the back of the garage on the first day and I asked him what he thought of JPM's tennis story.

'Total bollocks,' he laughed. 'My friend was at the same motocross event as him and he tried to ride a mini motorbike around a dirt track and crashed!'

Kimi loved the mischief he was causing because, for once, he wasn't at the centre of it all.

As the on-track rivalry between Kimi and Renault's Fernando Alonso grew, so did the competition between our respective teams. Our garages were positioned right next to Renault in the pitlane order and we'd already become good friends with most of their guys. As the season went on, we shared jokes and nights out together as a healthy respect developed between us. If ever we won a race, they'd all come to our garage and congratulate us and we'd reciprocate if the result went the other way. It was a nice way to go racing and definitely not something we'd experienced with Ferrari in the preceding years.

Renault had no qualms in not hiding their team's party spirit, which was great for anyone within their orbit. They were a breath of fresh air, performing fancy press stunts or wheeling out skimpily dressed models or A-list celebs, who'd then drape themselves across the car for photographs. It was proper eye candy and McLaren, as next door neighbours, had the front-row seats. It was a bit tabloid at times and went against a lot of what Ron Dennis stood for, and most weekends our garage was almost like a library in comparison.

Because of the boss's dislike of anything unordered, or beyond his control, music was banned from our garages on the official days of a Grand Prix, as, eventually, was chocolate and sweets, believe it or not. Ron reckoned our stereo system didn't give off the right image, and sugary snacks were unhealthy and unprofessional, but it used to drive me crazy. I loved music in the evenings, especially as we stripped and rebuilt the cars and although I wasn't a big sweet eater, they occasionally kept me going through the long nights when fatigue might have otherwise ground me to a halt. And apart from that, I was angry at the mere principle of having them taken away from our snack bowl as an option.

Luckily we weren't frustrated for long. Following a quick word with our noisy neighbours at Renault, who had by far the best sound system in F1, their tunes were cranked up a notch or two so we could share in their party atmosphere through the temporary walls – they were even taking requests passed on bits of paper between the garages. When they heard about our healthy food rations, they took pity on us and wrapped up covert 'Red Cross' parcels full of Mars Bars, lollipops and fizzy drinks to keep us going. We later learned that their flamboyant team principal, Flavio Briatore had enquired one day as to why his team had been playing their tunes so loud at the Singapore Grand Prix. When they explained our plight and mentioned how much Ron hated music in his garage, he apparently called over his personal assistant and directed her into the city centre where she was sent immediately to buy the biggest speakers available.

Following wins for Kimi in Spain and then Monaco, we headed to the Nürburgring for the European GP in May. McLaren were on a roll, eager to eat into Alonso's championship lead, and as the race got underway, things were looking good. Kimi led the race on lap one, but then a massive lock-up under braking heavily flat-spotted his right front tyre. The new rules for 2005 prevented us from changing tyres at pitstops, so the damaged Michelin had to stay in place.

Kimi continued to lead the race while simultaneously holding off Fernando, but everybody knew that the vibrations from the damaged tyre were causing significant problems elsewhere. Our technical bods were very concerned about the stresses, loads and vibrations going through the suspension components, they were being pushed well over their design limits. On the radio we discussed our options. Should we retire the car, or slow the pace to protect the car and concede position to Renault? Should we bring the car in and change the tyre anyway, with the idea we could later argue our decision to the stewards on safety grounds and therefore claim it wasn't a breach of the rules? (That would also mean conceding track position to Renault.)

Kimi was struggling out on the track. 'The vibrations are blurring my vision,' he shouted over the radio.

I believed him, too. Whenever our car went past we could hear the unique noise it was making and could see the shaking from the on-board camera, like the tyre was the shape of a fifty pence piece. In the end, the pit wall asked Kimi what he wanted to do.

'We keep going,' he said determinedly. Even if we'd ordered him to retire the car, I suspected Kimi would have ignored us and kept on racing anyway.

Somehow he held the lead, keeping Alonso well back in a brilliant drive, despite the vibrations becoming louder and visibly more violent. We'd been on the edge of our seats, but finally we headed into the last lap of the race with Alonso in second, closing slightly. All we needed was for Kimi to hold on to the finish line.

It would've been an amazing victory for us, but as Kimi hit the brakes for turn one for the final time, the right front suspension fell apart. I watched in horror as our car span off into the gravel trap on three wheels. My heart sank, I couldn't believe it. I was gutted. Gutted we'd taken a brave gamble and it hadn't paid off. It was exactly the decision we knew Kimi would've taken out on track and the one we'd have all taken too, but it had not only cost us the win, but gifted it straight to Fernando Alonso.

The truth is, I did feel those things, but not until much later. From the moment the car's front end had disintegrated, I'd been in shock. It was a reaction I'd never experienced before, but my mind had just seen the part of the car I was responsible for fall apart when leading the race on the final lap. Was it something I'd left loose? Was it something I'd forgotten to do, or installed incorrectly? Was Kimi OK?

I walked outside, to the back of the garage, and sat down against the wall, wracking my brains, consumed with a guilt I wasn't sure was appropriate. I smoked occasionally back then, as almost everyone did in the nicotine-flooded F1 paddock of the day, before the banning of tobacco sponsorship took away everyone's free supply of cigarettes. I must have sucked down five on the bounce, as one by one, fellow smokers came out, commiserated about the result, shared a ciggie, and left me to my next.

My paranoia was increasing. I'd by now learned that Kimi was OK, but it had been a big accident, significant in more ways than one, and the whole world had seen it. If the root cause later turned out to be my fault, how could I face the boys? How could I face Kimi? And how could I hold my head up in the pitlane, knowing the other mechanics had seen it too? I knew the vibrations had been serious, but my brain was placing far less significance on that in its assessment of the accident. Instead, I was desperately searching for the one thing I might have – *must have* – done wrong.

Eventually our Chief Engineer joined me as I wallowed in self-pity and insecurity. He explained that the vibrations seen in our data were so extreme that 'it was no surprise the pushrod had failed in that way; it had simply shaken itself to bits'. The relief was immense. Those reassuring words were all I needed to bring me back. Yes, I was still gutted, along with everyone else, but at least I hadn't let my team down, which would have been far, far worse.

We went on to win at the next race in Canada and then it was on to the single most bizarre Formula One race I've ever seen, and certainly taken part in: the 2005 US Grand Prix in Indianapolis.

11

F1 SUCKS

Plenty of Yanks didn't properly understand Formula One back in 2005, and I could see why. At Indianapolis, the F1 circus arrived and transformed their iconic track into something they barely recognised. Instead of driving the cars at insane speeds around a giant oval for 500 miles of IndyCar racing, we'd instead created our own twisty little circuit, with right-hand as well as left-hand turns in the infield. It was an alien form of racing to them. But when practice got underway on Friday things went pretty well for us on the track. Kimi seemed strong, but Ralf Schumacher had a big accident in his Toyota, coming off the high speed banking at turn thirteen. We all watched the monitors in horror as replays showed the enormity of his shunt, but other than it being a big crash, thought little more of it, once we knew he was OK, that is. A little later, though, rumours began circulating that the accident might have been the result of an unexplained tyre failure, which caused everyone to sit up and take notice.

Incidents potentially involving faulty tyres were treated very seriously, so a full investigation swung into action at both Michelin and Toyota to discover whether their hardware was at fault. A Michelin representative soon arrived to inspect McLaren's used tyres, checking for any signs of damage, and while nothing worrying was discovered, he explained that other Michelin teams were concerned about the integrity of their tyres. In fact, it turned out Ricardo Zonta had experienced a similar but less dramatic blow out at the same point on the track, which increased the severity of Michelin's problem: this technical flaw was no longer confined to just the Toyota cars. As Friday evening went on, Michelin were still unable to find a reason for the failures, and every now and then, our engineers would emerge from a meeting with the tyre experts. Having spent hours poring over analysis and shared data, their confused looks confirmed that we were still no closer to fixing the problem, although the root cause was becoming clear . . .

Turn thirteen on the Indianapolis track was a very high-loading corner on the tyres. It was banked at an angle, which gave the cars more downforce and grip. That meant they could go much faster than they would around a level corner of the same circumference. In turn, the extra speed caused a car's wings to generate even more aerodynamic downforce, which also massively increased the tyre loading. It wasn't a new corner; we'd raced there before with no problems, but it was a unique style of turn in F1. Michelin decided to cover themselves by flying in a completely different batch of tyres from their headquarters in France. Thousands of them, all to the specifications used and proven at the Spanish GP earlier in the season, were now on a charter flight across the Atlantic. On Saturday morning, all Michelin runners were instructed to run higher pressures to firm up and protect the tyres under the high loads, but as a last-ditch effort it didn't work.

While all this had been going on across Friday evening and Saturday morning, one or two people in the paddock had cottoned on to a potential scam. A few people speculated that there probably wouldn't be a solution to such a serious problem, not at such short notice anyway. Theories of what might happen should the Michelin tyres continue to cause safety issues became the chat around the track. We even joked about packing up early, or rescheduling the race for another weekend. 'What would the already-sceptical American fans make of that?' I wondered. But by Saturday lunchtime, after more Michelin failures in third practice, groups of gamblers up and down the pitlane were online, looking up the bookmakers' odds on a number of unusual outcomes for the race.

Hundreds of pounds were soon being laid, at mind-boggling odds, on things like 'A Minardi to score points.' Or 'A Jordan to get on the podium.' Normally, these were almost impossible outcomes, but if no Michelin-shod cars appeared in the race, that would leave just six Bridgestone runners to compete. Two Ferraris, two Jordans and two back-of-the-grid Minardis. I wasn't confident, or brave enough to jump on the wave of conjecture but plenty did.

At McLaren, we hadn't been told anything concrete on the race's chances of going ahead, because there wasn't anything concrete to discuss. The team bosses, tyre suppliers, the FIA, the circuit promoters, Bernie Ecclestone and anyone else who had an interest were desperately searching for a solution to what was becoming a very serious problem. Ron Dennis was down at Bernie's office in the paddock. He'd told us Bernie was doing everything he could to help, and that we should prepare for qualifying as normal. Other teams had speculated that the worst might happen. Friends of mine were saying, 'You've got to get your bets in now, before they cotton on. There's no way the Michelin cars can take part in the race tomorrow!'

Qualifying went well, however. The cars were all deemed safe enough to complete their single qualifying laps, even if Michelin couldn't guarantee their integrity for anything over a ten-lap stint, and Kimi had ended up second. Everybody was still in the dark as to whether the Grand Prix would go ahead, and on Saturday evening, we prepared our cars not knowing what the hell Sunday would have in store for us. Meanwhile, Ron and the management team were continually in meetings with the sport's stakeholders, trying to find ways to enable us to race. Solutions ranged from the idea of installing a makeshift chicane (to slow the cars down through the problematic turn) to making the Michelin runners take a pitstop every ten laps for fresh tyres on safety grounds. Someone even mooted the enforcing of a maximum speed limit for the Michelin cars through turn thirteen. None of them were very F1-type solutions, but these were desperate times with 100,000 people having paid for tickets, all of them expecting an F1 spectacle.

Meanwhile, by Saturday night, all bets were off. The bookmakers had shut the market down as news began to break of the significance of Michelin's woes, but by then many people throughout the paddock had plenty riding on what could be a disastrous outcome for Formula One. On the morning of the race we still continued as instructed as if everything was fine. It seemed impossible for the major parties involved to agree on a common solution, despite the best efforts of lots of people to try to make sure we were able to put on a show for the huge crowd. Kimi's attitude was, 'Let's just all get on with it.' And by then, we agreed. No one knew what was happening, so we got ready and went about our standard working procedures. By now, though, the rumours that we wouldn't be racing had amplified, but the party line from the boss remained: we had to keep going and assume we'd be racing. With half an hour before the pitlane opened and we could all head to the grid, Dave Ryan gathered us together. Ron, he explained, had rushed off to another last-ditch meeting and was still hopeful we'd be taking part in the Grand Prix.

I strapped Kimi into the car, still frustrated with F1's ridiculous politics and prepared to go to the grid. Both drivers were in their cars, the team was waiting to go, but we were being held in the garage for a phone call from Ron, instructing us to release everyone to the grid. When the pitlane opened, we watched as the six Bridgestone cars left their garages. Gradually one or two of the Michelin teams emerged, but still we waited. Dave Ryan, at the front of the garage, stared at his phone, as if willing it ring. We had no idea if we were racing or not. Then Ron burst into the back of the garage, out of breath and uncharacteristically flustered.

t: In the early years of my career, there was so much tobacco money in the sport that the marketing team had cook up all kinds of wacky ideas in order to get through it... such as promotional photo ops with the car and vid Coulthard in a zero gravity plane.

ht: McLaren fuel man Steve Morrow (AKA 'Forklift'), in 2002, sporting the controversial McLaren mechanics' eralls, which were effectively Babygros!

Top: A rare picture of the team testing new temperature-controlled race suits –
they never saw the light of day again.

Bottom left: Kimi Raikkonen's first ever win at the Malaysian GP in 2003 was a very special moment
for the whole team.

Bottom right: Dave Ryan (the Team Manager who delivered the message that my dreadlocks had to go),
with Ron Dennis.

Top: A James Bond villain's lair, or the McLaren Technology Centre?

Bottom left: Head shaved and working on the car ahead of the 2004 United States GP.

Bottom right: The working hours for an F1 mechanic were often punishing, and there was an obsessive demand from Ron Dennis to keep the McLaren garage spotless.

Top: Gathered round a screen, watching the 2005 British GP qualifying session unfold. We secured second for Kimi Raikkonen and fourth for Juan Pablo Montoya, who went on to win the race.

Bottom left: After concerns relating to the safety of the Michelin tyres, the 2005 United States GP slowly developed into a complete shambles.

Bottom right: Ensuring Kimi's brake pedal is rock hard in 2005.

Opposite: Celebrating with Kimi Raikkonen and the team after his 2005 Monaco GP win.

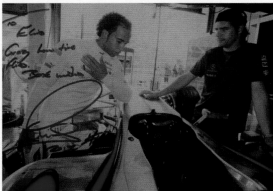

Top left: After car failure in the 2006 Monaco GP, Kimi Raikkonen heads straight to the jacuzzi on his boat while the race continues.

Top right: Kimi Raikkonen cleans blue dye off his hands after his final race for McLaren. The prank would land me in hot water with the McLaren senior management.

Left: Even while still racing in GP2, before getting into F1, Lewis Hamilton impressed the mechanics with his frequent enquiries about the technical intricacies of our car.

Bottom: A painfully uneasy press conference following the qualifying for the Hungarian GP of 2007. Earlier in the day Fernando Alonso had deliberately blocked Lewis Hamilton in the pits, sabotaging his final lap.

Top left: Spygate: Ferrari Technical
Manager Nigel Stepney was discovered
to have shared technical information
about his car with McLaren in 2007.

Top right: Mike Coughlan, McLaren
designer and the other key figure in
the Spygate scandal.

Right: Ron Dennis leaves the F.I.A
headquarters in Paris after the World
Motor Sport Council hearing. For the mechanics, the decision to strip us of
the 2007 Constructors' Championship
points was devastating.

Bottom: Celebrating a 1-2 finish in the
2007 World Championship following
the Italian GP. It would turn out to be
Alonso's last win for the team.

Top left: Lewis Hamilton celebrates with Ron Dennis after winning his first World Championship in 2008. A truly amazing moment.

Top right: The new British sporting hero dominated the front and back pages back home.

Left: 'Adrian's Wall' – You never knew who's watching! Screens were often wheeled out to prevent rival mechanics getting a close look at any of our top secret technical developments.

Bottom: Watching the race unfold in our team garage during the European GP at the Valencia Street Circuit.

'Go . . . *Go!*' he shouted, waving his arms frantically and gesturing us towards the pitlane.

The garage burst into life. We were off.

The grandstands at the Indianapolis Motor Speedway are enormous. America's hardcore F1 fans, plus a vast number of curious part-timers, had turned up in force and the seats were packed. I sensed they were relieved and excited to see all the cars arrive in their grid slots after the confusion and media speculation during the build-up; I know I was. I met the car as it arrived on the grid, helping Kimi out and resetting the belts, refitting the steering wheel and making sure the mirrors and aero screen were clean; I attached the data cable to the side of the chassis. The tyre heaters went on and the engine cooling fans went in; a fuel breather pipe was connected and laptops were attached to communicate with the car. With ten minutes to the race start, I strapped Kimi back into his seat. As ever, he just wanted to race – the surrounding drama was an unnecessary distraction. But as I reached in and connected Kimi's radio cable and drinks pipe to his crash helmet, Ron came and crouched down next to us. He leaned in towards Kimi,

'Kimi, I've just come out of a meeting and it's been decided that we'll do the formation lap and then peel off into the pitlane and retire from the event,' he said in his usual commanding voice. 'All of your immediate competitors will be doing the same. Do you understand?'

Kimi was furious. 'This is fucking bollocks, let's just fucking race. We're here to race, let us fucking race!'

'Kimi!' snapped Ron, angry that he was being disobeyed.

'If none of these other guys want to race, they can go home,' continued Kimi. 'But we're here to race, so let's do it . . .'

Any attempts to placate him weren't working.

'. . . It's a fucking load of bollocks!'

Ron quickly pulled rank. 'Kimi, I am speaking as your boss. You *will* pull into the pits at the end of the formation lap. *Do you understand?*'

Kimi sat in the car, shaking his head. I awkwardly adjusted the side of his crash helmet, pretending I was oblivious to the unfolding drama. Ron was enraged. I could sense it over my shoulder without even looking up.

'Kimi, that is an order,' said Ron.

He stood up and walked away. It was an interesting psychological battle and Ron had lost, something I'd never seen before. I gave Kimi a look as if to say, 'What the hell are you going to do?' He looked back, still fuming, but I could see a naughty smile revealing itself through the visor. I moved away from the car, the lights changed and the for-mation lap began.

The fans were going wild. Expectations were high as all the cars completed their lap, which was enough to satisfy any contractual obliga-tions the teams had when taking part in the event. The crowd knew nothing about what was going to happen and to be honest, despite having been inadvertently briefed by the team principal, I was equally in the dark. On the radio, The Reverend confirmed Kimi's instruc-tions and asked him to respond. Nothing came back. He tried another two or three times, explaining he wouldn't lose out to Alonso who would be doing the same thing. Still Kimi remained quiet.

As the cars made their way towards the end of the formation lap, we were told to expect both drivers back in the pits, though we should keep them in the cockpits, just in case. Options to restore some integ-rity to the race were even at that stage still being discussed behind the scenes. Anything could happen

'Box, box,' went out the radio call to pit.

As the pole-position car of Jarno Trulli peeled off towards the pit-lane entry, I genuinely had no idea whether Kimi was going to obey Ron's orders, or continue defiantly to the grid for the official race start.

He came in.

Kimi's radio burst into life again. There was more swearing – lots of it. He just wanted to race after all. He was angry at the farce he was being forced to participate in. We waited for the car to swing towards us in the pitlane and before we could even reverse it back towards the garage, Kimi had undone his belts, leapt from the cockpit and was striding back to his room in the garage. Montoya, in the other car, remained strapped in as Dave Ryan came on the radio again, this time confirming that we needed to keep both drivers in their cars with the engines ready to go. Apparently, Ron and the others were still in deep discussion and 'nothing had been decided 100 per cent' I keyed my radio and told him Kimi had gone and was probably getting changed by now.

Not that it mattered. The race eventually got underway with just six cars and I was embarrassed for Formula One. The crowd booed, some people even threw bottles from the grandstands and understandably so. They'd spent a lot of money on tickets; many had travelled a long way and they were being offered a dull six-car farce of a procession while we packed up our cars and garages in the background. It was a disgrace.

We spent the Grand Prix dismantling the garage as the six cars screamed past, over and over. Other than glancing up to see if anything interesting was happening, we took little notice of the proceedings. By the time the race was finished we were almost done, the cars were stripped and most of the equipment had been loaded into its containers. Leaving early was perhaps the only good thing to come out of the trip for me, but some Formula One folk were rubbing their hands together: an awful lot of money had been taken off the bookies that afternoon as the two Ferraris romped home in first and second, with a Jordan taking the unlikely third podium spot and both Minardis finishing in rare point-scoring positions. It was a bizarre feeling, but, rather than leave the circuit immediately with thousands of furious fans milling around outside, we were advised by the authorities to remain in the paddock until the angry crowd had dissipated.

When it was safe enough to go home, we finally drove out, passing one memorable race fan left at the gate all on his own, holding up a hand-written sign on a piece of cardboard:

'F1 SUCKS!'

On that day, I couldn't help but agree with him.

12

BLUE HANDS

I was pretty disappointed when Kimi announced he'd be leaving McLaren after the 2006 season, mainly because we'd so far failed to take a title with him and that would've been a fairy-tale ending to the magical story we'd all written together. Annoyingly, though we'd come very close to winning the World Title on two occasions, our cars and engines had failed him too often. I couldn't begrudge his move to Ferrari, though, after all the pay was pretty good and, well . . . *it was Ferrari*.

Kimi was one of the fastest drivers I'd ever worked with and the way in which he closed out the 2005 season was testament to that. After the American debacle, we won seven of the next ten races and did well to stay in touch with Alonso in his quick and reliable Renault. One race win, though, stands out for me as possibly the best and most celebrated of my career – despite it happening in Japan – one Grand Prix after Fernando had finally secured the 2005 title.

There was only the Constructors' Championship left to compete for at that stage, which was more than enough motivation for me, but our luck seemed to run out pretty quickly. The wet second half of qualifying had hindered the frontrunners' laps more than the back-of-the-pack drivers, who'd been scheduled to go out earlier when the conditions were more favourable. Alonso had qualified back in sixteenth, with Kimi one place behind and teammate Montoya another further back. It was a topsy-turvy grid, but those were the races that Kimi and the fans often loved the most: he had to fight his way through the field, but had a car more than capable of doing so.

He flew out of the traps like a bullet, picking off the back markers with a series of sensational moves, brimming with confidence as he moved quickly up the order. Montoya crashed out, which massively dented our ability to score Constructors' points in what was still a very tight battle with Renault, but Kimi forged on. It was thrilling to watch him advance, getting to within reach of the next batch of cars, and the next. He was doing so well, the pressure to deliver fast, smooth pit-stops became even greater as the race went on, but each one went well, thankfully, and Kimi's charge continued. After the final stop, he emerged from the pitlane just two seconds behind the leader, Giancarlo Fisichella.

This was it: a sprint to the flag. We caught Fisichella, but passing him was another thing altogether. The pair battled wheel to wheel; we could barely watch. Kimi closed at the same point on each lap, but the Renault driver was wise to the challenge and defended successfully each time. The laps ticked away and it looked as though we'd have to settle for second place; still an incredible achievement having started in seventeenth. But, going into the last lap of the race, Kimi put the pressure on again, and this time a small mistake from Fisichella meant our closing speed was just too much to defend. They went wheel to wheel, but Kimi was through and our entire garage erupted. We pulled away and led for the remainder of the final lap and brought home a very special victory. The second half of the race had been so tense, watching our man get closer and closer to the front, playing our part in the pitstops and then the drama of the final few laps. When he finally crossed the line in front of us all, hanging over the pit wall to cheer him home, the outpouring of emotion was almost overwhelm-ing and we went wild.

It was great way to cap off a brilliant afternoon's racing, though any hopes of winning the Constructors' Championship were short-lived. We entered the final race of the season in China just two points behind Renault but, sadly for us, Montoya suffered another engine failure, causing us to finish as runners-up again. Still, the relationship we had with the Renault boys was strong. We were genuinely happy for them, so much so that even Ron ordered us each to grab a bottle of champagne (especially prepared in case *we'd* won, of course) and charge next door. 'Let them have it,' he said and we duly obliged. It was a pretty cool moment actually and not something I've seen happen before, there was genuine mutual respect between us and I even remember congratulating Flavio Briatore who reciprocated with a giant champagne-soaked hug. The fight had been great all year and although we could reflect on the incidents and failures along the way as missed opportunities, so could Renault. They'd experienced defeat on fewer occasions and deserved their victory.

It wasn't just in racing terms I knew I'd miss Kimi, but on a personal level too. He was a cool guy and one of the only Formula One drivers I've ever met with no ego. He doesn't do politics, he doesn't do much in the way of socialising at races, and he barely does the interviews he's contractually obliged to do. What he does do, though, is drive fast, fair and ferociously when he needs to. When he was with McLaren, in the prime of his career and with a great team around him, I'd never seen a faster driver, nor had many people at the team. Kimi had an incredible ability to get an average race car around a track quicker than it ever should have gone. He didn't cave under pressure and he kept us all entertained on the team radio as he did it. Regularly, the garage would erupt into laughter during a race, because Kimi was telling the pit wall, in no uncertain terms, that he was indeed already pushing very hard, or that he didn't require any more of their advice, because he knew exactly what he was doing . . .

After the 2005 season, Kimi had flown our crew to Lapland on a private jet for a weeklong drinking and snowmobiling session at −28 degrees. He'd rented an impressive ten-bedroom house for us and several of his friends, which came equipped with chefs and cleaners. Not only was it huge fun, but it meant a lot to us too. On the last night of the trip, the jet dropped us off for a final stopover in Helsinki and we got an insight into the building blocks of Kimi's personality when we spent some time with his parents at their house and Kimi's enormous garage there. I'd met them before, but only in the context of work and never really got to chat to them much. This time we were treated like family.

Kimi's dad was a brilliant man: big, proud and intimidating, but ever the perfect gentleman and he was excited to show us around the garage when we first arrived, though it would be better described as a lavish aircraft hangar. It was full of boys' toys, with everything from a giant Hummer off-roader to tiny go-karts, motocross bikes and snow-mobiles and all sorts in between. One of our old McLaren Formula One cars was even housed there. His dad proudly presented his stacking red toolbox in the corner, calling us over to take a look.

'Go through the drawers,' he said, beaming with pride at the shining array of professional tools, all of them perfectly aligned and polished, McLaren-style. When we'd finished marvelling at his organisational skills, he gestured to the next drawer up, laughing to himself as I opened it . . . Inside was an equally impressive display, but there were no tools in this drawer. Instead it was stacked with different types of vodka, all still glimmering and as pristinely organised as the rest.

'This is a real man's toolbox', he said, giving us a wink and a heavy pat on the back as he walked off chuckling to himself.

Kimi's mum was a proper mum's mum – I really liked her. When we later went off nightclubbing, a spur-of-the-moment decision on our final evening, she waved us off, telling her son to 'be careful'. When we finally rolled back in around 4 a.m., she was still waiting for us, having stayed up all night, knowing the Brits had an early flight back to London and she was worrying about us being late. We were all given cups of tea and she made sure every one of us remained awake and got into our taxis for the airport on time.

Of course, Kimi's hospitality and generous spirit would count for nothing when it came to his McLaren send-off. If ever anyone left the race team after a significant length of service, either to retire or move on, it was our longstanding tradition to physically abuse that person after their last race. This would generally happen in a horrifically degrading manner, and often in front of the entire pitlane. Over the years I've seen people tied to the pit wall fence and covered with left-over food slops (which had been saved up during the week in preparation). People were doused in liquids that should never have been publicly seen outside of the human body. And I've watched, horrified, as one mechanic was set on fire before being hosed down with the enormous pitstop foam fire extinguisher.

One year, a test mechanic from our engine partner Mercedes, Archie, was moving up to the Race Team after the last test of the season. A legendary, but deadly, senior member of our Test Team, who shall remain nameless, spent the week building a full-size wooden coffin at the back of the garage. The box was then painted black and decorated with skulls and cross-bones. Of course it terrified Archie every time he walked past, and on the last night of the week, as we were packing up in the garage, out came the coffin, with its creator dressed from head to toe in black sheets, a white vicar's dog collar round his neck, and a pointy black hat. He was carrying an old-fashioned candle-holder, and the whole team had gathered round to watch his 'show'.

It didn't look good for our departing mechanic. 'RIP Archie' had been painted, ominously, on the front of the coffin in white paint, complete with horror movie-type drips from each letter. After a struggle, the powerless victim was forced inside; the coffin lid firmly screwed shut and propped up against the pit wall. Large breathing holes had been drilled near the top, or at least that's what Archie believed them to be. The reality was that they were to be used to slowly fill the coffin with a disgusting mixture of mouldy food slops, engine oil, brake-cleaner, old coffee and anything else offered up by the crowd. A repulsive, sloppy concoction quickly rose inside. It was truly horrible; I still remember the stink.

There's another story involving the same anonymous perpetrator, which took place well before my time, but it's now part of F1 folklore. One of the lads was stripped naked, tied securely to a tyre trolley and paraded up and down the pitlane as all comers were invited to contribute something to his dousing. He was painted in all the usual mess, but then our friend decided to raise the shock levels by a considerable amount. He set the trolley down on the ground, his victim lying on his back unable to move and then proceeded to take a shit on the poor bloke's chest. The parade continued until Michael Schumacher noticed what was going on, and, understandably disgusted, went to the circuit offices to complain about the 'savage McLaren team'. It didn't go down well internally and when Ron found out some serious reprimands were handed out.

Common across most McLaren leaving ceremonies, though, was 'the blue dye treatment', in which the victim was sprinkled with an intensely powerful powder and then soaked in water, the combination of the two leaving the victim resembling a bright blue Smurf. The dye was used in the car's engine cooling system, it helped us to spot any leaks easily, but it was so strong that a thimble full of the stuff could turn a small swimming pool deep blue within seconds. If it wasn't scrubbed off immediately it would stain the skin, even eyeballs in some cases. Days, sometimes weeks would pass before it faded away entirely, but ultimately it was harmless and non-toxic, though I remember when one bald-headed friend of mine left the team and was dyed on his final day. The stuff really took hold. His whole head was bright blue all the way back to the UK the following afternoon, and when he went for a hearing test two weeks later, the specialist was particularly puzzled as to why his ear drums were a strange blue colour, too.

And now Kimi was leaving.

When it came to reprimands, I had more than my fair share at McLaren. I was a good mechanic and I like to think always exemplary on the job, but I did perhaps enjoy myself a little too much sometimes away from the racetrack, let's say that. So by the time in my career when it came to going to Brazil at the end of 2006 for Kimi's last race as a McLaren driver, I'd already ticked off an official verbal warning and an official written warning, together with numerous unofficial varieties too, but there was no way I was going to let him get away without at least the threat of a traditional send-off. So I began winding him up from the moment he arrived at the Sao Paolo circuit and he hated every second of it.

'You know that whenever someone leaves McLaren, they get dyed blue, don't you, mate?' I said, darkly.

Kimi looked nervous and tried hard to mask his growing uneasiness.

'Ah, you won't get me,' he said. 'I get helicopter straight after the race.'

I just smiled at him. 'We'll see,' I warned, in a falsely confident fashion. I had no doubt Kimi would be jumping into a chopper as soon as he was finished with those pesky media commitments, and there were no real plans for actually carrying out my threats. It was purely designed to worry him a bit.

As the week went on, I continued my jabs; Kimi continued to bat them away in his uniquely nonchalant manner, but it was getting to him, and by race day no words were necessary. Just the subtlest of looks and a wry smile across the garage at him was enough to receive the middle finger back. My target had been wound up, *tight*. By that point, after all the bravado, I'd decided I had to carry out my threat. I'd run over the various scenarios a million times in my mind and, incredibly, somehow come to the idiotic conclusion that it was indeed a good idea to go ahead with this potentially career ending stunt.

Kimi was getting 'the blue dye treatment'.

My foolproof plan was this: on the grid, once Kimi had stepped away from the car to chat to his engineer or go to the toilet, I'd sprinkle some of the infamous powder into his race gloves. Kimi would then drive for two hours, his palms sweating in the Sao Paulo heat, and at the end of the Grand Prix, he'd remove his gloves to discover his hands had turned an alarming shade of blue. It was a bold (or maybe stupid) idea, and no chances were being taken in its execution. I even covertly checked with Mark, Kimi's trainer, as to whether he was allergic to anything in particular, or overly sensitive of skin. What could possibly go wrong?

I told only one accomplice of the idea, Barnesy, one of my most trusted partners in crime. To be fair, he strongly advised me against it, but as a true friend, still offered to aid and abet me because he knew that, one way or another, it would be hilarious to watch. So I went to the grid with a full kit of materials that Barnesy had prepared and loaded onto the team grid trolleys for me. There was a small bag of blue dye; a plastic spoon; rubber gloves for me, plus some wipes and paper in case of any spillages. While Kimi conducted his now infamous interview with Martin Brundle (in which he admitted the reason he was the only driver not to attend Michael Schumacher's Lifetime Achievement presentation with Pele at the front of the grid was because he 'was busy taking a shit'), I filled his gloves with blue powder. This was it. I'd gone past the point of no return. I was shaking like a leaf.

I strapped Kimi into the car, passed him his gloves and wished him luck for the last time as his mechanic. I was feeling incredibly nervous about what I'd done. It was madness and I knew it. What if he suddenly took his gloves back off for some reason? He'd see the dye and would worry about it for the whole race. What if he had some kind of reaction to the powder? I didn't dare think about it, but I was now regretting my move, though after a third of the race, I began to calm down a little. I hadn't heard Kimi screaming on the radio that his hands were burning, which was my biggest fear. If our race was affected by my actions, I'd be sacked for sure. What I really wanted was for Kimi to win the race and us all to have a good laugh about it together afterwards.

That didn't happen, however. We dropped back on track from second to fifth by the chequered flag, meaning my sadistic hopes of him unveiling the Smurf hands in front of the world on the podium, didn't materialise (which was probably for the best). The flip side of that meant Kimi came straight back to the garage, rather than being part of the press conference for the top three drivers and of course, with it being his last race for the team, everyone wanted to shake his hand. Ron Dennis, Ron's wife Lisa, Norbert Haug – Mercedes's head of motorsport – and his wife, plus a steady stream of other important people, all of them now wearing varying levels of blue colouring on their otherwise immaculately clean hands.

Kimi walked into the front of the garage. He was furiously wiping his bright blue palms with wipes. Then he looked over directly at me and pointed.

'You fucking bastard! I get you back!'

I tried not to look terrified and nervously laughed it off, but I was shitting myself. The can was now open, the worms were most definitely out, and most of the boys in the garage were learning of what I'd done. Disbelief spread through the garage, then hilarity as everybody began to witness the fallout. Unluckily for me, it was set to be brutal and as Kimi walked away, I heard Ron's voice from the other side of the garage's network of tunnels. He was furious.

'Whoever's done this has just lost their job!' he yelled.

My heart sank. I felt like a ten-year-old kid again, having just done something really stupid in class. Now I was about to be busted. I kept my head down and quietly got on with my work, all the while terrified I was about to be sacked. I kept well away from Ron, but there was an ominous atmosphere around the place and I could feel his presence everywhere I looked. The whole team had fallen pretty silent after his angry outburst and I'm sure most people assumed that my stunt would be the final straw. My inability to stay on the right side of sensible had finally gone too far.

After avoiding Ron for an hour or so, I noticed his right-hand man, Martin Whitmarsh, as he walked through the garage. I asked for a word. I had a good relationship with Martin. I'd been to see him over the years with various ideas to help the team innovate and become more productive. As a result, I'd earned a high level of respect from him. Years earlier, he'd also granted me that get-out-of-jail-free card after I'd shaved off my dreadlocks. That was a conversation I didn't think for a minute he'd remember, but if there was ever a moment to jog his memory, this was definitely it.

I owned up to Martin about the stunt I'd pulled. I tried to mitigate it with some context regarding my close relationship with Kimi. I also lied a little and told him I'd checked the ingredients of the dye (I hadn't) and ensured there was nothing in there that he'd be allergic to. I then told him I'd heard Ron shouting about the culprit being sacked and reminded him of our conversation all those years ago, in which he'd gratefully promised, 'If there's ever anything that I, or the company, can do for you, Elvis, even if it's years down the line, just come and see me and remind me of this moment.' Well, there I was, reminding him. Martin recalled his gesture, but I could tell he clearly wished he didn't. Holding his head in his hands, he closed his eyes.

'Leave it with me,' he said. 'Ron's pretty angry right now, so I suggest we wait until things have calmed down. Once we get back to the UK, I'll talk to him and see what I can do.'

It felt like the faintest glimmer of hope, but then Martin deflated my optimism. 'I can't promise anything, you understand, but let me try,' he said.

I continued to lie low around the garage as we packed up. It was the last day of the season so there was an air of relief and excitement up and down the pitlane. Our stresses were over for another year, but I wasn't part of that team euphoria, sadly. Instead, I felt sick. Word had got out and people from other teams began coming up and asking if the rumours were true. For everyone else it was one of the funniest stunts they'd heard of, but I couldn't be seen to be laughing about it. I'd landed myself in a serious predicament and I didn't want to give myself away to Ron, and so I got through the final pack-up of the year by lurking inconspicuously at the back of the garage. During the closing meeting before we left the circuit, Dave Ryan talked of the 'disappointing events that had overshadowed Kimi's final race for the team'. I was pretty certain that this had turned into my final race for the team, too.

By the time we got back to the hotel, I'd more or less conceded there was nothing more I could do and what would be would be. Sometimes, you've got to accept the consequences of your actions and this was one of those moments. I got showered, changed, and headed out to the end-of-season party where I intended to drink away my worries, but also to discreetly tout myself around to the various rival Team Managers and Chief Mechanics I knew, in the hope that they'd take pity on me and see fit to offer me the job I was sure I would need by the time we got back to England.

Red Bull, by now known as being the industry's leading party throwers, had gone to town for their end-of-season bash. They'd hired out a football stadium in Sao Paulo, not a small three-sided open-stand affair either, but Morumbi's 80,000-seat monster and completely revamped it to suit. The pitch was transformed into the most spectacular venue and there was even a record-setting 560 metres 360-degree projection around the top of the stands, which played films all night. It was an impressive sight and I dread to even think of what the whole thing must have cost, but that was Red Bull's marketing philosophy: if you're going to do something, do it big, do it spectacularly and get noticed for it.

When I arrived, jaw dropping though the set-up was, I went on a bit of a mission. This was a rare opportunity to have all the key players from almost every team in the same place at once in a more relaxed atmosphere than a Grand Prix. Before I got too worse for wear, which was definitely the ultimate intention, I needed to put the feelers out about a change of job for next season, and as I said hello to everyone, it became pretty clear that the news of my stunt had breached the McLaren garage and was now doing the rounds within Formula One as an unconfirmed yet already fabled tale. People were coming up to me, laughing, asking, 'Is it true that you filled Raikkonen's gloves up with blue dye today?' Then when I admitted the truth, they'd shake me by the hand, or pat me on the back. I hadn't really wanted to make a big deal of it, given the serious disciplinary consequences of my actions, but I couldn't help feeling a tiny bit pleased with myself in some twisted way.

After explaining the details of the prank, along with some contextualising and a description of Ron's angry reaction afterwards, to as many Team Managers and Team Principals as I knew, I came away from the evening with at least three fairly firm job offers. Some people thought it was hilarious. Others relished the thought of helping out the guy who'd managed to get blue dye on Ron Dennis's sterile hands. But they all knew that my years of experience at McLaren were invaluable. That's the thing about McLaren: it looks very good on the CV. The exacting standards required to work there are widely respected within the industry, so if a team's looking to up their game, or replace someone who's leaving, they might turn to a former McLaren employee first, hoping to benefit from their next-level attention to detail. At least that's what I was banking on.

The party was amazing, one of the best. No one ever escaped the season's closing celebration without the hangover from hell, but when the hosts were handing out Absolut Chambulls (Absolut Vodka, champagne and Red Bull), almost forcefully like they were perfume samples in an airport duty-free department, none of us stood a chance. The long flight home not only hurt, it gave me plenty of unwanted time to ponder my predicament. Moving teams, even if the alcohol-fuelled invitations did materialise, would have been a serious upheaval. McLaren were the only UK team that were based in the south of England, so if I had to switch, it would've meant taking my kids out of school, selling up and moving the whole family to Northamptonshire or Oxfordshire. Besides, I didn't want to leave McLaren, despite all their unique and often frustrating idiosyncrasies. They were a great team and I'd been incredibly proud to be part

of their longstanding history. I wished so much that I'd listened to
the little voice in my head that warned me so sensibly against my stupid idea.

I never spoke to Martin Whitmarsh again on the subject, but tried
to hide away when I got back to the factory. I was a quiet shadow of
my usual self around the race bays and felt as if a dark cloud was hov-
ering above my head everywhere I went. Everyone in the factory knew
what I'd done and thought it was the best thing they'd ever heard and,
of course, they all wanted to have a big laugh about it when I got back.
I wanted to keep up my false bravado and pretended I didn't really
care what Ron thought, so I joked along when I thought it was safe to
do so, but the last thing I needed was to be seen making light of the
situation, especially while senior management and HR debated my
future at the company.

I'd thought long and hard about the various outcomes, none of
which were good, though I had little choice but to wait for a decision
and take it from there. I hated myself at times like this. I'd always been
exactly the same ever since I was a kid, and the feelings I got just after
an idiotic prank were all too familiar. A sinking sensation and the
inevitable heavy heart, not to mention embarrassment, shame, regret.
I desperately wanted to turn back the clock and undo everything. The
waiting was just as bad. I was sulking around like a moody teenager,
while someone else decided my fate. It was awful.

I even spoke to Kimi, explaining what had happened and how
things had developed since my 'funny little gag' with his gloves had
backfired. I mentioned that I was now facing the sack. He thought it
was hilarious that it had blown up so massively, but assured me he had
no issue with what I'd done and would make sure Ron knew that – if
that might help. He also warned me that he would definitely get me
back at some point, before joking that if I did get sacked, I should go
and join him at Ferrari. It was an interesting suggestion.

After a couple of weeks, the day finally came and I was summoned
into Dave Ryan's office for the result of the disciplinary investigation.

I was terrified. Everyone on the team knew why I'd been called upstairs and was sure I'd be clearing my desk when I came back down. When I walked in, there was an HR representative in the room. I'd never been so nervous in my life. Dave had a smug demeanour, but that wasn't unusual. I was shaking, not listening to too much of his preamble, but intently waiting for the all-important words I needed to hear. The blurred, fuzzy sounds of his voice faded in and out of my consciousness and I only picked up snippets:

'Ron was not happy at all . . .'

'. . . This is a very serious matter . . .'

'. . . We have taken your relationship with Kimi into considera-tion . . .'

I was on the brink of crying.

Then it hit me.

'We have decided to give you a final written warning,' said Dave. My heart began beating again, albeit at 100mph. 'Understand how serious this is, Marc: it's the highest disciplinary action outside of ter-minating your contract.'

I knew it was heavy because he'd called me Marc and not Elvis, but nothing else he was saying was registering. My mind was too busy processing what I'd just heard. He went on to explain that I'd been fined a portion of my team points bonus, not for the first time, and talked about the process they'd been through in reaching the decision. There was no mention of Martin Whitmarsh being involved, but my sacrifice and outstanding commitment to the company did come up, so I could only assume he'd come to my rescue behind the scenes and I'd have to thank him later. What mattered right now was that I hadn't lost my job and it was all I could do to stop myself grinning like a Cheshire cat while Dave carried on deploring my behaviour.

I actually had a good relationship with Dave Ryan. He was a hard boss, dictatorial and strict, but he was there to uphold Ron Dennis's incredibly high standards, which was a tough gig. I had a lot of respect for the way he ran the team, but I also think he liked me. I was a good race mechanic, but I had a lot of fun too; and while professionally he had to play the hard-nosed and feared oppressor, I think secretly my always-at-the-limit cheekiness resonated with him in more ways than one. Once the formalities were over and the woman from HR had left the room, Dave changed his tone and smiled.

'Anyway, Elvis, don't worry too much,' he said. 'All the best people here have had final written warnings. I had one, and I'm pretty sure even Ron had one years ago, so they can't be all that bad, can they?'

So in a way I'd got away with it. Incredibly, I'd kept my job, much to the amazement of many of my colleagues who found it hilarious that I seemed to be able to survive the most hopeless of situations, like a cat with nine lives. The repercussions, however, were far from over, because when Kimi says he's going to get you back, he doesn't forget about it.

13

KIMI'S REVENGE

I had to watch my back; Kimi was coming for me and I knew it. After the formalities of his season were over, and what had been a stunning but frustrating McLaren career, we travelled to Finland for our now annual end-of-campaign bender in what was to be our final holiday together as a crew. This time we headed to Kimi's impressive coastal pad on the shores of the Baltic Sea, once Finland's most expensive residential property.

A couple of months had passed since the Brazilian GP and I hadn't seen Kimi since. I was slightly nervous about the prospect of some serious retaliation, but wasn't going to let him or anyone else see it. In fact, I was so outwardly cocky, I even arranged to have a personalised thank-you card made from us all. It was our way of wishing him luck at Ferrari, but on the cover I'd scanned an overhead picture of Kimi sitting in his F1 car and changed the image to give him a pair of bright blue comedy hands. I don't know if he'd actually forgotten about the incident (unlikely), but if he had decided to let it go, the piss-taking photo was enough to jog his memory, despite the heartfelt sentiments inside.

'Watch your back this week,' he said threateningly, as we walked through the airport.

Now I was really nervous. At the track it always felt like he was dropping into our territory. The team's garage on a race weekend was a place where I was comfortable and confident. Home turf. Now we were heading to *Kimi's* manor, with all of *Kimi's* mates, and there was a lot of alcohol flying around. I knew he wasn't going to hold back if given the slightest opportunity and so I had to be on my guard.

The first night was a big one. We all went in hard and had a brilliant laugh together. Halfway through the evening Kimi staggered out of the room and returned moments later with a bag. He didn't say a word, instead silently went into an adjacent bathroom, locked the door and remained there for some time. The rest of us carried on chatting until someone realised he'd been gone for a while and went to see if he was OK. The room fell silent for a moment, but we could all hear a muffled buzzing sound coming from the bathroom. Suddenly, the door swung open and Kimi emerged with a big grin on his face. He had no hair.

Things were often done on a whim with Kimi, and whenever he set his mind to something, a plan was often pushed into motion immediately, whether anyone else thought it was a good idea or not. Having silently left the conversation with his ruffled blonde locks, he'd returned just as quietly and sat down with barely a few millimetres left. The conversation continued. The British lads were in shock, we rolled around with laughter, but for the Finnish contingent, this was run-of-the-mill stuff whenever Kimi went on a bender. I began to worry, sensing the lawless mood he was in and stayed up as late as I possibly could, well into the early hours despite feeling so tired, not wanting to go to bed and leave myself vulnerable to attack.

Eventually, I caved in, barely able to stay awake, and went to my room sleepy and drunk, but aware enough to know that I shouldn't drop my guard for a second. To protect against unwanted intruders in the night, I locked the bedroom door and wedged a chair under the handle as extra insurance. Once I'd assured myself there weren't any conspiratorial whispers outside, I drifted into unconsciousness.

I can't have been out for very long when I was abruptly awoken by someone vigorously trying the door handle to my room and my heart began racing. I shouted at them to go away and, unable to open the door, the handle stopped moving and for a moment I assumed they'd given up. Unfortunately, Kimi's not the sort to quit easily and as I was cowering under the duvet, holding my breath, listening for signs of movement outside, there was the most almighty crash. The chair went flying across the room and the door literally came off its hinges, as Kimi and a couple of his mates kicked it so hard the frame broke apart. They were in.

After my experience with the dreadlocks all those years earlier, knowing Ron's disdain for anything other than a short-back-and-sides hairstyle, it had taken me a long time to build up the courage to grow my hair long again. I'd managed to subtly grow it out under the regular cover of a McLaren baseball cap at work and it was now almost shoulder length again and I quite liked it. So when Kimi leapt on top of me in my bed, holding his electric hair clippers in his hand, I fought like hell. We struggled for a few minutes, but it was no use; there were three of them, pumped up on the drink, and me, almost naked, half asleep and pinned down with Kimi kneeling over me as the other two held my arms. I had no chance.

Despite never giving up the struggle I was overpowered and less than two or three minutes after the ordeal began, Kimi had managed to shave what can only be described as a reverse mohican through the centre of my glorious long mane. That was it, he'd achieved his goal. Just one stripe was all he needed and with that he, his accomplices and the clippers were gone. I was devastated. I felt like I'd just been beaten up and robbed, my dignity stolen, and there was nothing I could do. I couldn't see the results of his assault, but I could feel it, my fingers confirming my worst fears as they went through the long, soft strands to the incredibly short, bristly section running from almost the front to the back of my head.

I could hear them all loudly laughing and joking downstairs, as they went back to their drinking and tried to shut out the noise by propping the damaged door back up against the broken frame to plug the gap – the last thing I wanted was to give them another reason to return, so instead of walking out and along the corridor to the bathroom, I decided to hide in silence under the bed covers. Looking in the mirror could wait until morning. After all, there was nothing I could do about it now.

When I woke up the next day there were two shuddering stages of realisation. The first was my hangover, an intense, blinding pain behind my eyes. It clanged like a church bell, but seconds later that was superseded by the sudden, yet fuzzy, memory of what had happened the night before. For a moment I questioned whether it had all been a dream, but as my consciousness returned, I noticed the hairy evidence around me: dark clumps scattered over my white pillow. Crawling out of bed, I noticed further reminders of the traumatic episode, shards of broken wood on the floor and a makeshift door propped up against the broken frame.

Lifting the door out of the way and creeping down to the bathroom, I couldn't hear anyone else awake, but I was nervous. I didn't know what to expect when I saw it, but also what everyone else's reactions would be either. What stared back at me, once I'd locked myself into the bathroom and faced the mirror, was pretty bad. It was a stripe, 5 centimetres wide, that went from just behind the front of my hairline right back to the crown; a shaved stripe so short you could see my scalp through the tiny bristles, which was obviously in stark contrast to the long, thick, dark, shoulder length hair all around it. The one saving grace, if there was one, was that he hadn't managed to carve the line right from the very front of my head and that meant I could almost hide the stripe from view with an enormous comb-over from one side to the other, such was the length of the rest of my hair. It was a small crumb of comfort, but at a time when everything else felt pretty depressing, it helped.

I stood, staring at my head in the mirror for a few moments, convincing myself the swept-over side parting didn't look *that* bad, and even managed a small smile. I'd been well and truly got, just as Kimi had promised he was going to do months earlier in Brazil, and I definitely deserved it. In the end I couldn't help but have a resigned chuckle to myself that Kimi Raikkonen, superstar Formula One driver, had done this to me. I knew I was going to have to shave the rest of my hair off, but hey, it would grow back. What a story this had turned out to be, I thought.

The first person I bumped into was one of my mates. He'd gone to bed early and had slept through the whole thing, but I was reassured and a little relieved when he didn't notice my new look at first glance. His reaction when I revealed the damage was priceless, though. His hand went to his mouth in shock, which was followed by a blast of disbelieving profanity, and finally, depressingly, a fit of doubled-over laughter. It wasn't long before everybody else was awake. All of them were revelling in my humiliation, none more so than Kimi, who collapsed in stitches. By now I was laughing too, calling him every abusive name I could think of before the pair of us fell into a drunken hug.

'You fucking bastard,' I hissed into his ear.

Kimi smirked. 'Don't fuck with me again,' he whispered back, only half jokingly.

My hangover swept in like a tidal wave.

14

THE PRODIGY

There was one driver I'd been familiar with for a number of years, even before his arrival in Formula One – we all had at McLaren. His name had cropped up regularly in speculative mechanic-chat about whom we might be working with in the years to come. His face appeared every now and then in articles across the team's company magazine, and in 2006, while I was tinkering with Kimi Raikkonen's car, making final Sunday morning preparations ahead of the afternoon's Turkish Grand Prix, this young kid in a GP2 car made the entire Formula One pitlane and paddock sit up and take notice of his impressive potential.

Our monitors in the race garage always showed the GP2 support races on a Saturday afternoon and Sunday morning. Normally the garage would stop working for the start of the event and maybe a lap or two, before cracking on with the regular routine of cleaning, checking, weighing and bleeding the brakes on the F1 cars. As mechanics at McLaren, we didn't necessarily follow the junior guy's progress closely or even take too much notice of the results, despite him being a distant part of our own team in the young driver program; we were all too focused on our own work at the weekend. One or two of our overly keen race fans in McLaren, or 'Bobblehats' as they were affectionately termed, were aware he was in a close fight with Nelson Piquet Jr for the GP2 championship that year, and with only one more event in Monza to go, they'd teed up the rest of us ahead of what would be a pivotal race start.

The two title protagonists lined up next to each other on the grid – neither could afford an error – and we all watched, as we did each week, hoping for some of the traditional crazy GP2 antics off the start line. Sadly for us, it was all a bit mundane. No spinners, no crashes and after watching most of the uneventful first lap, we went back to work. Only in lap two did things begin to come alive. Someone pointed out that one of the lead pair had spun and was facing the wrong way on track as cars whizzed by him and collectively we all looked up, made a few jokey comments about that being it for him and half of us immediately looked away. Those still watching shouted out as he spun his car round in panic into the middle of the oncoming field, and then we all stared at the screens. It was a crazy move, a dangerous move, but the kind of thing we all watched GP2 for. A collective gasp rang out across the garage and could be heard coming from the Renault garage next door too, as one by one a series of cars instinctively reacted and narrowly missed him. Somehow he'd got away with it.

The next forty minutes would announce a new driver to the F1 fraternity. He showed the world exactly what kind of competitor he was and, to some extent, the nature of his personality too. Looking back now, it was an early peek into how he would later approach his Formula One career when he eventually made it to the top.

The world had noticed Lewis Hamilton for the first time.

Now in eighteenth position, and with Piquet Jr in the top five, Lewis had nothing to lose and delivered one of the finest, most aggressive and most exciting recovery drives I've ever seen. Within a few laps there couldn't have been a single person in any F1 garage not glued to their TV screens on that Sunday morning as the prodigy carved his way through the entire field. He was desperate, probably angry at his earlier mistake, but somehow he managed to channel that fury and remained in control of his race car. His braking was later than everybody else; he positioned himself on the track in a manner that alerted the pack that he was surging through them, one way or another. Lewis hustled and chased them all down, picking his rivals off, one by one, and nobody seemed able to match his 'last of the late brakers' style. All they could do was watch him disappear down the track, wondering what on earth had just happened.

Lap after lap he made up places, eventually reaching the top eight point-scoring positions, McLaren and every other F1 team now clapping and cheering him on in disbelief as he went. To score after such a disastrous beginning would have been quite an achievement, and an exercise in damage limitation against his rival. But Lewis clearly wasn't thinking so conservatively. He pushed on and soon Piquet Jr, now in fourth spot, was in his sights. An epic battle ensued with both racing hard and fair and the positions changed hands two or three times. Eventually Lewis got by and pulled clear by a decent margin. Like fickle football fans we were definitely now right behind 'our' man. Lewis Hamilton was a young McLaren driver and we were proud of him. He raced on and in the very last lap managed to wrestle his car past another driver to cross the line in a jaw-dropping second position.

McLaren's future had arrived.

Towards the end of that 2006 season, Lewis would occasionally turn up in our garage to meet with various people and I warmed to him pretty quickly. Our first encounter was when he walked in one Friday evening. The garage was quiet and lots of people were away eating dinner in hospitality. Lewis came across as I was working away in the cockpit of Kimi's car with no engine or gearbox attached and looked around the chassis. He seemed like he was interested, but too shy to ask anything, so I said hello and broke the ice.

From that point Lewis opened up completely and introduced himself. He began asking question after question about the F1 car. I remember being fascinated at how keen he was to understand the technical aspects of everything. I eventually spent a good fifteen or twenty minutes explaining the intricacies of the car, from our high-pressure engine air reservoir to wiring harnesses and the various sensors, plus Kimi's specific pedal setup. Lewis was more interested in what we were doing to the F1 car than our own race drivers were, and yet he was just a goofy twenty-one-year-old, with a 'fro, who'd never even driven one in anger. I liked him, but didn't think anything more of the meeting as we went about our season and he disappeared again to go about his.

Of course, Lewis went on to win his GP2 title and reward came in the form of a McLaren F1 test at Silverstone, and the ripple effect had the potential to be significant. Ever since Kimi had announced his impending departure from the team and a pursuit of that elusive World Title with Ferrari, people began whispering the Hamilton name in regard to a possible 2007 F1 seat. Inside the team, we had no idea what might happen, but found it hard to believe the mighty McLaren would take such a huge gamble on a youngster with no Formula One experience. We were one of the biggest and most successful teams in the sport's history and prided ourselves on taking the very best drivers available. I just couldn't see Hamilton in one of our race cars just yet.

However, the Test Team had reported good things back from Silverstone and Lewis's lap times seemed to back up his ability. Even so, I think we all believed the drive would go to Pedro de la Rosa. Pedro was our test driver and had stood in at races that year since Juan Pablo Montoya left the team halfway through his contract in 2006 and headed back to America. He'd fallen out with Ron due to a clash of personalities and I was indifferent about him leaving if I'm honest. Because he seemed to associate the people in the team with his strained relationship with the boss, he didn't really open up to us, so we never got the chance to build that good a relationship. But Pedro was different, a thoroughly nice guy, even if he hadn't necessarily managed to match Kimi in the race car, but that was an extremely tough ask at the time. I think everyone thought Pedro deserved a shot after working so hard for so many years, developing cars, pounding round and round at test tracks without the spoils and rewards that the race drivers got whenever we tasted success.

Lewis's emergence and Kimi's departure were stories that had attracted lively debate in the media throughout the second half of 2006, and by the end of the year most of us in the team had no real clue as to what might happen over the coming months. In late November, the McLaren race team set off for a week of physical preparation and general team-building at the Olympic training centre in Finland. It was a new initiative at the time and part of McLaren's innovative push to improve human performance, as well as our technical excellence, and it gave us all a chance to relax and enjoy ourselves away from the racetrack and factory.

Pedro and Gary Paffett, another of our test drivers, were joining us for the week, but the big announcement was made just a day or two before our departure and we learned that Lewis would be racing alongside Fernando Alonso the following season, as did the rest of the world. This was huge, huge news; a shock to us all, and most people I'm sure couldn't help but feel massive sympathy towards the ever-cheerful Pedro. We all flew from London to Helsinki together, then hopped onto a small propeller-driven plane and headed north into the snow-covered forests of western Finland towards our destination. The mood was one of bewilderment.

After finally getting there and acclimatising, we were pretty surprised to hear that new-kid-on-the-block Lewis was making his own way out to join us. Apparently he wanted to get to know the lads a little and thought it might be a good way to integrate himself into the team. I remember thinking it was a smart play and was genuinely pleased he was taking that approach at such an early stage, particularly given that just a few days earlier his whole life had changed for ever.

We had a fantastic week. As well as the sports science aspect of the trip, which I found fascinating, we became involved in a number of team-bonding sessions where we were trained by Olympic athletes in shooting, skiing, swimming, and various track and field disciplines, even ten-pin bowling. It wasn't designed to be just work; the break was supposed to be fun and we functioned in groups where no one was more important than anyone else. That meant we all got to know each other pretty well by the end of it, including the new boy.

Lewis was shy. I imagine we could have been an intimidating group at first glance. We were a cocky crowd, self-assured in what we were doing, and we'd been mates for a long time. Formula One was a macho sport and we were a macho group of lads, super male-dominated. We weren't a retiring bunch, that's for sure. Lewis also knew that there'd been a lot of surprise regarding his elevation to the F1 team, and that Pedro had been very popular with the garage. But I soon became pretty impressed with his attitude. He got stuck in. No one pandered to him, or gave him any special treatment, but nor did he expect it from us. He soon became confident enough, but not so much that anyone thought of him as being arrogant, and we all got along well. So well, in fact, that by the end of the week I found myself, along with twenty or so others, including Lewis, Pedro and Gary, squashed – and I do mean uncomfortably squashed – fully naked, into a sauna made for fifteen people.

The trip also gave me a little more insight into Lewis's mentality. In a classroom session, a tutor asked us all to stare at a screen, which flashed up a series of images, each one comprising random groups of many, many coloured dots. Each image was only on show for a split second and carried a different pattern from the last, but we were all asked to write down roughly how many dots we thought had appeared on each slide. When we went back through the answers, most of us were some way off with our estimates, perhaps getting close on the odd occasion. Lewis was by far the most accurate over the whole test, nailing his answers on more than one occasion. I could never quite work out if it was just a case beginner's luck or an indication of the super-quick mental processing that takes place inside the mind of a successful Formula One driver. He was competitive with it too, refusing to ever give up on the physical challenges over the week, and his uncontrollable fist pumps if ever he came first in something were early signs of just how much he needed to win. It was exactly what we wanted to see.

He took the scientific and physical testing very seriously. I suppose he had to, since it was officially his first week on the new job. He also managed to have fun with the lads, though I'm not quite sure how he took the group Pilates lessons, desperately trying to hold the instructed poses, whilst a group of hairy-arsed truckies and mechanics farted and giggled all around him. He settled in well and we ate together, swam together, relaxed together and I found him to be an enthusiastic, polite and grateful young man. He could hold his own amongst the group by the end of the trip, and when we eventually headed home, I think most people appreciated that the journey to Finland had been a worthwhile experience, both in terms of what we'd all learnt individually, and in helping us all to bond together as a tight-knit team.

Little did we know that our unity would be tested to its absolute limits over the coming season.

After Christmas, as with every year, it was time for the race team to knuckle back down, leave the extra-long holidays behind us and focus on racing once again. This year, however, we had two new drivers behind the wheels of both cars, something most of us hadn't experienced before. When one driver changed between seasons, the crew of the outgoing driver inherited the new guy, and for continuity's sake, the other side of the garage remained the constant. This time, we had two crews of engineers and mechanics and two new racing drivers. One of those drivers was double and current World Champion, Fernando Alonso, the Renault star we'd been fighting against, and lost out to, for the last two years. We knew all too well just how good he was behind the wheel, and finally he was on our side. The other guy was Lewis Hamilton, a polite young rookie from Stevenage. Although some of us had by now spent some time with him, he was still a shock appointment and had barely even tested one of the cars, let alone raced one. Most of the lads figured a year spent working on his side of the garage was likely to be a long, tough struggle as he found his feet in the sport.

With Kimi having left the team, I'd been promoted from a Number Two Mechanic to the position of Number One Mechanic in charge of the T-Car. (Miraculous when you consider my punishment following the blue dye treatment.) That meant I was no longer directly assigned to either race driver, but was now responsible for the crew of guys who looked after the third car we used to have back then in the middle of the garage. As a consequence, I had no real opinion on which of the two race crews should be designated to which new driver. Instead, I could watch on with interest as the campaigning began to unfold.

There was a clear favourite in Fernando, of course, but politically it wasn't necessarily appropriate to be openly vocal about which driver you preferred to work with in the team. Moreover, it was even less politically correct to express a desire *not* to want to work with one of our two racers. But soon the mechanics' whispers, in small groups, began to get louder over the first week or so of the year. Senior team members began talking to me about it and were going to their race engineers for 'secret' chats about what, if anything, they could do to ensure their crew ended up on Fernando's car.

The feeling was that, not only did it look like we might have a very competitive car that year, but we had the man widely regarded as one of, if not, *the* best drivers in Formula One. Put those two elements together and this could be the moment the stars collide and that all-too-rare opportunity to genuinely challenge for the World Titles comes along. Fernando seemed to have everything: intelligence, a technical understanding of the car, obviously speed, and a Schumacher-style streak that meant he'd go to extraordinary lengths to win (a trait that would later cost us all dearly). As a mechanic or engineer, to be in that position is the stuff dreams are made of. Most in our industry never get the chance to be anywhere near calling themselves World Champions and it hadn't happened in our team since Mika Hakkinen in 1998 and 1999. It wasn't something that comes around very often, so I could understand the desperation of both sides of our team to get the shot at it.

As the new year's pre-season testing drew nearer, so did decision day. Dave Ryan had the final say and by now the whispers had become loud – really loud. It was an open secret that there was some serious jostling for position going on among the race team. At least one of the race engineers, the most senior members on each side of the garage, possibly even both, had been to see Dave personally, to state their case for running the Number One car. It was quite a controversial move and took the whole scenario into uncharted waters. It was one thing to discuss matters on the shop floor with mates, but officially approaching senior management to express a desire *not* to work on Lewis's car was a different ballgame altogether.

One crew, obviously, was going to end up assigned to Lewis, and everybody would know that they were unhappy about it. What questions might that pose further down the line should things not go so well? How would the crew feel if Fernando's side of the garage began to run away with the championship and yet they were working twice as hard to repair the inevitably smashed-up cars that a rookie has to go through during his inaugural season? And how would Lewis feel if he ever discovered his team's true feelings? Luckily, none of this got back to the drivers, and everyone made sure it stayed as internal garage politics.

It was a difficult and tense time for us all, which threatened to cause ripples amongst the team. The decision could have had a major impact to our next twelve months together as we travelled the world. Being in the middle of it all, I just hoped the call would be made as soon as possible so we could all get over it and move on. After all, I was running the spare car, something I was sure would be in constant use that year, what with an excitable young novice behind the wheel, so I was resigned to a busy season ahead, whatever the outcome. I just wanted the team to run smoothly and to take home the coveted Constructor's Title at the end of it all.

D-Day came and Dave Ryan issued the crews – Race One, Race Two and Race Three. R1 went to Fernando and R2 to Lewis, with R3, my group, looking after the T-Car. The news was taken quietly, but the reaction, of course, was split. Fernando's new crew was the same group I'd been a part of for the last few years and had enjoyed so much success with Kimi. It was also the team that had previously engineered several years of success with Mika. There was now a suspicion among many that the team looking after Fernando's car contained the individuals that had shouted the loudest to McLaren's powers-that-be about their preference of driver. Some considered it precedent-setting, or a confirming of a clear Number One and Number Two crew in status, something the company would be at pains to deny. It wasn't a policy we'd ever employed, unlike Ferrari, who even wrote into the contracts of certain drivers that they had to effectively play second-fiddle to their celebrated Number One, Michael Schumacher.

Fernando's team was naturally very happy and relieved; they retired to their race bays in the factory and got back to work. Lewis's side was, I'm sure, disappointed, but you wouldn't have known it. Paul James, their Number One Mechanic took a professional approach and led his team with their heads held high. Whatever he was feeling, he kept it to himself and rallied the troops, but this unfortunate process undoubtedly laid the foundations for a difficult season within the team. There'd always been a rivalry between both sides of our garage and I'd been fortunate to have worked on Kimi's for the last four years and we'd come out on top more often than not, but it was pretty much always good humoured amongst the lads. I didn't think for any reason the atmosphere would change that year, but the way things had played out had left Lewis's crew inevitably feeling slightly second-tier. To compound matters, everybody in the garage felt the outside world was thinking the same thing too.

The mess soon died down. Everybody got on with work as normal. Both sides of the team were behind their men as we moved into pre-season testing and despite a crash or two for Lewis, and some wider reliability issues, we looked quick. Things that broke on a fast car could be fixed and remedied, but trying to make a reliable yet inherently slow car *faster* was a different challenge altogether. Luckily, Lewis's pace looked promisingly strong in the build-up to the approaching opening Grand Prix of the year. He wasn't quite as consistently quick as Fernando, but no one expected him to be. If he could keep his car on the racetrack and score points in the early part of the season, while his teammate chased the victories, we'd all be happy. The hope was that Lewis could add to the all-important Constructors' points tally that we knew could be critical, come November.

In Australia, Lewis seemed a little overwhelmed before his debut GP, but all in an expected way. He worked smoothly with his team and the car performed well, but behind the scenes I could see how in awe of everything around him he was. Mind you, he never revealed this endearing greenness in public; his interviews and press calls were perfectly McLaren-like and highly professional, very different to Kimi's. Lewis was punctual and polite. He gave the media the time they needed and thanked all the right sponsors, which would've pleased Ron. He did well, though perhaps came over as being a little too McLaren-groomed at times, although that was the fault of the team, not him. I'm sure we'd have all preferred to see a driver saying what they really thought, but nevertheless, Lewis was living out his dreams in public and it was a joy to watch. He appeared so humble and grateful to us all for the opportunities he was getting and never stopped asking questions about how things worked; he couldn't help but let his excitable side show through once he'd escaped the press and was back inside the relative safety and sanctity of the McLaren garage.

On the track he was a very different character and the Australian race weekend was a huge success. Alonso qualified in second, with Lewis a competitive, and surprising, fourth. Ultimately, on race day, Kimi took the win on his debut with Ferrari, but our boys came home second (Fernando) and third (Lewis). It was smiles all round, an amazing result, and Lewis and his guys were over the moon. To finish right behind the reigning World Champ in the same car was impressive enough, but to take a podium on his F1 debut was some way for Lewis to announce his arrival to the world. Fernando was also happy, having made a great start to the season, and although Lewis had done really well, he was in his 'rightful place', just behind him. The celebrations under the podium were amongst the happiest I remember during that period. My mate Kimi was on the top step (even if he was wearing the wrong overalls) and McLaren were officially back and competing again. It would prove to be a brief moment of tranquility and cheer before a very ugly storm.

15

POWER PLAY

We were fired up for the fight ahead. The result in Australia had surpassed our expectations. Ferrari was our strongest rival, but Lewis had proven himself: he was fast enough to help the team in our collective fight for Constructors' Championship points and by the second race of the season, in Malaysia, his reputation increased even further. Alonso won his first race for the team, but Lewis was in his slipstream once again, following up behind, this time in second. The garage was a very happy place. Fernando and crew were ecstatic because they were 'rightfully' leading the championship in their self-assumed number-one spot within the team. Meanwhile, Lewis and co. were on top of the world, exceeding everybody's expectations at that early stage. Together, they were like grand master and protégé, with mutual love and respect; each one appeared to understand their place and no one contested the pecking order.

This harmonious vibe didn't last for long. Over the next two races I began to notice a slight shift in the team dynamic. In Bahrain for race three, Lewis genuinely had the better of Fernando all weekend, only by the merest of margins, but enough to out-qualify him for the first time. He later emerged on top in the race, finishing second with Fernando back in fifth place. As far as everybody was concerned, Bahrain was a minor blip for our reigning World Champ, but Lewis had announced himself as being more than an also-ran. Interestingly, after that round, both McLaren drivers, along with Kimi in his Ferrari, were level on points at the top of the leader board, something that hadn't gone unnoticed, either by the press or Lewis. He even laughed about it in the garage and couldn't believe he'd actually beaten Fernando in a Grand Prix.

He grinned sheepishly. 'Am I even *allowed* to be doing that?' he joked.

I think it was his way of expressing disbelief that, just three rounds into his debut Formula One season, the unbelievable had happened – *he was leading the World Championship*. He was like a kid at Christmas.

Spain was set to be Fernando's Grand Prix in front of an adoring home crowd. As a team, McLaren looked pretty competitive around the track and our practice sessions went well. Lewis had an upgraded air of confidence about him too, perhaps because this was a track he'd tested at before, but also because of the superb result in Bahrain. His excitement was palpable. The rookie had a spring in his step and was more vocal on the radio to his engineer. He was now starting to ask for specific technical changes to be made to the car rather than simply describing his problems and letting the crew work their magic, as he'd done up to now. He seemed much more comfortable as a Formula One driver and certainly more assured of his own ability.

I could sense Lewis was beginning to think of himself as more than just a number-two driver and his efforts on the track later confirmed my suspicions. He spoilt the Spanish party by finishing second; Fernando could only follow up behind in third after an early ride through the gravel trap, but there was a greater momentum shift behind the scenes. Lewis came away from Spain with the outright lead of the championship after just four rounds and his crew wore some wry smiles on their side of the garage and started to genuinely believe in their man. Suddenly, unexpectedly, the whole world was talking about Lewis Hamilton: the all-new British superstar and racing prodigy for the British F1 super-power, McLaren. This was the most explosive start to a career since the emergence of Michael Schumacher – but Lewis's results were *even more impressive*. The backstage bickering and political squabbles of pre-season 'Crewgate' now seemed somewhat churlish.

Ron Dennis revelled in the attention. I sometimes noticed him at the back of the garage, arms folded, watching over us silently as his team went about their business. In media sessions, he struggled to hold back an air of smugness and claimed he'd known for years about Lewis's potential, which is why he'd signed him up way back in 1998; he watched as the value of his stock rose with a slew of positive column inches that were being written with every passing week, and although these were early days, McLaren was back on top, exactly where we belonged and making history again with Formula One's latest rising star.

On Fernando's side of the garage, there was absolutely no reason to panic. I'm sure he was surprised by Lewis's results – we all were. I imagine he viewed his understudy as a bit of an annoyance back then, like a buzzing fly in need of swatting. But there was still nothing to suggest Lewis was going to threaten his overall superiority, and in Fernando's mind this was always going to be a comfortable season, with him as the clear number-one driver. Even if McLaren's policy was to never to state that publicly, he and everyone else knew that Lewis was there to learn the ropes, to look up to him. The only person not on the same page was Lewis himself.

The well-documented downward spiral that resulted in their soon-to-be tumultuous relationship began in real terms at the next round in Monaco. The 'Jewel in F1's crown' as it's known, was just that, one of the most special races of any season, though it could be a pain in the arse to work there at times, with its cramped, unique conditions, despite the newly built garages and pitlane complex. Still, to get a result in Monaco always felt a bit more special than anywhere else. Why? Because of the glamour and history there – a bit like lifting the FA Cup at a posher version of Wembley Stadium. (Prince Albert of Monaco even greets the winning drivers on the steps of his royal box.) But also, it's a Grand Prix where you can't make any mistakes as a team, or a driver, because if you do the car will invariably end up in the wall. So from the first practice session everything has to be perfect if you're to come out on top. The pressure's also high in the garage as a result, more so than anywhere else, and if time's lost during a pitstop it's very easy to lose track position on a circuit where overtaking and making the places back is almost impossible.

In the old days at Monaco, we used to operate from awnings attached to the side of our trucks, pushing the cars through the streets from the harbour-side paddock up into the tiny pitlane. The garages, if you could call them that, were more like large broom cupboards, so small that a whole racing car wouldn't even fit inside. We'd reverse them into position, with half a car sticking into the pitlane, which, if you were a front-end mechanic as I was back in the day, was fine unless it was tipping down with rain.

Pushing those cars up to the pitlane every evening to check them on the FIA flat patch and weighing scales was an experience too. It involved negotiating sections of the open public roads where the streets of Monte Carlo were awash with hundreds, maybe thousands, of lively, wealthy and drunken race fans. Typically, some thought it hilarious as they pretended to climb all over the car while we weaved through the crowded streets, contorting themselves into the most extraordinary positions to grab photos with their friends. We couldn't stop to help them pose, though; our priority was to protect the car and escape the potentially hazardous situation as quickly as possible. Lovely though I'm sure most of those people were, they were invariably tipsy and wobbly-legged. Trying to bend into a position worthy of the one and only photograph you'll ever get with a real F1 car (without getting run over, and more importantly from our side, without breaking anything on the car) wasn't easy. I'd love to see some of the blurred pictures taken over the years of people falling down, being dragged away and panic stricken, all the while desperately trying to look cool.

To give you a sense of the gauntlet we ran between trucks and pit-lane of an evening, one year I was pushing David Coulthard's car, along with the crew, up the hill towards La Rascasse corner, when a drunken fan threw a 1-euro coin inside our overhead air-intake. He found it terribly funny, as did his mates, but luckily I'd happened to see him do it so we knew it was in there and were able to strip the various parts off and remove it before firing the engine up again back at the awning. Had we not noticed, it would've sat on top of the engine's air filter and been thrown around violently when the car was on track. If it breached the filter somehow, it would've gone straight into the engine and destroyed it in an instant. On other occasions we had people fall onto the car and break front wings and bargeboards; cameras have been dropped inside the cockpit, and once someone even attempted to steal the very expensive bespoke steering wheel.

Despite the difficulties of working at the Monaco Grand Prix, it was a week I loved. Extended by twenty-four hours to accommodate the unusual Thursday, rather than Friday, practice sessions, you'd think it might have meant a rare day off on Friday for the race crew. But no, we somehow managed to fill an entire extra day with the standard workload of a regular Friday night at any other GP. It did mean, however, that we didn't work until the early hours on the Thursday night as we turned the cars around after FP1 and FP2, and that in turn meant we were able to party in the principality.

Hitting the town in Monte Carlo on GP week wasn't like most places. Nights out consisted of the somewhat surreal experience of hopping from one sponsor's super-yacht party to another, sipping champagne and cocktails alongside the very rich and incredibly famous. In fact, the bizarre reality was that, if we hadn't spent the night at those lavish but paid-for parties, a proper evening out in the exclusive nightspots would've been out of our financial league anyway, so we were left with no choice – honest!

It got better. Life at the Monaco GP wasn't just a heavy slog of boat parties, or remembering which vast, polished teak deck we'd left our shoes on. To sweeten the deal, McLaren kindly put us up in one of the finest and most vibrant hotels in town, the Columbus, which had been part-owned by our very own David Coulthard, back in the day. The hotel bar and restaurant were hubs for the beautiful people. It was pretty easy to spot our team mechanics amongst a Who's Who of the film, fashion and music worlds, not because we weren't well dressed of an evening, or suave and sophisticated individuals, but because none of us could really afford the hotel bar prices. Every twenty minutes or so, in staggered groups, we'd disappear upstairs to the bedrooms, refilling our drinks from the pre-bought supermarket bottles of Bacardi or vodka, before returning to the bar to mingle into the crowd.

There were no exact word-for-word rules regarding drinking on race weekends, nothing was written into our contracts, but that's only because it didn't need to be. It was pretty obvious we had a job, one which required us to be firing on all cylinders all the time as precision was everything and mistakes could be very costly indeed. Well, it should've been obvious anyway. It was accepted, even encouraged, that Sunday night was party time, but if we'd gone out late on a Saturday night, we'd need to sneak back into the hotel without anyone noticing, because if we'd been spotted and something had then gone wrong the following day, it would not have gone down well. Some teams began taking measures to ensure their crews behaved themselves and British American Racing (BAR) took it to a whole new level by bringing a breathalyser to the Monaco Grand Prix one year. When they sprung surprise tests on the Sunday morning, one or two guys were even sent home for being so far over the acceptable limit. It could've been any of us and was a stark reminder that times were changing.

Things were looking good for McLaren when we arrived in Monaco for the 2007 GP. We were leading the championship, the car was performing brilliantly, and our marketing team had pulled out all the stops to capitalise on the glitzy, glamorous occasion. Our diamond partner,* Steinmetz, had emblazoned the drivers' crash helmets with white diamonds for the event, and both Lewis and Fernando were given bespoke rings worth $10,000 as a gift. This wasn't a new idea; we'd done the diamond thing before. When I was the front-end mechanic on Kimi's car, both he and Juan Pablo Montoya had their names written in diamond-encrusted letters onto each side of their crash helmets. As a 'front-ender', the cockpit area came under my jurisdiction, so you can imagine my delight when it turned out that after two practice sessions, both drivers had knocked off a number of stones in the car and my opposite number on the other side of the garage had begun discreetly finding them dotted around his tub during the Thursday-evening checks. That night, I searched my cockpit more thoroughly than ever before and didn't find a single bloody rock.

Our two cars were utterly dominant in qualifying. Both drivers took turns in topping the time sheets and no one could get near them. When it mattered, Fernando came out on top, with Lewis right behind him, and the race itself was almost embarrassingly one-sided. McLaren's duo pulled out an unstoppable lead, their only competition was each other, and in the latter stages, with Fernando still ahead and starting to think about managing his pace to see out the victory, Lewis began closing in on him. His car was right up under Fernando's rear wing, clearly searching out a way past, something that isn't easy around the Monaco streets with the narrow track and close barriers. All of us began to feel pretty twitchy as we watched on the monitors.

For a couple of laps, Lewis put real pressure on Fernando, even coming close to making contact at one point, which brought shouts of horror from the team. It was getting uncomfortable and I could barely watch. Fernando began asking, 'What the hell is he doing?' on the radio and the engineers soon intervened, instructing both drivers to hold station and bring the cars home for a 1-2 finish.

---

* Yes, that's right: we had one of the world's finest diamond producers as one of our sponsors. Doesn't everyone in Monaco have a diamond partner?

It was the sensible play, particularly around Monaco's unforgiving circuit and especially given our commanding position in the race. Who knew what might have been at stake in the championship, long-term? It was a slightly controversial move, however. No one likes it when team orders are issued, it's a sporting event after all and nobody wants to see a result contrived; the fans want to see the drivers go at it, with the best coming out on top. It was also a very rare occurrence at McLaren, but that day, Lewis and Fernando were by far the fastest on circuit and if we'd let them do their own thing we could have seen some spectacular racing. From the team's point of view, though, there was a very real risk that one, or both of them, might end up not finishing at all and we couldn't allow them to jeopardise the perfect F1 team result.

Try telling that to the man in second place.

This was a new level of Lewis's uncompromising competitive streak; a driver not content with being second, who saw himself every bit as fast as Fernando and every bit as entitled to win races. Lewis seemed to ignore the team's instructions at first, we could almost sense his anger at the situation inside his crash helmet. He kept edging closer to Fernando, probing for a way past. The radio traffic was tense, Lewis was flirting with disaster, and we all knew it.

'What is he doing?' yelled Fernando. 'Have you given him the message too? This is crazy!'

Nobody could argue with his frustration. Had Lewis smashed into Fernando's rear, it would have been an unforgivable loss for a team holding the front two places. Lewis, on the other channel, was shouting at his engineer.

'I'm faster than him, let me get past,' he said, out of breath. 'Come on, I can win this race!'

Once again, he was told to hold his position, but Lewis's fighting spirit was undimmed. 'I'm here to race,' crackled the radio, 'not to settle for second!'

It was great to see this fighting spirit from such a young driver, but I couldn't help thinking his inexperience was showing through. Sure, he was faster, but only noticeably so because Fernando was seeing the bigger picture and backing off. He was preserving the car, which was a lot more fragile than the almost-indestructible, toned-down machines of the modern era. Our cars back then were highly stressed, and much more on the limit. We had fewer technical restrictions to work with so engines were revving up to 19,000rpm (even that was pegged back from the 21,000rpm machines of a few years earlier). In those days, it was one engine for one race and we could push it as hard as we wanted because performance was king, in today's rules each engine has to last for five races, so it's far more restrained. Pushing the limits of performance so hard meant every now and then, we'd see the rooster tails of thick white smoke pouring from the back of the car with an unexpected blowout; something we were very keen to avoid in Monaco.

Lewis continued with his pursuit, defying all instructions from the team, and continued with his reckless hunting down of Fernando. The frantic radio traffic on both sides became more angry and frustrated. This time, though, Lewis had crossed a line. Ron Dennis did not take kindly to anybody who defied him. Only the race engineers ever spoke to the drivers on their radio, it was part of the protocol so the instructional voice was always familiar and one less thing to process during a high-stress Grand Prix. That went out of the window though, and Ron pressed his rarely used button on the pit wall. His stern and unmistakable orders went directly into Lewis's ears, and mine.

'Lewis, this is Ron. You will drop back and you will bring home this 1-2 finish for the team. Do you understand?'

Lewis didn't offer a verbal response, but he backed off, though only by a fractional amount to comply. A clear message was being sent out to the team, and to the world, that he was quick enough to take on Fernando and win. As he followed home in second place, it was at a distance close enough to prove that he could have gone faster, if allowed. On paper it was a great result for the team, but a pivotal one in the relationship between both sides of our garage. Fernando knew without question that he had another rival and Lewis had learned he could match the World Champion. At the end of the weekend, despite saying the right things to the media after a strict briefing from Ron, both drivers retreated to their camps and privately declared war against the other, and as with most wars, the supporting armies, the mechanics and engineers, unquestionably pledged allegiance to their leaders. We didn't know it then, but this was probably the beginning of the end of our 2007 title hopes.

16

BUYING LOYALTY

Lewis was now in defiant mood and took a well-deserved opening Formula One victory at the Canadian Grand Prix, as Fernando became increasingly frustrated by a series of personal mistakes and unfortunate penalties. The maiden win was immediately followed up with another a week later, in Indianapolis, though his newfound confidence and elbows-out aggression caused several wheel-to-wheel flashpoints with Fernando. At the race start in Indy, with both cars jostling for position, a collision so nearly ended the GP for both of them. Our problem was that they were very similar in terms of performance and their cars were identical, so they often lined up close to one another on the grid. The rookie was on the up, though, and his rapid progression only widened the personal rift between the two. Before long, an unusual mood was brewing in the McLaren camp: both drivers were genuine title contenders and knew it, but both also understood the biggest obstacle in their path was the guy on the other side of their own garage. They weren't at the stage where a wall of silence had been built, but they were definitely avoiding one another behind the scenes.

For us in the team, this was uncharted territory. In the past, if we were lucky enough to be in contention for a championship, it was with one of our two drivers emerging as a favourite. It had happened with Mika, over DC, then again twice with Kimi. Never did the team employ Ferrari-style tactics of openly favouring one driver over the other; it was just the way the seasons had unfolded naturally, probably representative of the bigger talents at the time. The point being that in those situations, as a team, you close ranks and fight together against the opposition. Keeping secrets secret, protecting any technical or strategic advantage you think you might have found. The leading car crew needed the other driver to back them up, to take points away from the rival contenders, and everyone worked together as a team, proud to wear the uniform, fighting off challenges, wherever they came from.

The race between Lewis and Fernando would change all of that.

In 2007, the main challengers for the Drivers' Championship were wearing the same uniform, receiving the same technical updates and accessing the same information. No one quite knew what the protocol should have been in that situation. Sure, there was a rivalry, but at that point things were still friendly inside the garage, and amongst the mechanics it was light-hearted. Both sides were sharing the successes, so both had their chances to celebrate and also to deal with the inevitable disappointments along the way. Any ideas of a number one and number two crew had long since been put into perspective, although I'm sure the undertones of the pre-season mechanic allocation still resonated among one or two of the boys.

Watching on from the middle ground, I was seeing a tension from Fernando. Having been beaten by the young upstart for two straight rounds now, I got the impression he was feeling there was too much love for the local lad inside the British team. A couple of completely innocent strategy decisions had coincidently fallen Lewis's way, allowing subsequent safety cars or unexpected traffic to hamper Fernando's progress. I saw those events for what they were, *bad luck*, but it was clear that he saw them differently.* In his previous team he'd been

---

* I hadn't seen any sign of favouritism and I was fully involved on both halves of the team, listening to each side's radio communications and sitting in on meetings with both drivers and their engineers.

managed by, and had a close personal relationship with, Flavio Briatore, the Renault team principal, and had enjoyed clear number one
status en route to winning his two World Titles. He never said it out
loud, but he 100 per cent expected his position as the World Champ to
bring with it the same levels of respect and deferential advantages at
McLaren. I've no doubt Ron had explained that we didn't operate
that way when courting him for the team, but I imagine that he, along
with most other people, assumed Lewis wouldn't present any significant threat, at least initially.

They were wrong, and Fernando seemed to take it badly. Ordin-
arily, confidence oozed out of him, he exuded self-belief, and there
was never any doubt that he was *The Man* – a double World Champion. But with Lewis grabbing the plaudits somewhat unexpectedly,
Fernando seemed to shrink from view a little and to my mind it was as
if he needed a reassuring arm around the shoulder from someone in
his corner. There were closed-off meetings with his crew and he rarely
ventured away from his side of the garage; he viewed the wider team
as favouring Lewis and, as someone who was very much caught in the
middle as part of the T-Car crew, I was lumped in with that group.
Our chats stopped. If ever I needed him in my car to check his seating,
there was little conversation, and all of a sudden there seemed to be a
pressure on him, one that he probably hadn't experienced for a long
time.

The approaching British Grand Prix didn't help matters. Silverstone was a standout event on our calendar for a British team with a
predominantly British crew and most of us viewed it as one of our
biggest weekends. The crowd at Silverstone is like no other, it's certainly one of the biggest and most passionate, but the fans there seem
to be more knowledgeable and have a deeper understanding of the
sport than lots of other places we'd go. As a British outfit, it was impossible not to feel the love and support for McLaren as hundreds of
Union flags dominated the grandstand. It was stirring stuff.

That year, the hype was even bigger. Lewis had exploded onto the scene and had a serious chance of winning the Drivers' Championship, which was an unprecedented situation. It's no exaggeration to say that he was the biggest thing to happen in British sport at the time, and the press, somewhat typically, were building him up to be a superstar for our generation. By the time the media day had come around, all the attention was focused on Lewis, with Fernando almost playing second fiddle. When he *was* asked questions, half of them were about Lewis anyway and together with Ron's own media hype of his young protégé in the preceding week, I'm sure it only served to grate Fernando's nerves even more.

In any case, the World Champ kept his head, managing to finish second to Kimi and one spot ahead of the home hero Lewis at Silverstone. After that we headed to the Nürburgring for the European GP, where things took a divisive turn for the worse. Fernando dropped a bombshell that shocked most of us, in what I can only describe as as desperate call-to-arms to his side of the team.

When he arrived at the circuit on Thursday, before commencing his media obligations, he came into the garage as he usually did to say hi to his mechanics and engineers. This time, though, he had a surprise for them all. One by one, in a private space at the back of the garage, little brown envelopes full of cash were given out to those working on Fernando's side of the garage! The cash, €1,300 to mechanics and more for the engineers, was intended, I can only assume, to help galvanise the crew and encourage them to rally round their man during these tough times.

This was unprecedented in my experience. The official team stance was that McLaren's race team members shouldn't accept gifts from drivers, as it could be seen as unfair to the factory staff, who didn't have the same relationships. Despite that, I'd known drivers to give out gifts before. DC and Kimi had handed helmets to their crew; I've heard of drivers presenting watches, even paying off mechanics' mortgages in the past, but always at the end of a season. It was a way of saying thank you for everybody's hard work, and as long as we didn't shout about it, nobody had an issue.

This time was different, though. We were a team with an ever-increasing divide through the middle of our garage; a team where one of our two drivers, even if he hadn't publicly stated it yet, believed there was an air of nepotism towards the other from Ron Dennis, which naturally dripped down to the shop floor. There was an obvious Lewis Hamilton fairy tale playing out. It had begun when he boldly approached Ron at an awards ceremony as a child to say he wanted to drive for the team one day, to McLaren signing him up and guiding his junior career. Now, this kid was leading the World Championship in Ron's McLaren car. Fernando found it hard to believe he was competing on a level playing field and had decided to re-motivate his side of the garage.

The envelopes of cash quickly became known about throughout the team. Very rarely is a secret amongst that many mechanics a secret for long. The whispers began spreading, people speculating about 'bribes' and 'incentives' and wondering exactly what the intention was behind it. At a time when Fernando might have felt like he was losing power, was this his way of trying to buy it back? Either way, while the wider McLaren team spirit was becoming strained during an increasingly difficult season, this did little to pull both sides back together. In fact, the opposite was probably true.

When an envelope eventually reached one of the senior engineers on Fernando's crew, he realised the potentially incendiary consequences and went straight to Ron to tell him what was going on. I wasn't privy to the discussion, but from what I understand, Ron didn't look too favourably upon the news and so by the end of that same day, everyone had returned the envelopes and Fernando was making a substantial donation to charity. Meanwhile, the rest of the team prayed that the gathering storm would blow over quickly.

*

A Grand Prix can sometimes unexpectedly develop into mayhem on the track – and in the most unusual ways. At the Nürburgring, Lewis's Chief Mechanic had stayed at home to attend a wedding, meaning I had to step in and take charge of his car and car crew for the weekend. I had a good chat with Lewis on Thursday; we small-talked, discussing all the things we'd both been up to since the last race and then about the way we both worked and how we'd best operate together that weekend. He was relaxed and happy. I looked forward to leading his guys through another (hopefully) trouble-free and successful event, and come Saturday afternoon we'd all gelled well together as a crew. The mood was confident ahead of qualifying. Unfortunately, that was the last harmonious point of the weekend.

Utter chaos dominated the horizon until the chequered flag was waved on Sunday afternoon. In qualifying, Lewis's front wheel came loose and destroyed the suspension, sending him heavily into a wall. I watched in horror as our car left the circuit at high speed, Lewis unable to slow it down before smashing into the barriers. Watching a crash is an awful feeling as a mechanic, particularly while not knowing the cause of the accident; a whirlpool of questions always dominated my thinking. 'Is the driver OK?' Or, 'Was it something me or my guys did wrong that caused the accident?' Doubts and fears raced through my head and I desperately tried to find the answers I wanted to hear.

Luckily, despite a few knocks, Lewis was fine, and the failure was later traced to a faulty wheel gun. It had been used in the qualifying pitstop, right before the failure. The gunman had sent the car out from the pitstop thinking his wheel was attached correctly, but the faulty gun hadn't delivered the correct amount of torque, essentially meaning the nut wasn't tight enough. The incident rattled him emotionally. He was cut up and later became traumatised enough by the event that he was offered counselling by the team. Things like that can weigh very heavily on the mind of a mechanic and it proves just how passionate and invested in the cause we all are. The reality, however, was that the wheel gun had failed to do its job properly. With the pitstop equipment under frantic analysis to find a way to prevent any future issues, we set about rebuilding Lewis's car under the supervision of our *parc-fermé** steward on Saturday night.

We finished the final tweaks on Sunday morning and I ran Lewis through the work we'd done. He was very grateful, asking me to pass on his thanks to everyone else, something that was always appreciated, but on this occasion I thought it might be better if he went a step further.

'It might be nice if you said thanks to the guys personally?' I suggested. 'It would mean so much more to them coming from you . . .'

Lewis nodded and walked around the garage for a quick chat with the boys, which was a nice touch. He was starting in tenth place that day, winning was going to be a huge ask, but his little gesture helped as a bit of a rallying call. Everybody on his side of the garage was up for the fight, myself included. I was keen to ensure the weekend was a success and make my direct contribution to the Lewis Hamilton story.

The European Grand Prix that year was a memorable one, but for all the wrong reasons – in our garage at least. It chucked it down right after the start, and loads of people spun off into the gravel traps, including Lewis. Beached, he kept the engine running, stayed in the car and was craned back onto the track, where he re-joined the race just before it was red-flagged.† Chaos ensued, as it often did in these rare race restart situations as everyone was unfamiliar with the procedures. Back on the grid, engines off and sheltering under umbrellas, we shuffled the car backwards and forwards as Race Control decided the order that the now-out-of-position cars should be lining up for the restart. When we finally arrived at our grid slot, the car was checked over for any serious damage. It was a bit battered and bruised, the

---

* *Parc-fermé* is a closed space, normally the garage, where the cars are sealed up between qualifying and a race. Under the rules, cars in post-qualifying *parc-fermé* aren't allowed to have parts changed unless given permission from FIA stewards.
† This incident later prompted a rule change preventing mechanical assistance when getting the cars back into a race.

bodywork peppered in 'gravel rash', but otherwise it had survived a fairly bumpy excursion. A few minutes later, with everyone recomposed and back under control, standing at the front of the car I signalled to the gearbox mechanic at the back to insert the external starter motor and fire up the engine for a warm-up.

He disappeared down out of sight below the rear wing, as was normal, but moments later, his face told a worrying story on the way back up: something was very wrong. This wasn't a guy who panicked easily, he was calm and collected and highly experienced, so I knew the issue was serious. Trying not to alert Lewis, sat in the car, of any potential situation, I walked round to the rear, asking his trainer to lean into the cockpit and chat to him while we worked out what was wrong.

The starter shaft, a long, narrow tube that ran through the diffuser and into the gearbox (in which the half-metre-long starter motor probe was inserted to fire up the engine), was packed full of tiny stones. When the car had spun backwards into the gravel trap, the tube had filled with debris and I had no idea how we were ever going to get it all out. We picked at the stones with long-nosed pliers and screwdrivers, but while we were able to clear most of it, that wasn't good enough. If just one stone had been left in there it would've prevented the starter from engaging with the splines in the gearbox at the far end and we wouldn't be able to turn the engine over. This was now a real problem. Race Control announced there were ten minutes to the restart, our engine was cooling down to way below the optimum temperature and we still had no way of getting the thing going.

It was now clear to Lewis there was something wrong, so I leant into the cockpit and reassured him that everything was all under control (lies). I then explained we were just getting the last few stones (more lies), and would be firing up any moment (even more lies). Back at the rear of the car, desperation was setting in. Long makeshift tools were being passed over the pit wall from the guys in the garage and I updated everyone on the radio of what was going on in the calmest voice I could manage. Now the team had swung into action.

We had long metal rods, taped together, to reach the length of the tube. Balls of double-sided sticky tape had been attached to the end in an attempt to coax out the remaining stones. It was working, but there were still one or two stubborn pieces, each no bigger than 5 or 6 millimetres in diameter, right at the very end of the starter shaft and the clock was ticking.

With the three-minute warning on the start light gantry appearing, we became desperate. I told the gearbox mechanic to smash the starter probe into position so we could get the engine fired up. It was risky, as it might have badly damaged something inside, but we were in serious danger of not getting the car started, both because of the time left before the start, but also because the temperature was dropping below its safe, allowable limits (anything below that would have meant that the car would have difficulties starting; if it had, the process could've resulted in a lot of damage due to the precise clearance tolerances designed into an F1 engine). I knew it was a desperate measure, but I'd been left with limited options and somebody had to make the call . . .

'*Got it!*'

Someone emerged from under the car, his *Blue Peter*-style 'stone grabber' in hand – he'd removed the one remaining piece of gravel! Quickly the starter probe went in and we quickly but cautiously restarted the car. The guys from Mercedes Benz gently warmed the engine from its unusually cold temperature and I talked Lewis through what we'd done, while confirming that he was in good shape for the restart. I wished him luck and left the grid with just moments to spare. The relief was almost overwhelming, but the euphoria was short-lived. After all that drama, I felt sure we deserved a good race recovery, scoring a decent points haul for the championship fight would have been just rewards for our efforts, but it wasn't to be. A brave fight from Lewis, and a tactical gamble or two on tyres in what proved to be extraordinarily mixed conditions didn't pay off. We finished ninth, just outside the top eight scoring positions, in what was a disappointing weekend. Our adrenaline levels had spiked during the high drama, but the Nürburgring would prove a fitting stress test for our conflicts to come.

Everything blew up in a fortnight.

Fernando had won the European Grand Prix, closing the gap on Lewis to just a couple of points and his crew were in good spirits, if not a little disappointed to have had a 'grand in the hand' one minute, only for it to disappear the next. It seemed like some of them were buying into Fernando's theory and stoked the atmosphere of biased discontent. Perhaps it was only a vibe created by 'Nando himself, but if the others felt it, then it existed. Meanwhile, from across the garage, Lewis's crew saw the little brown envelope situation as an act of desperation, confirmation that they'd rattled the World Champ. Subconsciously, they gathered tighter around their own man in support.

Despite the rising tensions, anyone glancing at both the Drivers' and Constructors' Championships would have been impressed with McLaren's season by the time the Hungarian Grand Prix came around in August. We were looking good as a team, topping both tables, with a healthy lead over Ferrari. As I wasn't directly assigned to either of the two drivers, this position is what pleased me the most. To clinch the Formula One Constructors' Championship was a dream, but oh, how the Ferrari boys and girls in red must've rubbed their hands together with delight as we began to implode on that Saturday afternoon!

Qualifying used to be about everyone setting the fastest time possible in order to gain as strong a grid position as they could. During this period of time, though – as has happened at various points in F1's history – it became a lot more complicated than that. That season, the top ten cars making it through to the third and final part of qualifying had to fuel their cars for the following day's race before entering the Q3 session. Like most teams, our tactic was to set our qualifying lap time with the lightest car possible, yet still leave ourselves with the optimum race strategy, so everyone would fill up, then run around for fifteen minutes doing as many laps as possible to burn off fuel and lighten the car for a fast, flying lap at the end. The FIA would then allow those teams to replace a set amount of fuel for each lap completed, after the session, ready for the race start.

It was a bizarre system that hardly made for a great spectacle for much of Q3, but that was what we had to work with. Consequently, there was a premium for getting as many laps in as possible in the time available, as the resulting 'paid back' fuel could allow you to go longer into the race without refuelling and open up a series of strategic possibilities on Sunday. At circuits like in Hungary, being the car at the front of the pitlane queue to go out meant a driver could get on track for Q3 earlier and might gain an extra lap of fuel burning depending on where they were in the order. To make this fair, at McLaren we would take turns between our drivers in who would line up first at each event. At the Hungaroring it was Fernando's turn to go first on the clear track, his turn to try for that extra lap of fuel.

Lewis had been looking strong through practice and was dialled into the circuit nicely, his focus seemed to have reached new levels. It was no stretch to say that he honestly believed he could become World Champion in his very first season in the sport. Having safely sailed through to Q3 in dominant fashion, Lewis, controversially aided by his race engineers and mechanics, broke from the agreed plan and left the garage first to queue up at the end of pitlane ahead of the final session of qualifying. Fernando's team was angry and confused, but there wasn't time to discuss what was happening. Instead they followed suit and lined up behind him at the end of pitlane, waiting for the green light to start the session. There was lots of frantic radio traffic. Some people assumed it was just a mistake and that Lewis would move over, allowing Fernando past as they got going, but confusion turned to frustration as the lights went green and Lewis sped off into the distance.

He'd gone rogue.

It was difficult to calm Fernando down; Lewis wasn't playing the game, which chimed perfectly with his growing paranoia of a wider conspiracy against him. Instead he'd blatantly ignored numerous clear and increasingly stern instructions from the pit wall to switch positions.

'Lewis, this is not what we agreed!' he was told. 'You need to let Fernando through!'

The silence was deafening. Lewis's move gave him a race strategy advantage, with an extra lap's fuel, and Fernando knew it. His angry radio rampage continued and at the first pitstop for new tyres a slanging match broke out between Fernando and the pit wall about what had happened.

'What's he doing?' yelled Fernando. 'This is not the plan! Can somebody tell him?'

His engineer explained that Lewis had gone off on his own accord, and the first flying laps took place with the young upstart emerging on provisional pole position, but there was one more planned tyre pitstop for each driver before the final laps took place. Everybody knew that this was the best and only remaining shot at the pole spot, and I remember waiting in the pitstop area, nervous with the increasing tension in the garage, irate radio chatter burning my ears. I was part of the right rear wheel crew in pitstops at that time. Fernando's car approached and stopped accurately on the marks. The wheel guns fired. Wheels came off. New ones went on. The guns fired again and our job was done; it had been controlled and slick. Perfect, in fact.

We'd already told Fernando on the radio that we needed him to hold for twenty seconds after the change. That would allow us to release him into a clear gap. He would be on track at the fastest point in the afternoon, the last moments of the session. It was perfectly normal procedure and this window had been calculated with a typically McLaren-esque act of precision timing. I knelt a foot from the stationary car, the engine loud, the sound of it rumbling through my bones.

Heat emanated from the burning brakes and exhausts, cooking me through my fire suit. I was waiting, waiting, *waiting.* The radio in my ear began counting down: '10 . . . 9 . . . 8 . . .' The count was going directly into Fernando's ear too. '7 . . . 6 . . . 5 . . . 4 . . .' Lewis had arrived behind us, queuing for his pitstop as we knew he would, his engine growling. '3 . . . 2 . . . 1 . . .' The Chief Mechanic lifted the lollipop, releasing Fernando's car for his final run . . .

. . . But nothing happened.

The pit wall told Fernando to go, the mechanics beckoned him to get on with his lap. A few seconds passed – *what's going on?* Lewis revved his engine in the car behind, shouting on the radio. At first I had no idea what was happening. I wanted to lean in to Fernando and tell him to go myself. *Mate, what are you doing?!* Then it dawned on me: *This is deliberate.* Fernando knew exactly where Lewis was, he could see him in his mirrors. He knew exactly how long was left of the session and how long it took to get around the circuit to start a flying lap before the chequered flag came out. He waited and waited. *More seconds ticked away.* We could do nothing but wait and frantically wave at him to go. Eventually, a full ten seconds after the lollipop was lifted, Fernando screeched away.

Lewis's car was quickly serviced in the pitstop as he swore and screamed obscenities across the airwaves. All of us were aware of the time left in the session; we understood the cars would now be at their lightest, running on fresh, grippier tires. The circuit was at its most 'rubbered-in' and yielding the fastest lap times of the weekend so far. This was Lewis's last shot at a pole-position lap and everybody knew it, especially Fernando. The only question was: would he now make it to the start line before time was called on qualifying? The pitstop timings had been calculated with precision accuracy.

One radio channel fell silent, the other, Lewis's, was busy – *shouting, arguing, questioning.* The engineers tried to calm him down, to focus him on getting round his out lap as quickly as possible before the chequered flag dropped. Once that happened, Q3 was over, and with it

Lewis's chance for pole position. There was no time for the normal careful and meticulous tyre preparations, bringing the new rubber up to the optimum temperature with burnouts, weaving and heavy braking to generate the maximum grip needed; instead Lewis had to go all out to beat the flag. His head seemed to drop, he wanted to give up on his final shot, but the pit wall reckoned there was still time to make the cut; they wanted Lewis to get his head down and drive. We could discuss the brinkmanship afterwards.

They were wrong. Lewis didn't make it. Fernando crossed the line to start his flying lap with just one second to spare before the chequered flag came out. Lewis was two and a half seconds behind. On one level I was seriously impressed that a driver could calculate in his head, with that accuracy, the time needed to hold his teammate up, stalling for long enough to prevent Lewis from getting to the line in time, while still scraping through himself. On the other, I was appalled. Our drivers, the figureheads of our team, the guys we looked up to for leadership and inspiration, had behaved so childishly. Ron felt the same. His reaction was beamed across the world on TV screens, as Alonso's trainer, Fabrizio – the nearest cat to kick – bore the full brunt of his anger. I could see at times, the 'inner Ron' desperately tried to regain control in front of the cameras, but rage and anger was sketched across his face, he was on the edge of losing control and Fabrizio could surely have had no doubt about it.

Lewis returned to the pits while Fernando completed his lap. To add insult to injury, he stuck the car on pole, while Lewis was pushed back to P2. The reaction inside the garage was really strange. One half was delighted to be in pole position, though unsure whether to celebrate because of what had just happened. The other half was fuming. There was a sense of resentment and anger between the two groups, though nobody vocalised it yet. From that moment on, the two factions didn't mix, as they normally would. Instead they kept to their own sides, discussing the incident passionately among themselves. I normally liked to wander through the garage after qualifying was done, congratulating everybody, thanking them for their efforts, on both sides. That day, I didn't know what to do. Nobody did.

Lewis and Ron apparently had a stand-up shouting match about the incident, something I never imagined I'd see Lewis, or Ron for that matter, getting involved in.

'Don't ever fucking do that to me again!' Lewis had said, angrily walking past his boss.

Ron was not impressed. 'Don't ever fucking speak to me like that again!' he snapped.

'Go fucking swivel!' I'm told was Lewis's schoolboy sign off, as he stormed away.

Of course the media were all over us, desperately trying to uncover the story, looking for some insight into what had been said on the team radio and inside the garage. I was approached by two different acquaintances from the press in the paddock, digging for intel when they knew that talking to team members was off limits. Terrified of the magnitude of what was beginning to unfold at McLaren, we all tried to keep inside our own impenetrable walls and did our best to get on with the job. Even during the regular Saturday evening chats with friends from other teams, as we waited together in the pitlane for the cars to be released from *parc fermé*, we were unusually guarded about what was being said and done.

Later that evening the race stewards concluded that the incident warranted punishment and Fernando was demoted five places on the grid for deliberately impeding another competitor. None of us were surprised, disappointing though it was to lose the front row lockout. What was more shocking and even more disappointing was their decision to ban McLaren from scoring Constructors' points in the race, apportioning considerable blame to us, the team.

I was furious with both drivers. Lewis had started the childish spat and Fernando had taken the bait, but as a mechanic I wasn't interested in the drama or politics. All of us had worked so hard to create and develop an amazing car. We trusted them to use it wisely and deliver the results we deserved, but they were now screwing with us, playing fast and loose with a potential Constructors' Championship, a reward that the whole McLaren team craved. Lewis had cranked up the stakes; Fernando had pushed them even higher. Now everything we'd worked for was about to crash down around them, and us – *hard*.

17

SPYGATE

As well as the feud between Lewis and Fernando, an even larger story was unravelling behind the scenes as several simultaneous sub-plots converged in what is still regarded as one of the biggest scandals in F1 history: Spygate.

A couple of months earlier, whispers had emerged around the paddock, and then in the wider world, that a senior Ferrari employee, Nigel Stepney, disgruntled about decisions made within the team about his future position, had sabotaged his team's race cars before the Monaco Grand Prix. The team's former Chief Mechanic had reportedly wanted to leave the team because he was unhappy with the technical structure Ferrari were taking, but instead was placed in a new factory-based role and forced to see out his current contract. Apparently he'd poured some kind of white powder inside the car's fuel tanks and was sacked. At the same time Ferrari announced it was taking action against our own Chief Designer, Mike Coughlan, in a supposed espionage case involving technical information on the Ferrari car being passed between the two men. The pair were both fairly senior at their respective teams, but under normal circumstances wouldn't have normally been involved with each other on a professional level.

This was huge news. I knew Stepney to some degree from the

many years spent fighting Ferrari in the pitlane, and of course I knew Mike. He was a bumbling, technical boffin who would come downstairs to the race bays in the McLaren factory every pre-season, often to a barrage of tongue-in-cheek abuse from the mechanics. They'd jokingly complain about a technical part his team had designed that didn't fit properly, or had made our lives more difficult. We wound him up endlessly and although he was pretty switched on, he seemed to have very little in the way of common sense. He certainly wasn't able to keep up with the banter, which was a common trait among intellectual race car designers in my experience.

Although the story was the talk of the town for a while, it did seem to fade away, or at least it became overlooked, in the midst of the extraordinary season we were having. McLaren had immediately denied any wrongdoing and we were told, as everyone else was, that knowledge of the Ferrari information hadn't gone beyond Mike Coughlan's possession. We had no reason to believe anything else. When a meeting of the World Motorsport Council later found no concrete evidence with which to punish McLaren for any F1 crime, everybody assumed the matter was now closed. We were free to crack on with the matter of winning the World Championships.

Mike Coughlan was, of course, relieved of his duties. I was surprised he'd been so stupid in the first place, but there was something comically slapdash about the way in which he'd been busted. The story goes that he'd received somewhere in the region of 700 pages of Ferrari technical drawings and development notes on their latest car. The dossier came from Nigel Stepney in what appeared to be a very dodgy deal between the two, and Mike had then given the files to his wife to copy. Mrs Coughlan then walked into a copy shop in McLaren's hometown of Woking. The owner, by sheer bad luck, was Italian and naturally a massive Ferrari fan. Thinking it strange that official Ferrari blueprints were being copied in his shop, he immediately contacted Maranello – the home of Ferrari – to share his news.

What a low-tech way for the biggest international espionage case in our hi-tech sport's history to be blown wide open!

Despite the tabloid distractions that were now swirling around Spygate, the dramas of our Hungarian GP Saturday were far from over as it turned out. On race day morning, the hangover from the previous afternoon's qualifying debacle gave Ron a pretty serious headache. They took place well away from us, but you can imagine some heated discussions on Saturday evening between the various parties involved. Lewis was angry with Fernando, obviously. He was also angry with Ron, as their tête-à-tête clearly demonstrated. Fernando was angry with Lewis for going off-plan in qualifying, and fumed at Ron, as he assumed it was all part of a wider conspiracy against him. He was also probably quite angry with the stewards. Meanwhile, Ron was angry with both of them, like a parent annoyed with their kids for showing them up in public. And just for the record, I was bloody annoyed with it all too.

The dispute was an ugly mess and for someone like Ron, for whom mess was one of the most heinous crimes imaginable, this was a painful situation. Sadly, there was worse to come. While the behind-closed-doors meetings on that Saturday night must have been a horrible affair for everyone involved, I'm sure a lot of things were said that weren't meant – or at least shouldn't have been said. Somehow, and none of us knew the exact details, Ron and Fernando had apparently ended up in a shouting match. When they reconvened on Sunday morning, legend has it that Fernando said he wanted to end his contract with McLaren. When that request was denied, he supposedly then blurted out that he could take the team down if he wanted, thanks to the unfolding espionage case.

It appeared that, unbeknown to Ron, the Ferrari technical information had indeed been discussed beyond Mike Coughlan's singular involvement, and Fernando had the emails to prove it had actually been shared between a small but select few, including Fernando himself. The threat of taking that information to the FIA was too much and there's no way Ron was going to be manipulated. Max Mosley, president of the FIA, already had it in for Ron Dennis; they rubbed one another up the wrong way and nothing would have given him greater pleasure than to be able to convict McLaren of espionage at that previous hearing. At the time there had been no evidence to do so. It looked like there was now.

The point of no return had been reached.

It must have taken everything Ron had in him to inform Max Mosley that, actually, new evidence had been uncovered regarding Spygate. Fernando would deny ever making a threat, but in any case, I honestly believe Ron just felt that reporting it was the right thing to do, and I'm also sure the last thing he wanted was to allow Fernando to do it behind his back, so on the morning of the Hungarian Grand Prix, shortly after Fernando's outburst, that's exactly what he did. I can only imagine Mosley's delight. He must have thought all his Christmases had come al once. I'm sure he'd just happily watched the stewards as they demoted Ron's World Champion on the grid, while banning his entire team from scoring any Constructors' points and now he was learning that Ron's drivers were turning against him. Even more significantly, Mosely now had a trail to follow on Spygate.

This developing news had yet to hit the garage. We arrived at the circuit on race day with mixed emotions, determined by which part of the team you were in.

Lewis had been smart in recognising that Fernando would probably bear the brunt of any media scrutiny after Saturday's events. He'd delivered an almost Oscar-worthy performance in the post-qualifying press conference and his body language, demeanour and words all pointed the finger at the man, at that time, still sitting on pole position without actually saying outright whose fault he thought it was. Lewis was very deliberate in praising the team at every opportunity; he detailed what a wonderful job they'd been doing all year and how proud he was of everybody. Fernando, of course, did not.

This almost devious, under-the-radar sniping was a tactic Lewis would frequently use that year, mostly behind the scenes within our team, and it wasn't a trait many people warmed to.

In the garage, a lot of the lads became suspicious. Lewis's platitudes towards us were beginning to be treated with mistrust and the stuff he was saying in interviews and press conferences were taken with a dubious pinch of salt; we could see he had another agenda motivated by his feud with Fernando. I felt as if he was using us at that point to wind up Fernando and his side of the garage, and to drum up support amongst fans for his own cause. I remember seeing the press conference play out that day as we worked away in the garage, thinking it was like watching one of my own young children as they vied for attention by acting angelically, when the other one had just been in trouble for being naughty. The spat between our two drivers felt all too familiar, and became a feature of our season, but rifts were deepened even further after the Hungarian Grand Prix: Lewis led the race from start to finish; an increasingly frustrated Fernando came home fourth. But the Spaniard's revenge was about to impact on us all.

A month later, just before the Italian Grand Prix, the FIA announced publicly that they had new evidence in the Spygate saga. It seems, according to reports since, that Fernando did indeed pass on his emails, initially to Bernie Ecclestone, who then sent them on to an increasingly grateful Max Mosley. The case had been reopened and a date set for a new hearing in Paris, which just so happened to coincide with Thursday of the Belgian Grand Prix. Now there was genuine concern amongst the team. We hadn't known the scale of the infiltration of the Ferrari documents and their information until that point. Our own internal investigation had been kept within a pretty small circle and Ron had told everybody the same thing – the stolen documents had never entered the McLaren factory, and we'd had no reason to disbelieve him. I don't for a minute think he'd ever known anything about them himself and felt pretty sure that if he had, he'd have stopped it going any further. That level of underhand dealings over another team just wasn't his way . . . *Even if it was Ferrari.*

At this point I found myself in a fairly compromising position. The investigation was looking for further evidence of use, or knowledge, of the stolen Ferrari information and it had reached forensic levels. A cybercrimes unit had been tasked with searching the internal network at McLaren's Technology Centre and every company laptop was taken for a period of time to be analysed, including mine. Obviously I was in no way involved in the whole murky espionage dealings, but there was something on my computer from Ferrari that I didn't want my team seeing. Let me explain . . .

At the end of the previous season, after working with Kimi for so long, we'd grown pretty close. The pair of us worked well together and had become friends away from the racetrack too. Our little crew was pretty tight and together with Kimi's trainer, Mark Arnall, we helped him feel comfortable in a very corporate and restrictive McLaren team, one that he otherwise might have struggled to cope with. When he told me he was going to Ferrari for 2007, I was gutted . . .

Over the winter, our conversations moved onto the idea that some of us might go with him to Ferrari. Mark was going as he now worked directly for Kimi and for a while I actually entertained the idea. It would have meant relocating to Maranello, but I was looking into it. During this process I was put in touch with none other than Nigel Stepney who, unbeknown to me at the time, was the main protagonist on the Ferrari side in the Spygate scandal. A number of detailed email conversations followed, together with some phone calls, and I was on the verge of flying to Maranello for an arranged visit, when I'd finally decided to stay with McLaren.

Obviously, one of the first things any forensic cyber investigation would look for was the evidence of any communications with Ferrari, and specifically Nigel Stepney. My computer was full of it. None of the material implicated me in the scandal, but it was highly likely my team bosses were about to discover I'd been on the brink of leaving for our biggest rivals. Luckily, after an uncomfortable day or two, my laptop was returned with a wry grin and some knowing chuckles. The subject of my leaving was never discussed. But I knew that they knew, and they knew that I knew that they knew.

Our concern over Spygate was that there could be some serious sanctions against the team, punishments that could impact upon us all personally. The charges against McLaren were looking fairly bad. The emails between Mike Coughlan, Fernando and one or two others proved that, as a team, we technically knew about them and had discussed them. If Mosley and the FIA decided to throw us out of Formula One, what on earth would we do? I, like many others, had a hefty mortgage to pay, a family to support and McLaren was my only means of doing so. If the team went out of business, there was no way we could all find jobs elsewhere in the pitlane, and as an F1 mechanic, my skills weren't really transferable to many other industries.*

If an entire organisation folds, particularly in a small and specialised industry like ours, it results in substantial unemployment and that worried us all. Lots of the lads put on brave faces and claimed they didn't care if we got thrown out, that they'd had enough of F1 anyway. I didn't believe them. These were the same guys who said every year that this would be their last in the sport, that they weren't going to put up with the stress, long hours and constant travel anymore and would

---

* *You might think an F1 mechanic could easily go and work in a road car garage, even, perhaps, that those garages might be clambering over each other to get us to come and work for them. No. Firstly I had no desire to go and work on road cars, but secondly, and far more importantly, I don't know the first thing about them. It drives me crazy that my friends and neighbours all regularly approach me in the street, telling me about the funny knocking noise coming from their engine and asking me if I'd mind taking a quick look for them. If you are one of my friends or neighbours reading this, stop it. I barely ever open the bonnet on my own road car, I'm not sure I even know where the lever might be to do so, so I'm definitely not going to open yours! Just look at an F1 car. Does it look anything, anything at all, like your road car? I have a specific set of skills and experience, all of which relates to building, operating, setting up and optimising Formula One racing cars. I can change their wheels in two seconds, under extreme pressure, and help to make them circulate a racetrack as quickly as they can possibly go. I cannot, and will not, change a head gasket or ball joint on a Ford Fiesta! I'm afraid you'll have to take it to the garage . . . like I have to. Rant over.*

be leaving at the end of the season. They were all back in Australia every March.

As we approached the Belgian GP weekend, we had to prepare the cars as normal. Fernando had led home a brilliant 1-2 finish at the Italian GP two weeks earlier and only three points separated our two at the top of the table, with Lewis just in front. In the Constructors' Championship we were enjoying a substantial lead over our closest rivals, and Spygate adversaries, Ferrari. The weekend in Monza had been bittersweet, with the great result being somewhat overshadowed by an atmosphere that felt poisonous. A nasty war of words was brewing in the paddock with the media, who were stirring up the story; Ferrari claimed the incident was the lowest of the low and that they wanted us to suffer disqualification. Even the Italian police showed up with court representatives at our hospitality building to serve notice of a criminal investigation against senior management. Lewis seemed to be revelling in the fact that Fernando was taking most of the heat and turned up his 'team player' image to the media. In house, however, he appeared more and more self-centered, even underhand at times, as his press conferences and quotes became more divisive. I wasn't sure what to make of it all, but we had no choice other than to carry on, hold our own heads up high and attempt to win as many races as possible.

We arrived at the famous Spa-Francorchamps circuit in Belgium on Wednesday morning and set about our usual preparations. The track hadn't been on the calendar for 2006 and in the time we'd been away, a brand new pit garage complex had been built. It was huge, modern and state-of-the-art, making life a lot easier for us than it used to be in the old cramped facilities. Spacious garages meant we created a rabbit warren of rooms and corridors from our sponsor-adorned banner system. The team truckies, or hairy-arses, knuckle-draggers and lorry drivers as we fondly knew them, arrived in the days before us and painted the garage floor a delightful McLaren grey colour to look pristine and, of course, corporate. Then they'd put up the temporary partition walls and overhead gantries to delineate the various areas that each department needed. It improved our working conditions no end – we weren't on top of each other for one. It also meant, of course, that should we get thrown out of the championship at the next day's FIA hearing, we'd be taking it all down again before we'd even turned a wheel. That was something none of us could avoid thinking about as we began moving our cars and equipment from the team trucks. It was the last time all the teams would be driving their race trucks to a Grand Prix that season as Belgium was the final European race of the calendar, but for us, we genuinely had no idea if it would be the last time *ever*.

There was a nervous tension in the garage on Thursday as we made final preparations to the cars. Lewis was in Paris to give evidence with Ron, Paddy Lowe and the legal team, and their unusual absence in our garage made for an eerie vibe. We tried as best we could to stay focused on the job, but every time we set foot outside the garage doors, someone would ask us about the situation. What did we think was going to happen? What would we do if we were thrown out? Had we heard anything from Paris yet?

Dave Ryan had called a team meeting for that morning, to brief us all as best he could. The message was hardly ground-breaking: we were all to continue as if we were going racing. There was no news from Paris and we had no idea how long the hearing would take. We didn't even know if there would definitely be a decision, or more specifically a sentencing, that same day. The verdict, though, was surely a formality – we were guilty. The sentence, however, could literally be the difference between me keeping my house or not.

Dave told us that Ron had specifically asked him to hold the meeting and that he knew we were all concerned and worried. He admitted he had no idea how it would go, but tried to reassure us by saying that if we were expelled from Formula One, McLaren would just go and race in IndyCar in America instead. I don't think any of us believed him. How was that even possible? Were we all expected to move State-side with our families? I knew McLaren couldn't compete in that championship, not from the UK, even if they wanted to. It just couldn't work. Besides, none of us wanted to go into IndyCar racing, or had any experience in that field. It was different to F1 in just about every way imaginable. If McLaren wanted to race over there I'm sure at the end of the day they could, but none of us felt that was in any way reassuring. The meeting dispersed and we went into the pitlane for a somewhat subdued pitstop practice.

By early that evening, the garage, the two race cars and my T-Car were finished and ready for FP1 on Friday morning, and with huge uncertainty hanging like a black cloud over us, we left the circuit and headed back to our hotel for dinner. We got halfway there before my phone rang and Dave Ryan's number flashed up on the screen. The car fell silent in anticipation of news.

'We're expecting an announcement soon,' said Dave, somewhat anti-climatically. 'Ron would like us all to be here together when it comes. Could you please turn around and head back to the circuit?'

Apparently, he'd spoken to Ron from Paris. The hearing was over and now we were awaiting their decision. I was desperate, there were so many questions I wanted to ask, but Dave wanted to talk to us all together, so all three crew cars spun around and headed into the track for the second time that day. The cost of getting online using mobile phones whilst abroad in 2007 was extortionate, but it didn't matter. Everyone, in each of the three cars, was checking every website they could think of for news all the way there, but nothing had come through.

Back at the circuit it was a sombre scene, almost deserted. There was a bleak mood inside our garage, too. All the roller doors were down, just a few lights remained turned on, and the cars were under their covers. I'd had a similar feeling waiting outside the school headmaster's study as a teenager, my parents inside, after being apprehended for selling cans of beer to first- and second-year students. Back then there was no question I was guilty, I'd been caught red-handed; all that was left was to discover my fate at the hands of a terrifyingly strict and vindictive man in power. The two situations felt remarkably similar.*

Dave gathered us all together and recalled his telephone conversation with Ron. He'd said that the hearing had finished, McLaren had been allowed to put forward an honest and complete version of events and that Ferrari had done their best to discredit us at each step. Ron was proud that the team had done their best and that we should all remain hopeful for the most positive outcome possible. He expected the verdict to be delivered shortly.

For the team, it meant nothing. There was only one piece of news we needed to hear and until that came, even the most inspirational team talk from Ron, or anyone else, would fall on deaf ears. We waited. And waited. And waited. For over two hours we sat on tool cabinets, boxes, race tyres and on the floor, propped up against walls. The McLaren garage had never looked so untidy. Now able to plug in my laptop, I constantly refreshed the *Autosport* website pages looking for info, as did everyone else. A Google search of 'Spygate' brought up all sorts of public chat forums and unsolicited websites on the subject. Nowadays we'd all jump on Twitter, but in 2007 that wasn't the case. Every now and then someone would shout that they'd found something. Good news, bad news or no news, all of it was quickly dismissed as unreliable speculation and we waited for an official line, or another phone call from Ron in Paris.

Dave's phone kept ringing, the garage falling deathly silent with every call, each of us awaiting the news. He would give us all a shake

---

* In case you're wondering about my fate at the hands of the scary headmaster, I was suspended from school for one day, a punishment severe enough to elevate me to a certain level of infamy amongst student peers, yet not something that would affect the rest of my life. As is often the case with these things, though, and truly one of life's harder-hitting parenting tricks, the look of tragic disappointment on my father's face had far more impact on my remorse than my actual punishment.

of the head with every bleep or ring, confirming it hadn't been *The Call*. He'd then speak politely to whoever had rang him at such an inconvenient moment, asking them to get off the line while he waited for our inevitable sentence.

And then it arrived: *The Verdict*.

Dave's phone rang again, but this time he wasn't shaking his head. He'd stood up and we knew instantly it was Ron. Although it wasn't to deliver the news we were so desperate for, he said they'd been summoned back into the room to hear the World Motor Sport Council's decision and we would know the outcome imminently. The tension was unbearable. We scoured the internet ferociously, and after ten or fifteen minutes a story began to emerge across multiple sites. The source seemed to be a journalist who was present at the hearing, so it was the most believable news yet. It was also the bombshell we'd all been dreading. McLaren had been thrown out of the 2007 Formula One World Championship and we'd also been banned from taking part in the 2008 Formula One World Championship.

There was an air of disbelief in the garage as everyone crowded around the laptops. Others frantically searched for more corroboration on their phones. None of the big, reputable news sites had reported this story yet. *Was it true?* My heart had sunk but I wanted to see it confirmed before I fully believed and allowed the awful reality to take hold. I continually refreshed the respected *Autosport* website, hoping for a different outcome. I'm not in any way religious, and I'd never prayed before, but on that day I do remember muttering something in my head, just in case it helped.

Sure enough, it looked like somebody had been listening. Moments later, Dave's phone rang again. Everyone stopped talking and stared up at him, wide-eyed, like baby birds in a nest, looking up at their mother hoping for food. *It was Ron*. But we didn't need Ron for news: seconds into the call, with me still blindly refreshing the laptop – now habitually, compulsively – *Autosport* broke the real story. The earlier headline was wrong, and the first thing to hit home was that we would be racing that weekend, which ultimately meant I was keeping my job. The relief was immense.

There was bad news however. A $100 million fine, a ridiculous figure I couldn't even begin to get my head around, was to be imposed on the team, but in the end that wouldn't be my direct problem. That was one for Ron to work out. More damaging, though, was our expulsion from that year's Constructors', or team's, Championship. That really hurt. I think it took a day or two to properly sink in, probably because the bigger impact was definitely the overwhelming relief of McLaren being able to continue in the sport, but it stung like hell to miss out on a title – one I was sure we were going to win. It still hurts many years later. As a team, 2007 was *our* year. World Titles are indescribably difficult things to win, the opportunity doesn't come around very often, and after finally becoming an F1 mechanic, and after years of dedication and trying, that World Title was my dream, even more so in a year when I wasn't directly working with any one driver in particular.

When you work in a car crew, specifically with one driver, the job is all about making *him* – Kimi, DC, Lewis, *whoever* – a champion. As a mechanic or engineer in that small tight-knit team, that brings enormous satisfaction and kudos. Apart from anything else, it looks great on the CV. So for everyone in that situation, it's the one that matters. But car crews are a tiny part of any Formula One team, perhaps only comprising around ten or twelve people. That leaves many hundreds more in the wider race team and back at the factory who have no specific allegiance to one driver or the other. For most of them, they don't care which one of their team's drivers win as long as one does, ideally with the other one coming second. So taking the Constructors' Championship is their holy grail. Having worked on Kimi's car for years, I was finally in that situation. I wanted to be able to call myself a World Champion. With the best car and two of the best drivers in the world, plus a massive lead with just four races to go, it was the best opportunity we'd had in my entire career.

And now it had been taken away.

It was a difficult moment as Dave put the phone down and confirmed what we by now already knew. For Lewis and Fernando's crews, it was a great result. Their drivers had escaped any punishment in exchange for assisting the FIA with its enquiries and their intense title fight continued. They were laughing and joking around the garage like it was a completely insignificant result to them. Perhaps having been in their shoes with Kimi, coming so close to winning in 2003 and 2005, I could understand it. I'm sure I'd have been the same. But perhaps because of my previous experiences I realised how rare and treasured opportunities like the one just taken from us were. I was not happy, I wasn't laughing and joking with the boys that night, but cut a forlorn figure as we slipped away into the darkness and back to the hotel once again.

18

BREAKDOWN

The weekend was dominated by the Spygate story – it was *everywhere*. Newspaper editors and mainstream news channels led with our extraordinary and unprecedented fine as more and more details emerged from the investigation. Fernando's role in the sorry story was pretty damning, and everyone knew it. His position seemed untenable within the team, but come the weekend he was still a McLaren driver. Weirdly, because of the awful atmosphere in the garage prior to Spygate, there was very little change in the political climate at McLaren; nobody on Lewis's side of the garage needed any more reason to dislike Fernando, and vice versa – both groups had enough ammo already. The mood was sour. It's not very often that the cars and racing play second fiddle to the off-track headlines generated by an F1 weekend, but at Spa more revelations kept emerging from the case. Strangely the Belgian Grand Prix became a sideshow.

Lewis loved every minute of it and had returned from Paris smelling of roses, at least in the eyes of the public. We knew he'd played his part in forging the unrest within our team, but it had been worked more subtly than Fernando's Hungarian qualifying stunt. In the absence of regular good advice, with only his father as a constant presence,* Lewis capitalised on the bad press generated by his team-mate's behaviour. He was playing games to win support for his cause within McLaren and the angelic, butter-wouldn't-melt press conferences continued. He was really beginning to milk the situation, and I didn't like it one bit.

To be fair, he was young and inexperienced. I thought Lewis would have benefitted greatly if he'd received some sensible, effective advice; a figure to guide and reassure him, somebody to help him step back from the intense situation he was in. He only really had his dad, who was experiencing it all with him, so looking back, I guess the team could and should have done more in that sense. Lewis was just a kid and his world had changed almost overnight, and in so many ways. He'd been employed because he was a fast racing driver; now he was dealing with a series of competitive dynamics that nobody could easily negotiate, not without an experienced, supportive character in their corner. Truthfully, I can't imagine how anyone at that age could go through the emotional trauma of the insincere and fiercely competitive world of Formula One, on one of the biggest public sporting platforms in the world, and not emerge a different person. At the time, though, we were all immersed in that world too, but we'd been in it for far longer, so sympathy wasn't our initial response.

I'll admit I was disappointed he'd changed from the enthusiastic, humble and friendly young man we'd all got to know just a few months earlier. However, I appreciated it must be near impossible for such an intense situation not to make a significant impact on your personality. He now had people doing everything for him and the fans adored

---

* Anthony Hamilton, Lewis's dad, was a big character. He was there at almost every test and Grand Prix and we all knew him because he'd been around for a long time. He was a nice guy, but I don't think it was the right decision to have him as Lewis's manager because he knew him too well, and he wasn't familiar with the world of F1. It was as new to him as it was to Lewis and what Lewis really needed was a good PR Manager who could tell him what to say and do, or more importantly, what not to say and do. At times I'm not sure Anthony's advice behind the scenes always helped Lewis in the right way.

everything he did. He was also paid a fortune and found himself mightily close to winning a title in his very first season. It warped his outlook. He said and did things that didn't always put him in a good light and I know from media colleagues that there were one or two interviews with British TV that were never aired because even the broadcaster thought it would cause him major problems with his fans and sponsors. Rather than throwing him under the bus, however, they sent us the footage of what had happened and asked what we wanted to do. And that's despite our own PR person being alongside Lewis when the interview was conducted – they hadn't flagged it as an issue, perhaps intimidated by the momentum and aura that seemed to surround McLaren's impressive new star.

In Belgium, with so much carrying on away from the track, it was no real surprise when we didn't perform at the top of our game. Ferrari dominated the weekend. Not only that, but their 1-2 finish, with us now banished from the picture, was enough to seal the Formula One Constructors' World Title with three races to go – a championship we'd been leading by a mile up to that point. And so the knife twisted. Our two drivers fought each other during the race and we watched through our fingers as they almost made contact at the start, Fernando pushing Lewis off the track at turn one. It could have been a metaphor for the remainder of the 2007 season: fighting each other was the only thing they seemed concerned about.

Japan's race was being held in Fuji for the first time in thirty years and I looked forward to it as a welcome change after visiting the same depressing hotel in Suzuka for so long. As it turned out, the view from the window might have been different, but everything else was exactly the same. The room was so small that within minutes of checking in, the corridors were littered with chairs as everyone removed their furniture in order to create enough floor space for a suitcase or two. The entire bathroom was moulded from one single piece of orange plastic and you could brush your teeth, have a shower and actually use the toilet all from the comfort of its electronically heated seat, it was so compact. That's if you could decipher the hieroglyphic-style instructions for the toilet's ridiculously excessive number of functions: various temperature options; vibrations and bum-washing jets; backside dryers, music, lights . . . *action!*

With only three races to go and just two points separating our drivers at the top of the standings, things were tense inside the team. The relationship between the two sides of our garage had broken down almost completely. Communication between them was reduced to the bare minimum, with people like myself and the senior central engineering staff having to act as mediators at times. We were the team with the best car, the best two drivers and we were leading the championship, yet behind closed doors we weren't acting like a team at all. Focus had shifted so singularly to trying to outfox the guy on the other side of the garage that we began to forget the basics of motor racing. We'd been in close-run seasons before and the mantra was always to treat the last few title-deciding races exactly as you do the rest – *don't do anything differently just because the pressure's on.*

In Fuji there was very little to divide our two; nothing much separated them through the first and second practices, and both sides, as always, spent Friday night forensically searching their data for any tiny areas of improvement. On Saturday morning the weather was awful and after a much-delayed three laps, the third and final practice session was abandoned due to fog. The upshot was that any overnight changes after Friday's running couldn't now be tested before the afternoon's qualifying. Most people were left with two options: either go back to what they knew had worked from the day before, or keep their tweaks to a minimum so as not to be caught out when it really mattered. Fernando's boys went for the latter.

Over on Team Hamilton, however, the lure of a potentially advantageous but untried change had proved too tempting in their desperate fight with the enemy. Thinking they could achieve faster or more efficient gearshifts with a new gearbox software update, the team installed the system overnight, hoping to try it in morning practice. When practice was abandoned, having successfully shift-checked the car on our stands in the garage, they decided the risk was worth taking and opted to leave it in place for qualifying. But with half an hour to spare before the pitlane opened for Q1, the inevitable happened: further gearbox shift-checks revealed an issue with the car selecting reverse gear. This was potentially serious. Firstly, the car needed to have an operational reverse gear to meet FIA regulations, but also because anything outside of its normal operating parameters could cause destructive harm to the finely tuned and intricately delicate gearbox. Lewis's crew were very concerned. They tried again to get the reverse gear to work. Ron, Paddy Lowe and other senior engineering staff gathered around the back of the car, worried looks on their faces, as they discussed a series of ever decreasing options.

At that point, Tyler Alexander, one of Bruce McLaren's founding partners in setting up the team all those years ago and an all-round straight-talking American-in-F1 legend, wandered over to me from Fernando's side of the garage. Both of us looked over at the ensuing panic. Tyler really was a character, he's sadly no longer with us, but was a man in his sixties of unparalleled experience. At the time, he was working as the systems engineer for Fernando's car, and in his trademark dry, gruff Boston tone he surmised the sorry situation.

'Huh, ya know what, Elvis?' he said. 'Ya spend half the year wipin' your ass with one hand, then halfway through, all of a sudden ya start wipin' it with the other. It's no wonder when ya end up with shit on ya thumb!'

Tyler walked off, chuckling to himself, his shoulders rising and falling as he made his way back to his side of the garage. I tried my best to hold back my own laughter and look serious before heading over to see if I could help with the problem. These were anxious moments. I got my boys to start swapping the T-Car, previously set up for Fernando that weekend, over to Lewis's seat and pedal settings, just in case he had to jump in. Luckily, though, his race car was fixed by going back to the older, proven software maps and a relative calm was restored. Lewis went on to grab pole position, with Fernando second, and he later converted that into another Grand Prix win. When Fernando eventually crashed out, the gap at the top had been extended to twelve points with just two races to go.

This was a significant lead, with a race win earning a driver just ten points back then. All Lewis needed to clinch an unprecedented World Championship in his debut year was to finish within three points of Fernando or within six points of Kimi's Ferrari (who had steadily closed the gap from being twenty-six points behind earlier in the season). It was now Lewis's to lose and in that situation, I knew it was vital for him and the team to remain focused and calm. *Don't do anything differently just because the pressure's on.* Sadly, with both halves of our team, our approach to most races that year hadn't been great, we were fighting like cats and dogs and doing almost anything to get one over on each other. Communication was terrible, the workforce was disillusioned with the behaviour of both drivers, and trust had reached an all-time low. There were joint meetings because we had to have them, but that was it as far as the union went. In the past, both crews would have helped each other by openly sharing intel on the car across the garage, details on what was working and what wasn't, but that friendly vibe had come to a halt. With hindsight, a change in approach for those last two races may well have done us good, because it was exactly those idiosyncrasies which would cost us dearly at the Chinese Grand Prix.

Lewis was nervous that weekend – we could all see it. He tried so hard to give off an impression of nonchalance; a sense of having everything under control, but those of us who knew him could see he was feeling the enormity of what he might achieve that Sunday evening. He was hanging round the car in the garage, looking it up and down, asking questions and checking things had been done properly. That was our job, not his; we'd been there before, he hadn't. Lewis needed to stay focused on what he did best and not become distracted. It certainly didn't help that his engineers were clearly nervous too. They were worrying more than normal about the things that could go wrong and finding it hard not to interfere with the car. Lewis's inexperience in handling the pressure was showing; the anxiety had become contagious.

Despite the pressure, Lewis nailed his qualifying lap and put the car on pole, with the two Ferraris providing a welcome buffer between him and Fernando. Seemingly, history was set to be made the following afternoon and Sunday morning came all too quickly. The weather was awful again, which gave the engineers more headaches over tyre strategy as the race approached, and the last thing we needed was anything out of the ordinary to scupper a straightforward afternoon, like changing conditions. The atmosphere was just as unpredictable off the track. By now, Fernando was barely talking to anybody in the team outside of his own engineers. He was there only because his contract said he had to be and many of us felt little sympathy towards him. His lack of gratitude, or even manners at times, was hardly a motivating factor for a team of people busting their balls to keep his title fight alive.

Lewis was by now engineering his own car, while his actual race engineers seemed too intimidated, either by him or the wider situation, to overrule him. Outside of his own small crew, he'd been gradually losing a number of friends in the team over his apparently disingenuous and often arrogant behaviour in front of the media and behind the scenes. But then again, perhaps history shows that the big winners in this sport, people like Michael Schumacher and Ayrton Senna, require an edge of arrogance and self-importance to succeed.

The race got underway with the field racing on intermediate wet tyres and Lewis ran off into the distance. He pushed hard; his pace was incredible as, eventually, the track began to dry. But tyre wear quickly became an issue for him, much more so than for Kimi and Fernando, who'd both managed their pace more sensibly. In the garage we could see a pitstop was imminent, just from the way Lewis was struggling on his heavily worn intermediates, so we readied ourselves. The chasing cars, the more experienced title rivals, had closed right up to the back of Lewis, having preserved their tyres in order to make it to the forthcoming pitstop window. Frustratingly, we watched on from the garage as our lead car tiptoed round the track like Bambi on ice, trying to eke out a few more laps on his worn tyres, rather than stop too early and ruin the race strategy, and eventually he ran wide as Kimi and then Fernando whizzed by.

The new upended race order shouldn't have been problematic. If Lewis pitted for dry tyres (even though they would have been compromised on a still slightly damp track) it should have been enough to secure a safe third-place finish, and with it the only thing that mattered: the 2007 Formula One World Championship. It was such a no-brainer that several crew members in the garage were shouting at our own pit wall from under their pitstop helmets, urging them to bring him in. The problem was, though, for some of those people on Lewis's side of the team, in that adrenaline- and ego-fueled moment, the title *wasn't* the only thing that mattered.

Such was the fierce rivalry between the two halves of McLaren that the sight of Fernando racing past Lewis had been enough to bring down a red mist in the cockpit and on the pit wall. The long game was forgotten; the entire focus stupidly moved to getting back in front. Frantic conversations between the car and pits ensued. The engineers wanted to leave Lewis on track until his optimum pitstop lap for dry tyres, so as to not compromise his race strategy in relation to Fernando's. Lewis didn't know what to do, but was shouting that we needed to do something.

'Guys!' he screamed. 'My tyres are pretty worn out, what are we doing here?!'

We could hear the distress and panic in his voice on the radio. I don't know if Ron got involved, but it was no real secret by then that he wanted Lewis to win this championship. He knew Fernando would be leaving at the end of the season and if anyone was going to carry the treasured Number One on his car for 2008, he wanted it to be us, not Fernando taking it to another team. Perhaps he influenced the call in the end, I don't know, but the decision was made, after a lot of discussion and procrastination over the radio, to keep Lewis out for one more lap, an attempt to stay with Fernando and prevent him from gaining any strategic advantage by remaining on his intermediate tyres until the circuit was fully dry enough for slicks.

It proved to be the wrong call. Lewis lost something like seven seconds to Fernando on that extra lap as he desperately struggled to keep the car on the circuit. The tyres were so worn out that we could even see the canvas showing through on the TV screens, and when he eventually did manage to creep back round to the end of the lap, so little grip remained that he slid off of the track as he entered the pitlane and became beached on a tiny gravel trap in an embarrassing accident at around 30mph.

Half the garage, including me, held their heads in their hands, despairingly. We were ashamed to be associated with the unfolding drama. Mistakes like that hurt much more than you'd think when you're sat in the garage, watching along with the hundreds of millions of others globally as the ugly events develop. I had nothing to do with the decision-making process, but if I'd been in charge, I'd have done things differently. However, as far as the watching world knew, I was just one of those idiots in the McLaren team who had thrown away an 'easy' World Title. I know it's an old and overused mantra to say, 'We win and lose as a team together,' but we did. The defeats were just hard to swallow at times. Lewis knew he'd played his part in the disaster – it had been a joint decision to keep him out there in the end. In fact, I recently heard him interviewed about the incident and he rightly said that it had been a combination of him and us. The team was more experienced than him, he argued, so we should have brought him in sooner, which was fair. He also acknowledged that his lack of experience caused him to agree without question; he should have been stronger with his feedback. Either way, we'd cocked it up.

Of course, on Fernando's side of the garage it was a very different story. He eventually finished second, with Lewis's DNF the lifeline he never thought he'd get. Ironically, it turned out to be a gift from a team that he, by now, distrusted and was probably only reluctantly driving for. I had the feeling that, had Lewis wrapped it up that day, we wouldn't have seen Fernando again and he'd have repudiated us before even finishing the season. As it turned out, we headed to Brazil with Lewis just four points ahead of Fernando and seven ahead of a pesky Kimi, whose win in China had kept him just about in it.

19

THE BIG BLOW-OUT

I often found it difficult to look beyond the walls of McLaren's garage, such was the depth and intensity of any F1 season, let alone one as all-consuming as 2007. I'd almost lost sight of the fact that, despite the tumultuous, even poisonous, atmosphere within our own team, this was turning out to be one of the most exciting, controversial and record-breaking championships for as long as most fans could remember. For me and for many of my colleagues, it'd been a difficult year on so many levels, although with the car and drivers we had, on paper it should have been a relative cruise to a double World Title, something all of us had craved more than anything else. It'd been a long time since McLaren had been champions. A number of people in the team had never experienced it, but it had become the dream for all of us; over everything, it was the motivation that powered us through the long nights in the garage and months away from our families. The fact that our horrendous slip-up in China had taken the championship down to the final race may have been a source of embarrassment on our part, but for people following the sport, and of course Fernando Alonso, our mistake had served as a dramatic and welcome moment.

If by race sixteen of seventeen it was already a memorable season, the Brazilian Grand Prix of 2007 ensured its place in the history books. Returning back to base in between the final two rounds really hammered home the scale of what we were involved in. Formula One was even bigger news in the UK. The Lewis Hamilton story had reignited a passion in British fans that we hadn't seen for a long time and everyone was talking about the championship. Conspiracy theorists were having a field day too, as they had all season, coming up with wild accusations for why Lewis hadn't won in China. Even my mates back home took great pleasure in seizing the opportunity to ridicule our most recent team blunder.

It's not always easy holding an F1-based conversation with fans, especially if you're in a pub, or picking up your kids outside the school gates. Outsiders read the headlines and quickly develop strong opinions based on nothing more than newspaper speculation. I sometimes found that setting them straight, or at least trying to, was a fairly futile exercise, yet this became a feature of my week at home before Brazil. I hate to be too condescending, but I found it quite hard not to bite when someone said something incendiary like, 'So, why don't you lot want Lewis to win then?' Or, worse, 'It's so obvious Fernando has a clause in his contract that says he has to win the title this year!' I even found myself defending our ridiculous decision to keep Lewis on his worn-out tyres in China, armed with my insider understanding, but obviously that was just silly of me. There was simply no explanation for such a foolish strategy.

I travelled to Brazil with mixed feelings. The season was drawing to a close and the end couldn't come fast enough after the year we'd had. I'd had my 'nailed-on' World Constructors' Championship taken away from me by one or two idiots in my own team. I'd been embroiled in a massive espionage scandal that must have, in some people's eyes, labelled us all cheats. I'd lost a huge amount of respect for McLaren's own racing drivers for different reasons, and now we were off to the final race, where one of them was highly likely to become the World Champion, leaving with their dreams achieved. Whatever the outcome, though, I would fulfil none of mine.

As a mechanic in big moments like the title-deciding race of the season, all you can do is perform to the best of your ability. You leave race strategy to the engineering team and mathematicians; you leave the driving to the drivers, and you make sure your piece of the jigsaw falls into place without a hiccup. That means no mechanical mistakes, preparing the car perfectly, making sure the drivers are comfortable and at ease with their equipment, and trying to strip away any worries they might have before they can even consider them. It also means delivering perfect pitstops under extreme pressure.

The bad feeling between Fernando and the team over his attitude and the Spygate saga, not to mention Lewis's pretending to be angelic and self-perpetuated superstar-yet-rookie behaviour, meant a lot of people weren't as passionate as they should have been about either of them becoming champion. Fernando, if you believed the latest quotes, was still pretty vocal about the team being biased against him and that didn't go down at all well within McLaren. It put extra pressure on us to be perfect. Can you imagine if there'd been a problem on one of Fernando's pitstops and it changed the result? I certainly thought about the fallout from such an incident and that's the last thing I should have been thinking about. I could never imagine anyone in a pitstop crew deliberately sabotaging a stop for a particular driver. For starters, it's just not in our nature. Trying to do anything deliberately different in a precisely choreographed event that only lasts for a couple of seconds would likely be dangerous as well as obvious. We were pros and the team put the petty politics to one side and focused on our jobs. Whatever happened that weekend, we'd all be finished and on holiday by Monday morning. I think that was what kept lots of people up and down the pitlane going by that stage.

I liked the city of Sao Paulo, it's rough and ready; at night it felt edgy and dangerous, but we'd always managed to have a lot of fun there, and only once or twice did any of us ever get mugged – or shot at. We'd always get what we termed the 'Life Is Cheap' speech from Dave Ryan ahead of going, warning us about being sensible and how life was indeed cheap out there, so we shouldn't be going out at night or wearing our team sponsored TAG Heuer watches on the streets. We'd listen each time and nod in the right places, but there was no way we weren't going out to enjoy Sau Paulo. I think the fact that life was considered in that way gave the people a live-each-day-like-it's-your-last kind of attitude and I quite liked that. Meanwhile, the circuit was permanently in a state of near-completion, and even today that feels the same. We'd drive in on race day morning, past the huge queues of fanatical Brazilian race fans waiting outside in the street, to see swarms of workers in white overalls hurriedly painting walls and kerbs, or planting flowers and laying turf around the site. I always assumed Mr Ecclestone must've arrived the previous day and given them an almighty dressing-down, ensuring they worked through the night to make it look good for the TV cameras by Sunday afternoon. I imagined a 'Bernie Bollocking' would somewhat *focus the mind*.

Given our recent record of handling high-stakes pressure, I wasn't overly confident of a smooth weekend and by Friday afternoon we'd already made our first operational error. Lewis's side of the garage had used two sets of wet tyres in the first practice session, something the rules clearly forbade. It was a simple mistake and exactly the kind of thing that can easily happen when you forget the basics and become distracted by the bigger situation. We got away with a €15,000 fine and had to hand back an extra set of wet tyres, but with no rain forecast for the race, we were able to put the unfortunate incident behind us.

Ferrari were quick and lighter on their tyres, which would be a crucial factor on this track, but Lewis didn't need to win this race, so qualifying second, behind Filipe Massa for Ferrari, was a good start. Both his title rivals were behind him, but as the race got underway, that wasn't the case for long. All the talk in Sunday morning's briefing was about not repeating the same mistakes of China. Our drivers were to have a fair fight. The one in front, as was normal, would get first choice on pitstop strategy in the event of rain or a safety car, otherwise they were told to stick to the pre-planned fuel-load-determined stop laps. Because of the superior Ferrari pace it wasn't imperative to fight with them. If Kimi were to win the race, Lewis could even finish as low as fifth and still be World Champion. Fernando had a tougher job, but even so, the message from the team was to be sensible about things: 'Remember it's a long race,' they were both warned. 'Don't lose it in turn one!'

At first it seemed as if our drivers had heeded his warning. Three or four turns passed without incident, but on turn five the scrapping began. Lewis was overtaken by Kimi and then, infuriatingly for him, Fernando followed. Forgetting the morning's briefing, Lewis fought back hard, almost banging wheels with Fernando, and in the chaotic exchange he locked the brakes, his car spiralling off the circuit. The cock-up dropped him down to eighth position and once again the team in the garage had become a collective nervous wreck. We could barely watch. For once we didn't care about the damage being inflicted upon the cars – it was the last race of the season so we wouldn't have to repair them. But watching our two drivers come so close to ending their seasons on lap one was stressful. I'd sit through moments like that with my fists clenched and my knuckles turning white. I was fairly anonymous within the pitstop crew when dressed in all the gear, but beneath the suit my whole body was tensed and I barely breathed for what seemed like minutes at a time.

Lewis hadn't enjoyed the greatest of starts, but I knew it wouldn't be a major problem for him. In our hearts we all knew the Ferraris had the better of us that weekend, so it was always going to be pretty tough for Fernando to beat Kimi, who would obviously not be held up by his teammate, Massa, for the win. But Lewis had a car more than capable of passing through the field so finishing in the top five was well within his capabilities

But then the unthinkable happened.

The conspiracy theorists in the Lewis Hamilton fan club had already seen enough to give them plenty to work with throughout 2007. What happened next has kept them busy ever since, and during a typically tenacious fight back, with Lewis carving through the field, his radio burst into action.

'I can't select any gears!' shouted Lewis, frantically.

The nightmare scenario was happening; the TV pictures showed Lewis struggling to maintain his pace. For the entire season, our car had enjoyed the highest level of reliability I'd ever known. Now, during the crescendo of the championship, his grand finale, it was failing. You couldn't have made it up. Still, I sensed that not everyone in the garage shared the same levels of inconsolable disappointment as the frantic pit wall conversations conveyed, because of the strained relationship between team and drivers.

After desperately scrolling through various system modes on the steering wheel, devoid of any clear instruction from the team due to their own bewilderment at what was happening, and some frenzied pulling of the shift paddles, the car clunked into gear again. The systems engineers, furiously searching for reasons in both the garage and back in Woking, were as shocked, and pleased, as Lewis was to find the car mysteriously operational again. Confused, the pit wall told him to continue. This was an unnecessary instruction really. The kid was already well on his way, the bit between his teeth, but this time he was right up against it. Now down in eighteenth position, his situation had a much more desperate feel, even though the car was apparently functioning normally again. We'd all seen Lewis fight from the back of the pack in GP2 when his championship was at stake, but this was Formula One and he had a mountain to climb. The less sympathetic in the team had a disbelieving chuckle to themselves, shaking heads with incredulity as we all watched on, not knowing what to think.

It was rare for an F1 car of that era to experience such an issue, especially one that then disappeared immediately. At the time we didn't know if Lewis's frantic switch changes on the steering wheel had fixed the glitch and it was a particular mode that had the problem, or if it was a mechanical or hydraulic failure. The latter would normally cause irreparable, probably terminal, damage. Lewis's car might have been up and running again, but at the back of the garage people had crowded round computer screens, desperately seeking answers. For an F1 engineer, the only thing worse than a car or systems failure was not understanding *why* it had failed. We were all clueless. Even weirder was that the problem seemed to have completely vanished and, along with it, maybe Lewis's record-breaking championship hopes. He valiantly tried his hardest, fighting back to seventh place, but the gap was ultimately too large. Fernando didn't have the pace to challenge for the win either, so the Ferraris pranced home for a dominant 1-2 finish.

Incredibly, Kimi had stolen the Formula One World Title from right under McLaren's nose and I found myself feeling a strange mixture of emotions. I'd been swept along with the rollercoaster ride of the race and wanted Lewis to claw it back and complete the unbelievable story we'd all been part of. But there was also a hidden, spiteful streak in me that day: ashamedly part of me wanted both him and Fernando to have the opportunity of success snatched away from them, just as we'd had with the Constructors' title. But in the end I was gutted. There was a funereal, anti-climactic atmosphere in the garage and no one could quite believe what had just happened.

Outside in the pitlane, the Ferrari team went wild. A mob of them were cheering and running towards the podium, and despite the blood that had been spilt across our two garages, there was no bad feeling between the McLaren mechanics and our counterparts in red. I'd become friendly with a few of the engineers working on Kimi's car and I was genuinely pleased for them. I was thrilled for Kimi too. I knew how much he wanted it and was a little choked that we hadn't achieved it together. Interestingly, Fernando had finished third, but very few people were heading to the podium to celebrate as we normally would. My conscience got the better of me and I grabbed a few of the team and told them to come to the end of the pitlane; we had to show some support for our man. I knew it might be the last time that Fernando appeared in one of our cars. I felt we should gather together under the podium for one final time. It might help prove to him how dedicated we'd been to his cause all along.

Lewis later returned to the garage with his head held high. He was proud of his inaugural season and had every right to be. As the F1 rookie, he'd smashed all expectations, even our own. In the end, he'd gone down fighting hard, a characteristic that would later define his career and I was pleased he'd reacted that way. I know that a few McLaren people were worried that he might throw his toys out of the pram and become critical of the team, but he handled the situation diplomatically. Fernando was pragmatic in defeat too, though I think he took it harder than Lewis. In his mind, he was fighting against more than just the opposition that year. He believed the odds had been stacked against him from Monaco onwards. Still, he walked round the entire team that evening, as we were packing up, stopping to say thanks to us all and we had a brief chat, looking back on the highs and lows of our season.

'Let's hope next year's a better one!' I said optimistically, but we both knew that whatever the following season brought us, it wouldn't be together, even if it hadn't been announced yet. That was the last time I spoke to him.

The final night of the championship was always a big one. Every team packed up as quickly as possible, throwing the entire contents of the garage into boxes with far less care and attention than we'd done it back in Australia, before gangs of engineers and mechanics then went out to the end-of-season parties. That year it felt more appropriate to douse the lot in petrol and leave the cremated remains of the championship right there rather than pack it up, but I thought better of it in the end.

There was a reflection of the season in the way we all partied that night. Fernando disappeared, never to be seen again. Lewis gathered together his own ever-growing entourage in an exclusive private VIP area – none of us from the team were invited. Instead, we drank the night away with the new Formula One World Champion somewhere in Sao Paulo. I say *somewhere* because I really can't remember much about it. I do know we ended up at Kimi's hotel, the sun rising, none of us able to stand or talk, but it was so nice to finally be able to share part of the incredible achievement with him. I couldn't help feel that, even though he was no longer driving for us, in our own inimitable, chaotic, McLaren way, we'd made a substantial contribution to his World Championship season and a tiny part of me had to laugh about that.

20

A NEW ERA

After all that controversy, scandal and infighting, 2007 couldn't finish soon enough and Fernando somewhat inevitably returned to Renault, which felt like a fresh start for us. So with one side of the problem gone for 2008, McLaren suddenly felt like a new team. Heikki Kovalainen, who'd previously driven for Renault, arrived as Lewis's teammate and no one expected the same kinds of issues. He was yet another Finn, of which we had substantial prior experience, he was also a nice guy, and, perhaps crucially, he just wasn't quite as fast as Lewis. But then, it was becoming apparent that not many were. Meanwhile, Spygate had pretty much come to an end and the $100 million fine (give or take, after deducting the value of our Constructors' points) had been paid up.

I remember being in the McLaren gym one day, late in 2007, where I was chatting to the Commercial and Finance Director, John Cooper. He casually mentioned that, 'Today was the day for coughing up.' I'll admit that I couldn't get my head around paying such a huge figure with a simple bank transfer. In most people's views, the punishment was as much about the personal vendetta between Max and Ron as it had ever been about McLaren's 'insider' knowledge or use of another team's data. A point that was demonstrated almost embarrassingly by the unbelievable fact that the Renault team escaped without any recognisable punishment whatsoever after being found, later that same year, with secret McLaren technical drawings and intel in their computer system. Apparently, it had been embedded and used in their company network after an employee had moved between the two organisations and stolen the files on his way.

For me, things had changed again as the new rules brought in for 2008 had banned the use of spare cars on cost-saving grounds, so my trusty T-Car crew was disbanded. I'd also met the girl who would later become my wife, and it turned out she loved a stupid practical joke just as much as I did.

She was working for a production company that broadcast Formula One around the world and we went through an exploratory spell of testing each other's limits through a series of ridiculous flirty pranks. After I'd soaked her by leaving the shower nozzle (which was attached to the hotel room's bathroom sink) pointed in her direction when I left the room early for work each day and she'd sleepily turned the taps on to clean her teeth, she then filled my trainers with water before bedtime. In the morning I had no choice but to grouchily pull on the sodden footwear and squelch my way into work. Unbowed, I later individually super-glued the entire contents of her makeup and washbag to a hotel's marble bathroom top, and then I think it's fair to say she took things too far. In an outrageous stunt, she conspired with my teammates to zip my pitstop fire suit up, tying the legs and arms closed with knots, and stuffed the inside with raw tuna from our catering crew. My pitstop bag had then been left in the sun to 'ripen' for two days and stunk like hell when I finally opened it to get ready for pitstop practice. I'd met my match and incredibly we're still married today.

With no T-Car that year, the garages were reconfigured to house two cars instead of the three we'd previously used, and while one of my guys had managed to get a spot on Lewis's race car crew and another had been able to take a role back in the factory, in my position I was left jobless. Luckily for me, a new role was created to accommodate my experience and seniority after so long with the team. The job was fairly fluid in its remit and it didn't even have a job title at first, but my main task was to oversee the boys in the garage and to ensure there was consistency between the two halves of the team and their cars. After the challenges of 2007, I was there to smooth our lines of communication, to ensure that everyone was working to the same high standards and to foresee and overcome any potential issues before they arose and caused us problems.

It was pretty tricky at times. Some people couldn't help but see my appointment to the new role as a sign that our management was casting doubt on their abilities to do the job properly themselves. It took a while for me to rebuild the various relationships after they'd been dismantled during the turbulent year before. In reality, it was another example of McLaren leaving no stone unturned in their relentless pursuit of performance and reliability. But as is so often the case in many walks of life, resistance to change can be the initial, inherent response from some of those it affects. Thankfully, in the cars, the drivers were both happy. Heikki was a lovely guy. He was relishing his big chance with a top team. He wasn't expected to beat Lewis in his first season; instead he was encouraged to learn from his new teammate and the McLaren crew, and to bring home the points we needed to win that elusive Constructors' title. Meanwhile, Lewis was happy because he was now the main man, the de facto Number One, and knowing he had no immediate major threat from a team-mate meant that he had the full support of the garage. It was now down to him to win races and the Drivers' Championship. The public mind games that had upset so many people within the team in 2007 had stopped and most people rallied behind our man as the new season got underway.

There were some hiccups of course, but it wasn't enough to derail our efforts. During a pre-season session in Barcelona, a small but very vocal contingent of the crowd racially abused Lewis with banners and gestures. They'd gathered in the trackside area opposite our pits, but the outrageous incident just brought us all a little bit closer. There was an instinctive feeling this was a direct and appalling retaliation from a gang of Fernando Alonso fans, enraged at the perception of his mistreatment by Lewis and the McLaren team. While it was quite rightly met with an appalled response from the F1 media and beyond, the abuse only served to strengthen the resolve inside our garage. Figuratively, we felt an urge to gather around and protect our driver. Any bonds that had been broken in the past, or were yet to be established between Lewis and the team, were quickly forged and strengthened. The Lewis Hamilton story was back on track.

Testing had showed us to be pretty quick and reliable, something that hadn't always been the case on day one of a season. Traditionally, one of our biggest strengths had always been our ability to out-develop the opposition throughout a campaign, so an unsteady start was rarely deemed a disaster back then. But in 2008, everything was looking pretty encouraging and it was the boost we'd all needed to help overcome the pain of the stressful year before. It's an amazing feeling when your car rolls out on the first day of a new season in testing – *and it's fast*. The sense of relief and excitement is palpable, both within the team and around the factory. Sensing we had a great basis to work from gave everybody a boost. The acid test of that first race couldn't come soon enough.

It started with a bang. A supremely confident Lewis dominated the Australian GP and got his first victory of the year, confirming to us that our car was indeed as competitive as we'd hoped. I remember feeling proud of him as he crossed the line, which was an emotion I hadn't experienced for some time with Lewis, and I knew we'd played our part in the win. Our pitstops had been sharp, efficient, and he commented on what a good job the team had done in helping him to victory during a post-race interview. He gave props to some excellent strategy calls too, and this time around I believed his acknowledgements came with some sincerity.

Heikki had also put in a solid performance, qualifying in P3. He would have later finished the race in fourth had he not attempted to remove a helmet visor tear-off as he began his final lap. Disastrously, as he did so, he accidentally hit the pitlane speed (PLS) limiter button on his steering wheel. The car slowed right down on the straight, and by the time we'd got him to rectify the situation, Alonso had breezed past, demoting him to P5, albeit with the fastest lap of the race. It was quite an embarrassing incident for poor Heikki in his first ever GP for the team, so in true F1 mechanic style, we seized the opportunity to jokingly remind him of his blunder at every opportunity. At the next event, his PLS button was temporarily modified by his mechanics with a comedy oversized label, just so he couldn't miss it this time.

After race one, all was well in the McLaren world again, the mood in the team was refreshing; the cars were performing well and as we left Australia, we were leading both championships. It was a great start. But any premature thoughts of World Titles were soon squeezed as Ferrari won the next four races on the trot. It took us until Monaco with its mixed conditions and a couple of favourable safety cars before we were back on the highest step of the podium again. Lewis was on top of the world and not just because he'd won the race. The Pussycat Dolls singer Nicole Scherzinger had flown in that day to watch the GP from our garage, which turned a few heads amongst the lads, I can assure you. (Without resorting to tabloid-style gossip here, the pair of them were getting on *very* well indeed at the post-race Amber Lounge party.)

Their relationship unsurprisingly ended up being a fairly well documented one, but over time it also became a fairly on/off one too. Analysing everything, as we do in Formula One, the next few years proved there was a tangible correlation between Lewis and Nicole's relationship status and his race performance levels. So much so, that by the time he'd moved on to the Mercedes team for the 2013 season, his new mechanics joked with me that they reckoned there was more lap time gain in focusing on keeping the two of them together than there was with anything they could do to the car. Gags aside, it highlighted a part of Lewis's character that I think might have distracted and held him back on certain days; on others it could be the genuine difference between him and the rest of the pack. I'm talking about the passion and emotion he has in abundance as part of his personality. There are rare occasions when personal, family or relationship issues have clouded his focus on a race weekend and his driving has suffered. Luckily, though, there are plenty more examples of the fire inside him taking his performance to an extraordinary, unbeatable level. His explosion onto the scene in 2007 was an early indicator of that.

By the time we got to the British GP of 2008, things weren't going perfectly for Lewis. He'd struggled in a number of races and made a couple of very public mistakes on track, which resulted in a few penalties. Perhaps he was distracted by events elsewhere in his life that we weren't aware of, or perhaps it was just bad luck. It could have been easy in that situation, when errors were being compounded with punishment, to feel as if the world was starting to gang up against him, and I'm pretty sure that was exactly the way he did feel at times, but instead of getting down and sulky about it, which we'd seen on occasions before, he gritted his teeth and vowed to fight back. His rhetoric in the build-up to that weekend had been defiant and it was quite inspirational to see as part of the team. He'd taken on the role of team leader and wanted to rally the troops. Lewis felt that McLaren had been through a rough season and wanted to make 2008 a great one; as far as he was concerned, 2007 was done. Forgotten. We felt the same way.

I still had every faith that he would win the British Grand Prix on Sunday, despite the fact that he'd qualified in fourth spot – I honestly couldn't see any other outcome; he was so determined. More than anything, Lewis wanted to win in front of his passionate army of home fans and I could see it driving him on throughout the weekend. He'd duly overtaken the three cars in front of him, including Heikki, by lap five of the GP, charging on to take his home race by over a minute, one of the largest winning margins for years. The enormous crowd, largely there to cheer on their new British hero, went mad, and as part of a British team, with a British driver, we couldn't help but get swept along with the euphoria. I can only imagine what it did for Lewis's confidence and patriotism. I honestly think that weekend was a turning point for us all, not necessarily in terms of outright results, although we did win the next two races, but more in the way it galvanised the team around both Lewis and Heikki. We felt proud to be McLaren; we felt proud of Lewis. He had a bigger understanding of the car and what it was doing; Lewis was leading technical changes from the cockpit now, but working together with the engineers to fine-tune them. In his first season he was more like a PlayStation driver at times. His strategy was often to get to the front on turn one and the experienced drivers would get out of his way knowing he could spin out at any moment. In 2008, he'd matured. He was calmer, more sensible, and we were taking on the world again.

Everything was drawing together for a final few climactic Grand Prix races. The closing events of the European leg of the season saw the Brazilian Filipe Massa in his Ferrari pulling together a string of good results and he emerged from his charge just one point behind Lewis in the Drivers' Championship as we left the comfort and familiarity of our team trucks and paddock hospitality buildings. F1 was headed east again for the final batch of races, and once more, McLaren were in another definite title fight. I felt excited and privileged to be in that position once more, but while I revelled in the challenge, I knew all too well from experience just how easily it could slip through our fingers.

Next on the calendar was the first ever Singapore Grand Prix and all of us were pretty excited about it. McLaren had sent a crew to recce the venue a few months previously, as had most teams, and the reports were pretty good. Although nothing had been finished at that stage, for a street circuit the facilities were shaping up to be very impressive indeed, and the city looked like great fun. Even more intriguing was that this was to be Formula One's first ever night race, which we knew might give us a logistical migraine or two.

Our hunch was spot on. We arrived in Singapore with a plan to deal with the change to our regular schedule, by working normally for the first day or so, then gradually shifting our time zone throughout the week, moving towards the early afternoon starts and early hours of the morning finishes as we approached race day. The strategy was to try and minimise the effects on the body of jet lag, whilst still being able to utilise the local infrastructure of facilities and services we needed to operate throughout the week. No one had done this before, so there were varying schools of thought up and down the pitlane as to the best approach. Some opted to remain on the European time zone from the moment they landed, getting up at lunchtime and heading into work for the 'day' and there were differing degrees of success, as we learned when talking to guys at the other teams.

As the years have gone by, teams, locals, hotels and race organisers have all found ways to make the night race schedule work smoothly at Singapore. Now, most teams prefer to stay on European time, with hotels adapting their services to suit. F1 personnel are put on dedicated floors with effective black-out curtains, where cleaners are ordered to stay well away until the afternoons. Breakfast is served just for them, at lunchtime, and the restaurants stay open well into the early hours of the morning to accommodate the demand when pit crews return from the track. It works well and Singapore has turned into one of the sport's favourite venues. Back in year one, however, we were all finding our feet and no one quite knew what to expect, but one of the things Formula One teams do best is adapt to change. We overcome problems. Whatever happened, the show was going ahead and it looked like it would be a good one.

The atmosphere was very cool, despite it being over 30 degrees. Being at the track, with the grandstands brimming with excited spectators under the pitch-black skies, felt like a whole new experience. *Singapore was a special event.* There was a real buzz about the place, not just in the stands, but up and down the pitlane too, and when we walked onto the grid before the race on Sunday, we got a real appreciation for just how effective the trackside lighting was. Projectors, 1,600 of them around the entire circuit, cast an almost eerie brilliant white light across the tarmac and it felt like we were on stage.

As the race got underway, we knew it would be a difficult track to overtake on because, like Monaco, the streets were narrow and it was a relatively slow and tight lap. Also like Monaco, the walls were close and unforgiving so there was a strong chance of a safety car or two, and our race strategy had to factor that in somehow. It was that very safety car in fact that went on to shape the race and cement its infamous place in F1's history books.

Fernando Alonso made an intriguingly early pitstop on lap twelve, which left him right at the back of the field, on a track where it was very difficult to overtake. At the time I thought it was a fairly strange move, but I later put it down to him having some kind of issue with the car or tyres. As a strategic decision, it seemed suicidal, but it got somewhat overlooked what with him not being a major player at the time in the title fight, in a car that'd been off the pace all season. But two laps later, with a refuelled Fernando at the back of the field, his young Renault teammate Nelson Piquet Jr lost control and hit the wall at turn seventeen.

Out came the safety car.

Everyone, other than one or two cars on an alternative one-stop race strategy, had to react and dive into the pits for fuel and tyres. The theory being that you lost less time making your pitstop behind the safety car, while the rest of the field was being led around the circuit slowly, than if everybody was running at full racing speed. Of course, Fernando didn't need to pit and so while the bulk of the cars came in to the pitlane, he was catapulted from last place into the lead group in just three laps.

I remember returning to the garage after making our own pitstops, boosted by the fact we'd just seen Ferrari make a hash of theirs with Felipe Massa, as he'd left the pits with his fuel hose still attached to the side of the car. I settled down to watch the race develop on the garage TV. After digesting everything that had happened, knowing we were now in a very good position with Lewis in relation to our main championship rival, I watched the train of cars trundling around in procession.

It was one of the other mechanics in the garage that first pointed out Fernando's extraordinary net gain after the safety car and pitstops, but despite a few of us casually joking about him probably demanding that Piquet Jr crash on purpose to help his cause, nothing more was said on the matter. I don't think any one of us honestly believed that to be the case. But as the rest of the night race worked itself out, the one-stoppers inevitably had to pit, leaving Fernando with enough space in front to open up a lead and eventually take an unlikely win from fifteenth on the grid.

For us, the story of the day was that we'd taken the lead in the Constructors' table, with Lewis extending our gap over Massa after the Ferrari pitstop error. When their fuel rig was ripped apart as the car sped from the box prematurely, it was another stark reminder of how one or two wasted split seconds in the pitlane could often be the difference between winning and losing races. It might have been so much worse for Ferrari. Had the fuel spilt by Massa ignited, there could have been a very different outcome. Moments like that certainly unsettled me as a mechanic, and despite being happy about the result, I couldn't help but spare a thought for the guys in red and the narrow escape they'd had. Of course, the other headline accident was the one suffered by Piquet Jr. He later put his crash down to a simple driving mistake, but not everyone was buying it.

It wasn't until well after the race that night that a few people in the paddock began to speculate on the Renault accident. It was clearly an odd decision to pit Fernando so early, one that without the lucky break of a safety car would have likely seen him languishing near to the back of the pack all evening. With hindsight, his teammate crashing just two laps afterwards seemed incredibly fortuitous. The rumour mill was now on overdrive, recalling the heavy gossip of some internal threats by Renault to pull out of the sport because the team had been so unsuccessful in recent times. They hadn't won a race for almost two years, despite pumping hundreds of millions of pounds into the oper-ation. It was suggested that perhaps Flavio Briatore, their team principal, and his colleagues had conspired to engineer a good result to appease the board. Had Nelson slamming into a wall been part of the plot?

Despite a few raised eyebrows up and down the pitlane, I'm pretty sure most people didn't want to believe that this could have been the case. No one in this high-profile global sport would ever sink so low as to try and fix the result of a race by ordering a driver to deliberately crash, surely? Apart from anything else, what if he'd been hurt? What if another driver had been harmed? What if a piece of debris had flown into the crowd and caused an unpleasant injury? What about the marshals, risking their own safety in coming onto the track to assist the stricken car? There had been plenty of examples when teams had been caught bending the rules to gain the smallest of advantages. Some had even cheated outright. But the idea that some-one would crash deliberately sounded like a conspiracy theory too far. I couldn't believe anyone would be so reckless.

I was wrong. The conspiracy theorists had been right, and it later transpired that Nelson Piquet Jr *had* crashed on purpose. It's reported that he himself eventually blew the whistle the following year after being unceremoniously dropped by the team after the Hungarian GP, and the murky details emerged. When the investigation was con-cluded, Renault was handed a two-year suspended sentence, with a potential disqualification from the sport to follow should they become embroiled in a similar situation again. Their opportunistic, shocking and frankly dangerous stunt proved to us all the lengths an F1 team would go to win in such a dramatic sport. Nothing, it seemed, was off limits.

21

GLORY

Japan was a scrappy Grand Prix. Lewis was overly aggressive turning into the first corner after losing his pole-position advantage off the start line and ran himself and Kimi Raikkonen off the track, dropping us back through the field as a result. Lewis was later hit and spun around by Felipe Massa and both, for their respective separate incidents, received drive-through penalties. Neither McLaren nor Ferrari were having a good day, but by comparison theirs turned out to be a bit less rubbish than ours: Massa finished seventh, while Lewis finished outside the points in twelfth.

I'm sure many of us in the garage were having nightmarish flash-backs to 2007 and our title slipping away at the last moment. Lewis was showing the first signs of being flustered, reacting badly when things weren't going his way, so we had to keep everything within our control as simple, and as calm, as possible. That meant maintaining the garage as a happy and relaxed place and making sure that everything was operating as it should; we took even greater care (if that was possible) to ensure the car was 100 per cent correct in terms of his seat, belts, pedals, steering wheel and the various settings he needed. If his emotions were running high, which we knew they could under pressure, he needed everything around him to go smoothly. Following Japan, the final race of the season had been set up in dramatic style, with Lewis five points ahead of our Brazilian rival, Felipe Massa, as we headed on to his home event in Sao Paulo.

All the pressure was on us. After the Friday practice sessions it became pretty clear we were at a performance disadvantage. Ferrari was stronger than us. Once again their car better suited the design of this fast, sweeping, hilly track. We knew if we were to win the race, then we'd have to really earn it. There'd be no room for mistakes, not even a fractional error could be tolerated, and the smallest tactical oversight might be enough to hand the trophy to the red team. With our points advantage we only had to finish in fifth place if Massa won the GP, meaning we had to think our way through the weekend. Meanwhile, Ferrari had nothing to lose. They had to win the race. Going for it was their only viable strategy.

Luckily, we had experience on our side. After the horror show of the previous season, the team was well aware of what it would take to win the title under these circumstances. We were sensible, we took deep breaths before making big decisions, and our heads overruled any unduly passionate ideas or theories. Allowing our hearts to control our minds in 2007 had cost us dearly and we weren't going to repeat those mistakes, so when Massa qualified in pole position with Lewis in fourth place, everybody remained steady. Since Lewis had the second-fastest car on the track, the odds of finishing in P5 or better were still stacked in his favour.

And then Mother Nature played her part.

The weather in Sao Paolo could be notoriously aggressive. When it rained, *it really rained*, and torrential storms often struck without much warning, with squalls of horizontal drops quickly forming treacherous rivers across the undulating track. On the afternoon of the Grand Prix, the Brazilian climate was in typically unpredictable mood, hurling rain down heavily just before 3 p.m. local time, delaying the race start. Anything out of the ordinary I thought was bad for us: we had a car and driver more than quick enough to deliver the result we needed, so we just wanted a straightforward afternoon. But when the race did get underway, the rain eased and the track began to dry quickly as Massa pulled out a lead from pole position. By lap eleven everyone was back onto dry tyres with Lewis running a comfortable fourth.

One of Lewis's great attributes was his ability to assess and mentally record the strengths and weaknesses of the drivers around him as a Grand Prix developed. There were occasions when, in the melee of a hectic race, he'd notice a rival was continually experiencing oversteer through turn three and inform our pit wall of the minor details, just in case the information presented some tactical advantage ahead of time. I'd always think, 'Bloody hell, how did you see that?'

Fourth place was fine and even though Sebastian Vettel was chasing Lewis down later in the race, even fifth would secure us what we craved so badly. Towards the closing stages steady rain fell once more and everyone except Toyota's Timo Glock made the seemingly obvious choice to dive into the pits for wets again. With Glock gambling on the weather and staying out on dry tyres, he moved up to third, pushing Hamilton and Vettel back into fourth and fifth respectively after the pitstops were completed. It was OK, fifth would still do it.

In Sao Paolo, Lewis was paying attention to those cars around him, but instead of noticing the deficiencies of his rivals, he was convinced Vettel's car was coping far better with the tricky conditions of the day. He may well have been right, although only marginally at that stage.

'The car's undriveable, I'm all over the place,' he said. 'Sebastian's in far better shape than I am, I don't know if I can hold him off . . .'

We tried to calm him down and keep him focused, telling him he was doing a great job and that we were in a good position. Shivers of concern rippled around the garage. As a team, we looked to our drivers for inspiration; their leadership engaged us behind the scenes, so when somebody like Lewis freaked out a little, we all took notice. After all, nobody understood the car as well as he did.

A short time later, in the closing stages, the rain came down harder and the balance changed again. Now Sebastian's car really did look much more stable than ours in these wetter conditions and Lewis, desperate to stay ahead, ran wide with just a lap and a half to go, slipping back one vital spot as a result. We all held our breath. Nicole Sherzinger screamed at the back of the garage and I turned round to see her with her hand over her mouth, staring wide-eyed at the TV, as one of our marketing girls comforted her. No one could quite believe what was happening as Lewis regained control of the car as the now-fifth-placed Vettel pulled away up the road. We were sixth. Massa was starting his final lap and was going to win the race. It looked over. The mood in the garage had completely changed from one of tense excitement, to sombre disbelief in a moment.

'OK, Lewis, just get your head down and let's see what you can do. It's not over yet,' came the calming voice of the race engineer over the radio. There was no response.

We watched as Lewis tiptoed his way around the final lap, pushing as much as he dared, always on the brink of spinning off again. It was horrible. There was no grip at all, but he wasn't giving up and he chased Vettel hard. We could hardly bear to look. I was gripping the edge of my chair so tightly my hands hurt when I finally let go. I don't think any of us took a breath during that lap, apart from an involuntary gasp as the cameras showed another driver sliding off the wet track. Was it one of the five cars in front of us? No. Our title was slipping away. There was no way we could pass Vettel in these conditions from this far back.

I remember becoming angry and shouting at the screen as the TV pictures turned to show us in our garage, now with pitstop helmets removed and with desperate looks across our faces. I didn't want to see *that*, I needed to see the cars. Massa crossed the line half a lap ahead of us and took the chequered flag to win the race. He'd done it. We watched him celebrating in his own car and his Ferrari team in their garage. Our hearts sank. It was like the life had slipped out of our own garage in that moment and everyone breathed collectively. The pictures turned back to our battle as Lewis balanced his car over the edge of the grip limits right behind Vettel. He was close, but getting past was impossible: Seb was simply faster and more in control. I couldn't quite believe how this could've happened again, no one could. It was such a depressing moment.

The cars came around the final corner and up the hill towards the line, Vettel fifth and Lewis sixth. Still pushing right to the end, they passed what everyone assumed was a struggling back marker going incredibly slowly, when suddenly commentator Martin Brundle dropped the bombshell.

'Is that Glock? Is that Glock? It is, it's Glock!' he shouted, getting louder and louder with every word.

Both commentators went crazy. Timo Glock, who'd earlier taken the massive gamble to stay on his dry tyres, rather than make a final pitstop like everyone else, had been running somewhat inconspicuously in the top five with all eyes on our battle. But now that the heavens had opened even more on the last lap, he had absolutely no grip whatsoever, barely staying on the racetrack. Vettel and Hamilton drove past him through the final turn. In a heartbeat, we were fifth.

The garage erupted. People leapt out of their chairs. We screamed, shouted and jumped around euphorically. But even then, some people weren't completely sure what'd just happened. Ferrari were celebrating, so were we. I wanted to be absolutely sure before running outside into the pitlane and I tried to see the television through the chaotic crowd. Then it was confirmed over the radio . . .

We'd done it.

'Lewis, you're the World Champion!' came the words he needed to hear.

Lewis was crying as he keyed his radio switch on the steering wheel; no words came out. But I remember seeing the moment the Ferrari boys realised the result and how distraught they all were in their garage and couldn't help feel for them. Someone grabbed Massa's dad and told him what had just happened. I'll never forget his face. One of their mechanics was so angry at the news that the cameras caught him punching the red partition wall in frustration – part of it fell off. But this was our moment and I ran, jumping up and down, into the pitlane, hugging everyone within range. It was the most incredible feeling of my entire career.

As we leapt around, Lewis managed to shout and scream across the radio, as he realised the enormity of what he'd achieved and I was thrilled for him. He was a fighter and had never given up, even on that last, seemingly hopeless lap. Finally, he was able to put some heartfelt words of thanks together for the team and this time around, this year, we all believed him and were right behind him. The mess of 2007 was a distant memory in that moment and we'd all pulled together to help him achieve the dream.

'You've all been amazing this year, all year. Thank you, you all deserve this so much,' he said, with a slight wobble in his voice.

We'd bloody done it.

Lewis pulled up in the *parc fermé* area and jumped from his cockpit into a crowd of mechanics. Nicole, with her fancy nails, hair and dress, was stuck in amongst the boys, most of them desperately trying to protect her in the swaying throng that had swarmed around her man. Not that she seemed too bothered. Nicole had settled into what was probably quite an intimidating environment for a pop star, and she was lovely, always taking the time to talk to people. What really came across a lot was that she was genuinely passionate about the races, taking it terribly when Lewis had bad weekends and going crazy whenever he won. This time was certainly no different. They made a good couple, and while some people thought it was simply a showbiz relationship, I got the impression she was head-over-heels in love with him. As the celebrations kicked off in Sao Paolo, she was very much in the thick of things.

There were more hugs, more emotional outpourings and lots of champagne. When Lewis saw his dad, he jumped into an emotional embrace, the pair of them in floods of tears. For them, more than anyone, this was the endgame in what had been a long and challenging journey. Ron was in tears too and understandably so. He'd taken a punt on Lewis when he was just thirteen years old and helped to develop his career. This was one of his greatest successes and he struggled to hold back his emotions, which was something not many of us had witnessed before. I think it proved to the world just how much Ron truly cared.

I was reeling from the result too. As the whole team gathered together for a group picture, an enormous wall of photographers, like nothing I'd seen before, had penned us in to the entrance of our garage. The sight was overwhelming: what seemed like a mob of hundreds, squatting, standing, balancing themselves on chairs; the crowd stretched back for a few rows, their flashlights popping as we savoured a very, very special moment. Not only had we won the coveted F1 World Title, something so indescribably difficult to achieve – very few people ever manage it across a generation – but we'd done it in the most dramatic fashion imaginable. Lewis Hamilton, after all the controversy and emotion-stirring theatre of his first two seasons in this incredible sport, had become the youngest-ever champion at the last corner of the last lap of the very last race of the season. We couldn't have been prouder to be part of the story.

The party went on long and hard into the night in Sao Paulo. Lewis DJd for us all, Nicole sang on stage (in fact Lewis and Nicole sang a duet together at one point), but we all fully deserved the celebrations. The hangover the following day was fitting and only then did things really begin to sink in. I don't think anyone could ever remember a championship finishing like that. In fact, that level of drama was rare across any live sporting event. We'd been part of something special. For me it'd happened after many years of trying, of chasing a dream, firstly by getting into Formula One, and then trying to win a race and eventually allowing myself to hope that one day we might get ourselves into the position of being the best of the best.

My time with the McLaren F1 team had been fantastic, a challenge, a life experience, and a hell of a lot of fun. But there'd been sacrifices too. The travel back then was relentless, so too the hours spent working either in pitlanes around the world, or if not, back at the team's base. Family suffered, friendships outside of F1 too, and I woke up one day and realised that my entire life was centred around the job. For me, since separating from my ex-wife, I'd found it far more difficult to spend enough time with my young children and for the first time I pondered the previously unthinkable idea of an exit strategy.

I always knew that if I was ever to bow out from F1, I wanted to do it on a high, and it didn't get any better than one of our cars winning the World Championship. Lewis's success hadn't just made it to the back pages of the national newspapers at home; it was splashed across the front pages too. I began to realise that maybe my time in this life-changing job had reached a fitting and suitably dramatic endpoint.

There were doubts, of course, lots of them. What if this was the beginning of a run of success for the team? What if I missed out on the next amazing experience? The next prodigious driver? The next unbelievable place F1 were to visit? But I knew that's exactly how so many people had become trapped in the Formula One life: the lure of winning just one more championship hooked them in, and when they failed, they assured themselves, 'One more year, just one more year . . .' After lots and lots of very careful and difficult consideration, I eventually decided that this life couldn't be for me anymore and I needed a new challenge. I'd worked in the F1 pitlane for almost a decade and loved every minute of it, but I also knew that hundreds of young kids in exactly the same position that I'd been in all those years ago would give their right arm to get the chance. It was right that I allowed them that opportunity. When I returned to the MTC in Woking a couple of weeks later, I went to see Dave Ryan for 'the Chat'.

'I think I'd like to stop travelling, Dave,' I said. 'I can't see us ever being able to top the feeling in Brazil, and, as you know, my situation at home changed some time ago too, so life on the road's become even more difficult. I know there's a massive demand for the jobs we do, and I feel very lucky to have been part of this team for so many years, but I think someone else should have a go. I hope you understand?'

Dave looked shocked. 'Blimey, that's a bombshell I wasn't expecting,' he said. Overall, though, he understood my position, and together we worked out a new role for me where I'd work from the factory as a link between the MTC and the Race Team, ensuring that everything operated perfectly on the road, from a logistical perspective. I really appreciated it. It wasn't something McLaren had to do, they could've just let me go, but Dave and Martin Whitmarsh both assured me my loyalty and dedication to the team would not be forgotten and that was a nice thing to hear. At first, I was really happy, the atmosphere in the factory during the pre-season of 2009 was pretty much the same as during any other pre-season I'd been involved with over the years. But when the first Grand Prix rolled around, I hated it, I became envious as I watched my former teammates and friends packing up for Australia with a nagging sense that I was being left behind. I realised that while I'd embarked on a new chapter in my life, I needed something to give me the adrenaline buzz again. The buzz of competition, of meeting impossible deadlines, of getting the car out whatever it took. More than anything else, I needed the overwhelming adrenaline buzz of a Grand Prix pitstop. Years of F1 had taken my boredom threshold to insanely high levels. Being in the McLaren factory day in, day out just wasn't going to cut it.

I don't know why I started writing. One day in 2009 I decided to post a blog on a Wordpress site. It was nothing too spectacular, just some insight into what an F1 team's preparations were like for a new season, but the feedback from the few people that read it was encouraging enough to convince me to do it again – and again, over the following months. Once Twitter began to take hold and I was able to spread my work around quite freely, I found that my blogs were getting more and more traction with F1 fans and were being shared far and wide. Over the next couple of years, I began being paid to write columns and features for various industry magazines and websites, and really enjoyed the process. I realised I had a unique perspective amongst fans and even most experts in F1 about the inner workings of a team. Without giving away any embargoed secrets, I could help people to more fully understand our complex sport. It also meant I could work from home at my own schedule and enjoy all the freedom and benefits I'd missed out on by being at the beck and call of the team for so many years. Eventually, with things ticking along nicely (although without earning anything like the salary I'd been used to at McLaren), I received a call from one of the producers at BBC Radio 5 Live in 2012.

'Look, this is great, Elvis,' he said. 'The insight you're giving here could work really well on the radio. How do you fancy going into the British GP as a pitlane reporter for us?'

I said yes without even thinking about it, even though I had no idea what I'd be doing. Once I'd agreed, I was sent to Silverstone where I was given a microphone and radio kit to roam the paddock on the Thursday media day.

'Off you go,' said the producer. 'If you find anyone interesting chat to them.'

I couldn't have had a greater baptism of fire. The first 'person of interest' I'd bumped into was the Godfather of Formula One, Bernie Ecclestone. Though I obviously knew of him – it was impossible not to – I'd never spoken to Bernie before and it took all the courage I could muster to approach him. Despite his diminutive size, he cuts quite an intimidating figure, an understandable side effect of the power he wielded in our sport at the time. As I looked down at him and he looked up at me, it must've been clear to everyone around us that I was shaking like a leaf. Luckily, the interview was being broadcast on radio, so nobody would have seen me quaking with fear, but even if they had, I'm sure my trepidation would have been greeted with a certain level of sympathy. This was the man responsible not only for creating the modern Formula One empire as we knew it, but also for ruling it in his own inimitably dictatorial style that we all were so well aware of. I also knew he'd once been part of an F1 team, so figured we at least had that vaguely in common. I shoved a microphone towards his face. As Bernie realised I was considerably ill at ease, he led me calmly through the interview, and though I can't fully recall what was said, the rush was incredible. Later that day I was asked to interview my old pal Kimi, and by Sunday I was reporting live from the pitlane on events unfolding in the race. On my way home that night I realised I'd found my new calling. I spent the next few months pestering anybody who could give me a working opportunity in the broadcast media, much as I'd done when I'd first banged on the doors of Formula Three and 3000 as a kid.

As the work increased, with Sky Sports, the BBC, ESPN and Fox Sports in America, and I commentated on, reported and analysed Grand Prix after Grand Prix, I loved it more and more, though it was slightly strange seeing my mates in the paddock – at McLaren and the other teams – talking to me differently in my new roles. When I'd worked in the garage, it was subconsciously drummed in to me that the media were the enemy, always up to something, and never to be trusted. Once I began chatting to people behind the scenes, old mates and acquaintances, on and off the track, I found people weren't quite sure whether to talk about stuff that they would have happily opened up about the year previously.

In a way I couldn't blame them. When I worked for the team, we referred to anyone working on the media and marketing side of Formula One – as 'the Cake Eaters', mainly because, as we saw it, stuffing their faces was all they ever seemed to do, when they weren't quaffing champagne in the hospitality paddocks, that is. All of a sudden, I'd joined an elite group of people that I'd long regarded as being fairly detached from the hard-working aspects of F1 – hangers-on, types that didn't want to get their hands dirty – and I was taking a fair bit of light-hearted stick from my mates as a result. Their biggest laugh came from the fact that, in disciplinary terms, I'd sailed fairly close to the wind on a number of occasions, and now I'd been given a job with the

Cake Eaters, and TV producers were pointing cameras at me while I spouted endless opinions into a microphone. Most of my friends found the whole thing hilarious and I'm sure still do.

Joking aside, my former teammates were really happy for me and the new career I'd carved out for myself, and I had an element of pride in the fact I'd gone on to do something very different. I had a lot of support from them and the team in this new world I'd found myself in, which I still really appreciate. When I'd first joined McLaren, there were one or two lads who were forever complaining about the job, the lifestyle, and the travelling that came with it. Those same guys were still moaning when I first walked the pitlanes with a camera crew trailing behind me all those years later. Nothing had changed. I'd always promised myself that I'd never let myself become like that and although I could never claim to have not moaned at times, I always loved my job at McLaren and appreciated how lucky I was to have it. Moving in a different direction, while staying in the same sport, certainly helped to keep my enthusiasm and adrenaline high. The challenge of working in live sport TV brings with it many similarities to working for an F1 team and I've no doubt my experience in the pitlane helps me today. It also saved me from turning into a grumpy old cynic.

The world of a Formula One mechanic's changed a lot over just the short period of history I've been involved in it, and today, when I walk the pitlanes and paddocks, I occasionally struggle to recognise the atmosphere and practices that take place in some teams. Sure, those BAR breathalyser tests that had caused so much controversy back in Monaco never really caught on, but a new level of professionalism was in play, one that put many of our old antics to shame. Typically, Ron Dennis was well ahead of the curve when he'd first placed a greater emphasis on increasing the human performance of his pit crew, and now teams are encouraging their mechanics to run laps of the racetrack once their working days come to an end in an effort to keep them leaner, fitter and more productive. During the years when I first came into

F1, a fitness regime would never have been entertained because it would have reduced our hours spent drinking in the local bar.

It's obvious why so many teams wanted to change the game in this regard though – if it increased performance standards then it was a beneficial progression. From a personal point of view, I think it would have made my life a lot different had it been introduced to the level it is today during my time with McLaren. As much as I was passionate about cars and engineering, I was also keen to see the world and experience new cultures. The way we worked was bloody hard, but at the end of a day, we were able to let our hair down, see the country we were in and relax a little. We had a balance. These days, things have changed so much in modern Formula One teams that the drinking and excessive partying culture barely exists. But that's a reflection of the modern world in general and even I can't argue its merits. We were just around during very different times.

Much of that had to do with the disappearance of tobacco sponsorship, and the modern F1 cars and garages are currently adorned with the logos of investment banks and tech companies. Cigarette brands had a much more rock'n'roll vibe at the start of the twenty-first century. Their ethos was to set themselves up as being a little bit wild; a business that tended to live on the edge. That attitude was mirrored by some of the behaviour behind the scenes, and while the money still flowed into Formula One following their departure, it wasn't quite in the quantities that allowed us to hire zero-gravity planes for promotional stunts, or hold extravagant parties to quite the same level. Meanwhile, the advent of mobile phone technology twinned with a certain sensitivity to the corporate sector's public image meant that a huge sponsorship contract was only ever one drunken Facebook post away from being torn to shreds. Formula One's solution to all of that was to ensure the crews and drivers towed the line in their downtime. The party was well and truly over.

I couldn't help but be slightly chuffed with my fortuitously timed departure. Working with McLaren had coincided with the tail end of one of F1's more hedonistic eras and I'd revelled in both the decadent atmosphere and extravagant lifestyle that accompanied it. But I also loved the experience of working, and enjoying success, with one of the most exciting and game-changing teams in world sport. My new life in the television media of both Formula One and now Formula E, the world's first fully electric single-seater race series, means I can now watch all those technological and innovative changes that had me hooked on motor racing in the first place, from my privileged box seat. I've somehow managed to move from one adrenaline-charged chapter to another and feel incredibly lucky to have done so. The buzz is still most definitely there, as strong as ever.

And I can't see myself slowing down any time soon.

ACKNOWLEDGEMENTS

I'd like to dedicate this book to my wife Clare, and children, Lexi, Leo, Rex and Ginger, who've all made significant sacrifices to enable me to follow my dreams in both of my careers. You've had to put up with me being away for long periods over the years and committing huge amounts of my life to what I do, but you've all been incredibly supportive all along the way and I would never have been able to do the things I've done without you all. I love you all more than I can ever tell you and I owe you the world.

I also need to give a big shout out to everyone working in this weird and wonderful world, as well as those left behind at home, because without you all going above and beyond the regular call of duty, the F1 show just couldn't happen. Respect.